PRAISE FOR

B & Me

"By turns charming [and] obsessive . . . *B & Me* frequently wonders if reading is closer to lust than to love, but it finally comes closer to this truth: that to be good readers, we must learn to be deeply interested again in things which we can neither love nor befriend."
—*Pittsburgh Post-Gazette*

"Unabashed enthusiasm and wit about living with a deep relationship with books . . . I fell in love with Hallman's book."
—*San Francisco Chronicle*

"Audacious . . . Hallman ranges deep and wide in this passionate . . . wildly intelligent, deeply personal, immoderate exploration of Nicholson Baker's entire oeuvre, reading in general, and the state of modern literature."
—NPR

"To say that *B & Me* is an odd book doesn't quite do the project justice. . . . As provocative as this material is, Hallman's inquiry has a deeper agenda. It's a love letter to the book as a physical object, a source of intellectual ardor, and a form of emotional salvation."
—*Salon*

"Incisive and chummily inviting . . . Hallman is concerned about all books and all reading . . . and some of his most passionate, insightful writing arises in sections where he considers the bigger picture."
—*Los Angeles Review of Books*

"It's about the most fun reading you've experienced in years. . . . Thank the good sweet lord for [*B & Me*] . . . Give us something messy and unfilmable and weird and slightly embarrassing. Give us J. C. Hallman. Instead of some artfully rendered enactment of cultural sensitivity that flatters my own sophistication, Hallman has written a book that's both enthralling and unnerving. Praise be." —*Quarterly Conversation*

"Calling the book creative criticism, though, doesn't do justice to *B & Me*'s inventive narrative. *B & Me* is a love story and a look into the writings of Nicholson Baker." —*Interview Magazine*

"Nearly 25 years after *U and I*'s publication . . . *B & Me* aspires to more than mere reiteration . . . Hallman has set out to take the next step." —*The New Republic*

"Mr. Hallman is clearly a smart guy and an engaging author . . . sounding more than a little like George Carlin. . . . This is a great book to read if you love reading books and are worried about their future; and it's a great book to read if you love words and love to see them gainfully employed, often with humor." —*Washington Times*

"Hallman is an intelligent, passionate critic, and his fecund mind leads readers in many directions worth following. . . . *B & Me* morph[s] into the deeper contemplation of literature and life that he chronicles with candor, humor and insight. . . . [A]n original, at once quirky and thought-provoking—a book in love with books and the power they can and should hold." —*BookPage*

"A bright, funny, and expansive account of a rewarding and investigative personal journey." —*Litkicks*

"A labyrinthine odyssey . . . *B & Me* is a great love letter to literature itself, and a reminder that the writer's job is to push further with each generation, to reorient our moral compass, and take back criticism from the critics." —*World Literature Today*

"J. C. Hallman has written his best, funniest, and riskiest book, one that flirts deliciously at the edge of obnoxiousness before darting off into deeper, sager truths. Every writer or would-be writer will find much to relish, wince at, and identify with here." —Phillip Lopate

"J. C. Hallman's *B & Me* is a daring book. Its ostensible subject is the virtuosic and uncategorizable writer Nicholson Baker, but Hallman, borrowing a page from Baker's book on John Updike, *U and I,* transforms appreciation into autobiography. The fact that Baker has already played this trick only raises the stakes for Hallman: What can he say about Baker that Baker hasn't said about Updike? But the fact of the matter is that Hallman pulls it off. He reads Baker brilliantly and compellingly, and at the same time, he tells a moving personal story about love and fame, envy and admiration, which says as much about what it's like to be a writer now as *U and I* ever said about the writing world of the 1970s and '80s." —Paul La Farge

"Witty . . . Hallman is a talented writer . . . *B & Me* is a wide-ranging and idiosyncratic career survey for Nicholson Baker's work, a love letter to the act of reading, and a commentary on the modern novel. It's difficult to do Hallman's work justice, but this is a book that readers will absolutely adore." —*Publishers Weekly* (starred review)

ALSO BY J. C. HALLMAN

The Chess Artist

The Devil Is a Gentleman

The Hospital for Bad Poets

In Utopia

W^m & H'ry

The Story About the Story (editor)

The Story About the Story, Vol. II (editor)

B &
ME

A True Story of
Literary Arousal

J. C. Hallman

Simon & Schuster Paperbacks

New York   London   Toronto   Sydney   New Delhi

For Catherine

Simon & Schuster Paperbacks
An Imprint of Simon & Schuster, Inc.
1230 Avenue of the Americas
New York, NY 10020

First Simon & Schuster trade paperback edition March 2016

SIMON & SCHUSTER PAPERBACKS and colophon are registered trademarks of Simon & Schuster, Inc.

For information about special discounts for bulk purchases, please contact Simon & Schuster Paperbacks Special Sales at 1-866-506-1949 or business@simonandschuster.com.

The Simon & Schuster Speakers Bureau can bring authors to your live event. For more information or to book an event, contact the Simon & Schuster Speakers Bureau at 1-866-248-3049 or visit our website at www.simonspeakers.com.

Interior design by Ruth Lee-Mui

Manufactured in the United States of America

10 9 8 7 6 5 4 3 2 1

Library of Congress Cataloging-in-Publication Data is available.

ISBN 978-1-4516-8200-7
ISBN 978-1-4516-8201-4 (pbk)
ISBN 978-1-4516-8202-1 (ebook)

IMAGE CREDITS
22, 85: Courtesy of the author; 42: Permission of Jimmy Cohrssen; 84, 106, 133: Permission of Abelardo Morell

Am I becoming a critic? Fine, I don't mind.

Nicholson Baker, *The Anthologist*

B &
ME

1

WHAT SEEMS ODD NOW, AT A REMOVE, IS THAT I FELL IN LOVE AT
pretty much the same time I forgot how to love books. Or maybe
that makes perfect sense. Several months after my photographer-
girlfriend, Catherine, and I seduced each other with sexy letters
bridging the three-hundred-mile gap between our homes, she came
to join me, packing her belongings into a U-Haul and moving into
my dinky apartment in a small city where for the few years previous
I had worked toward building a "life of the mind," reading many
books and producing a couple of my own, and to pay the bills
working as a "tenure-track" instructor of undergraduate literature
and writing.

On the relationship side, this was a glorious time. The transition from our racy scribblings to real life was imperceptible at first,
and when Catherine and I weren't living out epistolary fantasies,
people stopped us in the street to tell us how happy we looked together. As though we needed to be told! On the book side, however,
I experienced a dark turn of mind. This actually began before Catherine hauled her life north, even before we began our portentous
correspondence, and it's probably more accurate to say that a sickly,
preexisting blot on my soul had begun to grow. What happened—I
think—is that immersion in teaching and publishing exposed me
to the literary world's dark, institutional inner workings, and truth
be told even a quick dip into those inner workings would have been
enough to trigger a crisis of faith. The exact nature of my dilemma
had remained opaque, but it was clear that an essential innocence
had been lost.

I got my first glimpse into the nature of this crisis one night a few months into that happy but troubling time, when Catherine and I went to a nearby university to hear James Salter read from his work. Many years before I'd read and greatly admired *A Sport and a Pastime,* Salter's homage to sex and France, and Catherine had read the book just recently, and she loved it too, and so while Salter can't be said to have inaugurated our intimate life—that was sui generis—it is fair to say that he was there right from the start, bobbing in our imaginations as we laid the foundational bricks of our union.

This had as much to do with France as with sex. After graduate school I had almost moved to France—I picked New Jersey instead, a sore point still—and Catherine had lived in Paris any number of times: to this day France is essential to her identity and aesthetic. Neither of us particularly enjoys hearing writers read from their work—far too often the physical presence clashes with the on-page self—but when we heard that James Salter was coming to town we knew we had to go. Because of sex and France, yes, but also because Salter had just recently written a blurb (kind words intended for use in publicity materials) for a book I had edited, an anthology of "creative criticism," published about a month earlier. It seems obvious now that editing this anthology was among the earliest expressions of my crisis. No one edits anthologies for money, and I had edited mine in a spirit of gasping desperation. Salter's blurb was auspicious for two reasons: one, because I'd never met him, not once, not even to shake his hand; and two, because he was widely known as a writer who didn't blurb. Not ever. When you get a blurb from a writer who doesn't blurb, well, that's a particular treat, because he or she has selflessly sacrificed a kind of hallowed status. That meant that Salter's blurb for my anthology really meant something. So of course we had to go to his reading.

Sadly the event was underattended: sixty or so undergraduates and teachers spread thin through a lecture hall built for three hundred. Salter was unfazed by this. Standing there reading, he was the precise opposite of fazed: a model of calm serenity. I realized that I enjoyed Salter's on-page and off-page presences equally well. He had had an amazing life, full of adventure and literature and amazing dinners—before the reading began, Catherine and I stopped at the vendor table and bought a copy of *Life Is Meals*, a book of days Salter had produced with his wife, Kay—and you could see all of it on him: Mustached and dapper, he looked like a seasoned explorer holding court at an adventurers' club. When he finished reading and the time came to answer a few questions, Salter let the initial awkward silence pass for a moment, and then pivoted theatrically on his feet to present us with a flattering three-quarter portrait of himself. He elbowed the lectern, and huffed a swaggering Dean Martin impersonation into the microphone: "Well—here I am."

I *loved* that. I loved that he said that, and for me that was all he needed to be. But other people actually wanted to ask questions. For a time, Salter batted away the usual student queries about influences and work habits, but then he stumbled—and this was the crucial moment of the evening—when a man off to our right stood up and posed a question into a wireless microphone, speaking in an Eastern European accent.

"What is the purpose of literature?"

"What?" Salter said. "What's the question?"

"What is the purpose—of literature?"

Salter squinted and shook his head, stepped away from the lectern. He cupped a palm by his ear. "What? I can't—"

The man was young, dark-haired, thin to the point of emaciation—he might have walked out of Kafka—contrasting in every way Salter's sturdy, octogenarian vigor. There was some additional back-and-forth, and after the young man repeated his question two or three more times he began to grow embarrassed: Perhaps his English was not as good as he thought. But it was. Everyone in the audience understood the question, and that began to look suspicious. Might Salter's inability to even *hear* the question indicate that it was a particularly penetrating question? Could he have been dodging the question, like a politician, because it was the only good question? In any event, the audience wasn't going to let the miscommunication stand. A couple of helpful people sat up in their seats and repeated the question in raised, insistent voices, and were you to have walked into the lecture hall at just that moment, you might have thought they had an interest in the young man's cryptic query, that they were converts to his cause.

"What is the purpose of *literature*?" "What is the purpose—*purpose*—of literature?"

To be fair, the young man's accent was fairly thick, and Salter's ears were probably not what they once were. As well, Salter had been going on for more than an hour by then, and what is sometimes true of reading even enjoyable books—there comes a time when you simply want them to be over—had long since become true of the event. So most people didn't mind when Salter, having finally grasped the question, flicked it away with the back of his hand and mumbled something about his pay grade.

"You need an expert for a question like that," he said. And of course he meant a literary critic.

I nearly leaped out of my chair at this. Which was fine, because that was what everyone else was doing, leaping out of their chairs. It was the final question Salter took, and it was time to head for the doors. But I was raging inside. An expert? James Salter, you're the expert! Quite unwittingly, and entirely accidentally, I'm sure—because recall he'd just blurbed my anthology of writers writing about literature, the anthology that had inadequately addressed my blooming crisis—Salter had lent public support to one of the most deeply rooted problems of modern literature, namely that we leave it to scholars to preside over its most vexing question: what it's for. Catherine, holding my hand, could tell that I'd wandered off into a mental snit. As happy as we were in those days, she knew that some part of me was suffering, and her response so far, and this was simply lovely of her, had been to buy me books. Once, during a visit before she moved in, she left me two books by Roland Barthes on the kitchen table: *Roland Barthes by Roland Barthes* and *A Lover's Discourse*. I needed the latter more than the former, but I read the former right away, immediately incorporating it into something I was working on.

As we got in line to have Salter sign *Life Is Meals,* Catherine gave my hand a few quick squeezes in that way that newish couples have of communicating understanding during moments of stress. These squeezes offer a wise piece of advice: *Hold it together until we're out of earshot.* I was grateful for that. But there was also something Catherine didn't know. In response to my inward rage, a name reflexively popped into my head, in the way that solutions to puzzles appear suddenly in the mind, that kind of organic unveiling. I thought, *Nicholson Baker.*

I kept thinking this over and over—*Nicholson Baker, Nicholson Baker*—as we edged toward the front of the line. Catherine, my ballast, my rudder, kept squeezing my hand—*Hold it together, hold it together*—and when we finally reached Salter he was incredibly charming, a truly dashing off-page presence. I reminded him about my anthology, which he politely recalled. We handed him *Life Is Meals,* but before he signed it, in the nick of time, Catherine spotted Salter's wife a few steps away and asked her to sign the book as well. I practically burst into tears at this. Catherine had been thoughtful and quick-witted at a moment when, for all practical purposes, I was stunned and thoughtless. And for a moment after that, for just a flash of an instant, the four of us stood there over the now doubly signed book, Catherine and me and the Salters, like friends.

2

WHO IS NICHOLSON BAKER? THAT'S AN EXCELLENT QUESTION, AND I can honestly say that at that moment I didn't know. Which isn't to say I hadn't heard of Nicholson Baker. Of course I had. Obviously he was a writer, and that's why his name came to me on hearing a plaintively posed question about the purpose of literature. But that's all I knew. And that's perfectly normal. I'd heard of Nicholson Baker, and hearing of writers has always been essential to the experience of being a reader.

I can remember being a very young reader—not actually a child, as I came to the world of literature late (sometimes the institutions of literature appear to work like the institutions of chess or math or music: Unless you've had professor parents force-feeding you books from the age of four, you're forever behind in your ability to intuit the fundamentals of language)—and thinking of it in just this way: you begin to read, you become a "reader," and you begin to hear of writers, to discover the writers you must take in. The *essential* writers. A close friend, a near mentor, explained further: You don't have to read everything by those writers of whom you've heard and must take in; you just have to read their representative work. Kafka? *The Trial* and *The Castle* will do you fine. Nabokov? *Lolita*, and you're done. Woolf? *Mrs. Dalloway* and *To the Lighthouse*, and toss yourself into the river! Opinions differ on precise texts, but that's the basic theory behind what's commonly referred to as "the literary canon."

I had started my reading—my canon-dabbling—and I loved it. I loved reading the greatest hits of the essential greats. But I also became aware of another category of writer, those of whom one has heard but need not necessarily read. The noncanonical. This, I knew, was not the category that most writers aspired to when they took the vows of the writing life, yet it was by far the more populated field. And truth be told you can't completely ignore the noncanonical category of writer, as a critical facet of modern literary life is participation in awkward cocktail party conversations about obscure authors. For the most part, a cursory investigation into these writers' careers will suffice: passing acquaintance with a few book titles, a plot summary for emergencies. There are many, many nonessential writers, and for me Nicholson Baker was one of them.

I don't even remember the first time I heard the name "Nicholson Baker." The world works like this. We hear new names, every day we are more or less inundated with new names, some of them belonging to writers we haven't heard of. From a book-marketing perspective, this is probably science. The whole goal, I'm sure, is to provide exposure for the names of writers we haven't heard of, to plant names subconsciously into the minds of populations of potential readers (because we're forever unconsciously recording the names of writers we haven't heard of so that we don't appear underread during awkward cocktail party conversations), in the hope that someday, after the planted names have taken root, after some saturation point has been reached, at least one of them—one name—will make the magical leap from being a writer we've heard of but need not necessarily read to being a writer we've heard of and must read.

After the Salter reading, that's about where things stood in regard to Baker and me. I did, in fact, wait until we were out of earshot to rant to Catherine for a while about how it simply couldn't be left to literary critics to decide what the purpose of literature was. But I didn't say anything at all about Nicholson Baker. And actually it wasn't the first time, of late, that Nicholson Baker had popped into my head. A number of times in the weeks before the Salter event, I'd wound up thinking about Nicholson Baker, usually in response to seeing his name in an advertisement or hearing it on the radio, but sometimes, as at the reading, experiencing a spontaneous outbreak of Nicholson Baker in my mind. This was curious. Wouldn't it have been wise for me to have already acquired at least a passing Nicholson Baker familiarity? It would—yet I hadn't. Why not? The obvious answer was that Nicholson Baker had not yet been canonized. Baker was a quite popular writer—that's why I'd heard of him—but he was not a writer whom everyone had heard of, a writer whom everyone must read. Rather, he was a writer *many* people had heard of, a writer whom people *should* read. That's why I hadn't read him.

Then, maybe a month after the Salter reading, something changed. I began to worry that somewhere along the line I'd made a mistake, that some part of me had prevented another part of me from doing what I should have done a long time ago: read Nicholson Baker. These sorts of moments (e.g., epiphanies, inspirations, revelations, etc.) are often described as a kind of biological "click," followed by a sensation of "release." That's what happened. I clicked and released. And suddenly I began to feel a certain literary attraction to Nicholson Baker, an attraction that, viewed from the perspective of my crisis, loomed with the promise of an antidote. A salvation. In other words, Nicholson Baker had become a writer I needed to read. He had entered my personal canon. And in response to that, I did what I'd always done when I realized there was a writer I needed to read. I ordered one of his books, *U and I*, which I realized I knew a little bit about: it is a fretting, hand-wringing exploration of John Updike. I'd learned of this book while editing my anthology, but here's the thing: I hadn't read it then, and I didn't read it now, either. I stopped myself. Or wait, that's not quite right. Here's what really happened.

The book arrived in the mail—as is all too frequent these days—and I unsheathed it with Christmas morning verve. The paperback had a happy blue cover—the blue of French artist Yves Klein, Catherine observed—and I passed my fingers over the slick, glossy surface and placed the book on my nightstand. One night I opened it. I liked it. I thought it was great, in fact. I didn't know if it was Nicholson Baker's greatest hit, but I thought it was very funny and good. Then, for some reason, I stopped reading. The next night I started again—and stopped again. *Because* I liked it. This is what happened. I clenched. Then I seized. I clenched and seized. So the real truth is less that I stopped myself from reading Nicholson Baker than experienced, every time I picked up *U and I*, a mysterious cycle of clenching and seizing. It seemed I was torn on the subject of Nicholson Baker. I had some kind of pent-up resistance. From somewhere came the fleeting thought that I had ordered the book not because I was genuinely attracted to it, but because some clever marketing campaign had succeeded in planting in my brain a desire to read it. How could I know whether my attraction was true? I was stuck. I couldn't read Nicholson Baker because I had to. It seemed to me that Nicholson Baker might be a writer on his way to canonization, and where once this would have triggered in me a desire to read him, it now left me paralyzed, unreading. I was forced to ask myself anew: Who is Nicholson Baker?

2

I HAD NO IDEA! HE WROTE *U AND I* AND SOUNDED ENGLISH, IS ALL
I could have told you. "Nicholson Baker" sounded to me like an
English writer, and for some reason that repelled me. This made
no sense at all. There were, it's true, a number of English writers I
studiously avoided (e.g., Julian Barnes, Graham Swift, Martin Amis,
etc.), but there were also a number of English writers I absolutely
cherished (e.g., George Orwell, Bruce Chatwin, Geoff Dyer, etc.).
So why had I lumped Nicholson Baker into the category of English writers to avoid? Probably because of his name. It sounded to
me like an heirloom name, and no one but the stiff-upper-lipped
English (those with names like Julian, Graham, and Martin, as opposed to George, Bruce, and Geoff) would pass along a name virtually guaranteed to earn black eyes in prep school quadrangles. The
impulse to name a child "Nicholson" could belong only to a sentiment dangling from the last frayed threads of empire, a sentiment
that perceives such suffering as character building and therefore
healthy (in other words, fascist), and what, I asked myself—now
that I seemed to be on the brink of actually reading Nicholson
Baker—could such a gene pool really offer me by way of wisdom,
particularly when that sad, beat-up, Harry Potter of a writer (or,
to allude to another thin British allegory, "Nicholson" is the name
of a hobbit!) eventually chose to put his full name, as opposed to
"Nick," as he was surely known to his friends, on the front of his
books? The humble-sounding surname aside, it seemed I had been
wise in thus far avoiding all work by Nicholson Baker because even
a fool could tell he was snotty.

Or scratch that, because it was me who was being snotty. Snotty all around, in fact. For I've actually enjoyed books by Julian Barnes, Graham Swift, and Martin Amis (*Flaubert's Parrot, Waterland,* and *The Information* are in my opinion the canonical works), and truth be told Nicholson Baker wasn't even English, a fact I discovered when I glanced at the author's note in my copy of *U and I.* He was an American writer, born and bred. This revelation hit me less like a sensation of click and release than a devastating psychological crumbling in the face of the uncanny. How could I not have known this? I'd heard of Nicholson Baker, and apparently I had a very faint acquaintance with his oeuvre, but how could I have been in possession of even a fraction of the knowledge one should have of a nonessential writer and still not know what country he hailed from, particularly when it was my own? Looking back at it now, that's when it became clear that there was something peculiar about my relationship with Nicholson Baker. Something that could not be explained solely by marketing efforts launched on behalf of an author for whom I'd begun to feel a mysterious draw.

4

THE AUTHOR'S NOTE ALSO INFORMED ME THAT NICHOLSON BAKER was only ten years older than I was. This annoyed me. Nicholson Baker published his first book in 1988 at thirty-one years of age, and since then he'd been more or less regularly banging out tomes. He was a writer, in other words. As a writer myself I had a somewhat later start, and I was admittedly far less essential, less canonical. I had to allow for the fact that I was intimidated and jealous. After all, I'd been reading—seriously reading—for roughly a quarter century, and I hoped that in that time I had canon-dabbled my way to a certain level of expertise. But then, all of a sudden, here comes this guy who was only ten years older than I was, and he was already, magically, absolutely essential to me, while I was completely *inessential* to him.

This is part and parcel for writers these days. Writers who magically become essential have the added burden of breaking down walls of pent-up resistance in fellow writers. For example, I was also annoyed—for no good reason—that I had no idea what Nicholson Baker looked like. If I had known what he looked like, then perhaps I wouldn't have been repelled by the thought that he was English. Was Nicholson Baker hiding? His author's note was cagey, but I believed that the eye on the right side of the cover of my copy of *U and I* (a clever double entendre by the designer) belonged to Nicholson Baker. The image was a bit out of focus, but he appeared to have a beard. A beard that probably indicated insecurities of his own, for obviously it was a mask (and I won't even discuss the roundish Harry Potter–like spectacles). I recognized John Updike, of course, who was clean-shaven and apparently had good vision, and I even knew where John Updike hailed from—I've read the canonical Updike—but Nicholson Baker, by comparison, appeared to be hiding, appeared to be reluctant to step out from behind, let's say, the bars

of his book cover. Nicholson Baker's author's note was cagey because he was *caged*.

And doesn't that begin to get at how it feels to be on the brink
of giving in to a newly essential writer these days, to transcend-
ing your own selfish concerns long enough so that you can open
your soul to the soul of another, to a writer's soul? Gone are the
days when one could hear of a book or a writer and experience the
slow, delicious process of a long-building sensation of attraction:
an initial, casual familiarity that gradually becomes a crush, which
accelerates into longing, and which then, very suddenly, becomes
a satisfying splurt into the freedom and joy of reading. It doesn't
work that way anymore. We've been blurbed, book-packaged, key-
worded, and target-advertised into a kind of prison-camp oblivion.
These days, why does anyone read the writers they read? Do readers choose books, or do marketing departments choose readers?
Are we truly satisfied by whatever winds up on a celebrity's book
club list? Do we browse or surf? Do we read or scroll? It's not that
we're brainwashed. We know what's happening. We've all become
savvy—all too savvy. Anyone who picks up a book in a bookstore
knows full well that they might be being duped by its campaign.
Even a gut-level attraction to a writer of whom we've caught an enticing glimpse seems suspect to our new cyborgy selves.

Of course my crisis—and this was my crisis—was nothing new
at all. Gone are the days when people were not saying things like
"Gone are the days . . ." Still, I think there's something unique to
the current state of modern literature, to today, this moment, right
now. These days, it's not you, the reader, who is set free by reading, it's the writer. By reading, you free the writer from obscurity,
from the cage, the prison of his or her book. But even that's been
said before, most notably by Samuel Butler, who said, "Books are
like imprisoned souls till someone takes them down from a shelf

and frees them." Which proves my point, for I did not pull Butler down from a shelf and quote him. Rather, Catherine, who had been watching me serially pick up and put down *U and I* for weeks, lovingly gave me a copy of photographer Abelardo Morell's *A Book of Books,* full of inspiring literary quotations and wonderful photos of old, decaying codices. Butler was in there . . . and so was Nicholson Baker. He'd written the introduction. That's why Catherine gave it to me, as a gentle prod to go ahead and read a writer I clearly needed to read. Baker's introduction—I skimmed it—describes the "impenetrability" of books, their prison-like "rectangularity" and "thickness." He didn't quite say it, but he implied it: These days, we break *into* books.

That was true on a larger scale too, I thought. Libraries, long a core institution of the literary world, are no longer libraries—they are *correctional* institutions. Many, many books are incarcerated in libraries, serving life sentences, as it were. Of course this is troubling, in that it suggests we have imprisoned our soulfulness. But it does create an opportunity for romance. These days, readers must recognize when an author needs to be rescued, needs to be sprung from the prison of his or her book, held in the prison of a library. In the end, it's all prisons within prisons.

2

SPEAKING OF PRISONS, DID I MENTION THAT I TEACH? THAT AS I was trying to launch a career as a writer I was a teacher of undergraduate literature and writing? I broach the subject again because it's relevant to my thinking about Nicholson Baker.

The truth about writers teaching literature and writing is bleak:

These days it's rare for writers to pursue almost any other sort of work. There may be noncanonical writers here or there who do something other than teach to put bread on their tables, but more likely than not you haven't heard of them. As a general principle, writers teach. Essential writers may teach only cursorily—leasing out their names to diabolical institutions, limiting their contact to responsive graduate students—but nonessential writers teach undergraduate courses like galley slaves, and the problem of course is that to be a teacher, to be shackled deep in the hull of some slave ship institution, is to not be a writer at all.

The psychological effect of sacrificing writing for teaching—and this was the other part of my crisis—trickles down onto students, who quickly come to seem like a bane and a vice. In class, as the teacher, as the "professor," you sit there among them, trying to talk about books with the sort of sustained ardor you would need to produce a book of your own, and some of the students are sneezing, and you can see the snot dripping from their noses because they're not yet old enough to have developed any kind of refined sense of nose etiquette (thirty is the new twenty, we're told; twenty, therefore, is the new five), and some of them are covered with pimples because they still haven't figured out that regular washing is generally a good idea, and some of them are asleep because they've decided that they would rather be vampires than people and so they stay up all night long to try to make this come to pass. From your perspective it's frustrating, because even though you evilly relish these shallow and mean-spirited thoughts about students, another part of you is actually quite fond of the students. Too fond, perhaps. For example, you completely identify with your male students, the men, the man-boys, who remind you of yourself at that age, even the ones who are clearly more masculine or athletic or intelligent than you were back then. And then of course there are the female students, the women, the girls who, because your frustrations with teaching have left you lonely and in a state of perpetual inner rant, provide you with material for escapist fantasy. There are women in your classes that you actually can't wait to get home and masturbate to, the memory of how they cock their head when you've gotten off some really interesting point about Alice Munro's *Lives of Girls and Women* (her greatest hit, incidentally). Of course, some of these women think about you when they masturbate, too. You *know* this to be true, you can see it in their eyes sometimes. That girl with her hands under her desk as she gazes steadily before her, appearing to be completely ignoring everything you're saying, she's not sending a handheld electronic device message to her stupid eighteen-year-old boyfriend who wouldn't know cunnilingus from scratch and sniff— no, she's in a state of thrall, and she's thinking about *you,* she's masturbating right there in class while you make some quite interesting, and apparently arousing, point about Alice Munro's *Lives of Girls and Women.*

And that's the state of modern literature in higher education these days: It's all about masturbation. The "professor" is always masturbating to his female students as soon as he has the chance, and some of his female students really are masturbating to him in turn, and virtually all of the man-boys in class are masturbating too, though not to the teacher or the girls in the class, but to the tiny porn stars they call up on their own handheld electronic devices, a more or less constant activity in the modern classroom. The impact of handheld electronic devices on higher education is a subject deserving of significant attention, but for our purposes it will be sufficient to note that a good portion of a teacher's job these days is to inspire students away from their handheld devices—to rouse them, even to *arouse* them. The trick is that one must accomplish this without either annoying students to such an extent that they exact petty, late-adolescent revenge on course evaluation forms that are of ever-increasing importance in the modern academy, or violating sexual harassment policies that are inconsistently interpreted but enforced with draconian zeal. Complicating matters, many canonical texts are quite lurid, so masturbation comes up as subject matter fairly often, but even on those rare occasions when a "seminar" seems to be about something other than masturbation, it's still *intellectual* masturbation in that a public conversation about an event intended as a private encounter between two souls amounts to masturbatory activity. By which I mean desperate and craven.

Which isn't to say masturbation is bad. It isn't. It's how we learn what our bodies like, and our sex lives go on to be either good or terrible to the extent that we learn how to communicate this information to others. That kind of communication, intimate and intended to generate physiological reaction, is exactly how reading once was and ought to be, but no longer is. And my crisis, to the extent that I had begun to understand it, had a great deal to do with the fact that these days a significant portion of the world's literary commerce is conducted in classrooms. More often than not, people begin to read not because they've become attracted to a writer and long to have a kind of virtual sex with him or her, not to have an experience that echoes the multivalent intensity of physical love, of two people made metaphorically naked by a willed suspension of ego, with only the silky membrane of the parchment, the page, between them, like a bedsheet—no, these days, most people begin reading with books assigned to them in the modern classroom, and they read these books dutifully, for "credit," and then participate, because they're graded on this too, in the exhausting but unsatisfying circle jerk known as "class discussion."

6

ALL THIS MIGHT SOUND RADICAL OR SHOCKING. BUT IT SHOULDN'T. Here's why.

"Creative writing" began as an attempt to use language as a technology of intimacy, as a way of sharing intimate passions, thoughts, and sensations with strangers. Creative writing is a fetishization of self, a self that is stacked up and tied up in the book—*bound,* after all—and presented for sale so that many people across time and space can share and savor that preserved self. Or scratch all that. Because creative writing did not begin that way at all. Literature did. Or that's what literature became after oral and written storytelling transcended overt historical and journalistic utility. "Creative writing," on the other hand, began another way. Not long ago a prominent and well-intentioned critic claimed in the highly esteemed and often well-fact-checked magazine *The New Yorker* that creative writing first came into use as a phrase in the 1920s. He was wrong only by about eighty years. The first to use the phrase was Ralph Waldo Emerson in "The American Scholar," a lecture delivered at Harvard in 1837. What did he mean by it? Well, if we make the assumption that Emerson was not trying to establish the modern definition of creative writing—a catch-all for the agreed-upon genres of literature—then a question naturally arises: Why did Emerson think we needed to be told that writing could be "creative"? Why indeed, unless the world had arrived at a moment—the first faint hints of modernity, say—when it was opting for language that was stale, dead, and insipid. For Emerson, creative writing wasn't a loose allusion to creation, to *pro*creation, to the grand scheme of two people coupling to make something beautiful out of nothing, it was a direct citation of it; "-ive" is the operative portion of the phrase; "-ive" is the suffix of similization. In the end, creative writing means "writing that is like fucking." It's from the Greek. Or the Latin. Long story short, Emerson refetishized the self (he got a leg up from Montaigne), Whitman borrowed it (along with a great blurb) and installed it in a "body" of work shrieking off the page, and for a good long time after that everyone happily fucked the body electric.

Which brings me back to Nicholson Baker, to what was beginning to look like my plan for him. But there was a problem— or rather, two problems. Because when a teacher of literature and writing begins to form a plan for a writer, his or her first reflexive thought is to incorporate the writer's work into a course. That was problem one, because it's generally held that in order to teach an author, a "professor" really ought to have at least some level of familiarity with the author's work. I had not read Nicholson Baker, and I had a pent-up resistance to doing so. I could get through that, surely—I had a plan for it—but even if I succeeded I would run afoul of problem two: teachability. I can go on for hours about teachability—ask Catherine, I have—but, in short, a teachable book, in academic terms, is a "good" book. And a good book has two main features: one, it can be understood even if students divide their attention between it and the much more important tasks that need to be completed on their handheld electronic devices; and two, it does not say anything that might discomfit a typical eighteen-year-old's sensibility, which means it resembles television. Teachability was a problem because, at least on this scale, I didn't think Nicholson Baker was a particularly good writer. True, I was guessing. I hoped for the opposite, in fact. Because privately—and this was core to my crisis—I knew that

good, teachable books were actually bad books. And beyond not
having read him, I couldn't teach Nicholson Baker because somehow I knew that he was a terrible writer who was actually a great
writer. What I really wanted to do with Nicholson Baker was have
Emersonian sex with him, rather than try to masturbate to him
with a bunch of kids who didn't know the first thing about pulling
themselves, or me, off.

7

SO I WAS BACK TO SQUARE ONE—NOT THAT I'D EVER REALLY LEFT
it. To read Baker or not to read Baker. To B or not to B.

Actually it wasn't all that bad. Once I decided that teaching
Nicholson Baker would be an abomination, I composed a few musing, meandering pages about one day possibly reading Nicholson
Baker. Then I set them aside and went about my life, choosing for
my courses the least bad teachable books I could think of. Class sessions proceeded with all due masturbatory rigor.

During this time, my paperback copy of *U and I* performed
an odd transformation. Day by day I monitored a gentle curling
of its cover stock, a slow metamorphosis as the pristine, tightly
bound book borrowed moisture from the air and twisted the cover
into the shape of a question mark, a question mark asking me why
I was not deliriously consuming this book I would so obviously
enjoy. But my pent-up resistance held, and I was able to keep
the book at bay. In the meantime, Nicholson Baker kept on with
the job of being a writer, traveling, giving talks and readings, and
probably doing a whole lot of reading and writing. As a result of
all this activity, I began to notice an uptick in the frequency of

Nicholson Baker appearances in my life. By now I'd grown accustomed to regular but infrequent thoughts about Baker, but now I experienced an acceleration of Baker materializations. They marked off an almost pulsing rhythm, a primal drumbeat of Baker that made him seem unshackled, unimprisoned, and utterly essential.

For example, I stumbled across a reference to Nicholson Baker on a prominent literary blog. Baker had appeared recently at a Canadian book festival, an event that the blogger claimed was woefully underattended, like Salter's reading. Apparently, Canada was filled with people who had no real knowledge of Nicholson Baker, like me, or who had heard of him but felt no pressing need to see him in the flesh. In any event, Baker provided a nugget—via the blog—of spot-on Australian-style wisdom: "Writing," the blogger said Baker said, "was a process of 're-engaging our excitement in the world around us by going out on a long journey,'" which he likened to the path of a boomerang. Precisely, I thought. Provided you can embark in the first place. Then I learned, via another blog, that the original manuscript of a short story by Nicholson Baker was being auctioned off for charity. I was too late to make a bid. The manuscript sold for $51. Drat!

These few appearances proved to be only the first wet mists of an approaching Nicholson Baker wave. There were further mentions of Baker in online forums, he sneaked into my hometown to give a reading while I myself was doing a reading in another city, and he wrote a piece for the *New York Times,* a review that was accompanied by one of those pencil-sketch caricatures that high-end publications produce so that you have at least some sense of what a writer looks like, and that are probably the very best indicator of when a writer has reached the absolute brink of canonization:

CREDIT: JOSEPH CIARDIELLO

When this image made its appearance in my life—via my hand-held electronic device—I was struck by two things. First, I was struck by Nicholson Baker's Santa Clausian mien and the fleeting thought that if Nicholson Baker were actually canonized he would literally be St. Nick. Second, I was struck again—truly whacked this time—by the fact that Nicholson Baker was still only ten years older than me. To illustrate this whackedness, here's a picture that Catherine took of me with her Hasselblad just after we shared an on-the-fly cheese and sausage lunch in the Italian market in Philadelphia, right around the same time Nicholson Baker was sneaking around our hometown:

It was also during this period that I received an additional reminder of my own writerly status, as compared to that of Nicholson
Baker. I received a review—a remarkable review. Wonderful! But
what was most remarkable about it to me, beyond my being flat-
tered and affirmed by all the flattering, affirming things it said, was
that it began with a preamble about the state of modern literature
that only too well captured my professional predicament: I had
failed to establish my writerly significance.

> In this age of perpetual presence . . . it's all too easy to lose track
> of those writers who appear only when they have something par-
> ticular and finished to share. Strangely, my two best examples of
> this kind of writer both go by their initials. The first is journalist
> D. T. Max, who will appear in *The New Yorker* or elsewhere once
> or twice in a blue moon, always leading me to think: *oh yeah—*
> *that guy! I* love *that guy! Where's* he *been?* The other writer is J. C.
> Hallman, whose work always excites and intrigues me—when-
> ever, that is, I am reminded he exists.

Ouch. The most remarkable thing about me, it seemed, even ac-
cording to those who remarked on me, was that I was not more
remarkable.

Which left me sort of sad and overcome. The in-all-other-
respects-positive review wreaked havoc on my ego, but it did wonders
for my pent-up resistance to Nicholson Baker. I could feel myself
steeling, heart-hardeningly, against him. Which was timely because I
was soon awash in a whole new tide of Nicholson Baker appearances,
a breached-levy flood of praise and events that made him seem less
alluring and necessary than kind of tiresome, like a down-on-his-
luck uncle who doesn't know when to quit sleeping on your couch.
What had initially struck me as a sweet and seductive campaign to
murmur the sweet nothing of Nicholson Baker's name in my ear

now seemed like a pharaoh's effort to chisel the glyphs of Nicholson Baker's entire itinerary into the sandstone of my brain. This led to a grim conclusion: These days, books are not only imprisoned, readers righteously monitor the cell doors. If once upon a time we happily waited for books, stood vigil for their arrival, then what we did now was stand guard against their escape. Even worse, I had begun to conspire against myself. No longer was I merely waiting for Nicholson Baker to appear in my life. One night I actually broached the subject of Nicholson Baker, mentioned that I'd put together a few rambling pages about him and had begun to toy with some kind of vague plan.

Catherine and I were at a bar that night, having a beer with a close friend, one of those meaningful, hugely substantial friends you have who reads not just from the canon, but even writers like Nicholson Baker, simply because he loves writers and books. He agreed that Nicholson Baker might soon be canonized, but he nonetheless claimed that Baker was an *under*appreciated writer. Certain literary innovations, our friend said, often attributed to other already canonical authors, had first been introduced by Nicholson Baker. For example, a recent trend in using footnotes to create parallel narratives echoing the mind's layers of consciousness (e.g., David Foster Wallace, Junot Díaz, etc.) had initially been employed in Nicholson Baker's first book, a novel called *The Mezzanine,* which our friend said was about a man going on a short escalator trip after purchasing a pair of shoelaces. I admit it: I enjoyed hearing this. I was entirely tickled, in fact. I was tickled because I pregot the clever jokes: escalators and levels of consciousness, shoelaces and footnotes. It was evidence that Nicholson Baker was not just an underappreciated innovator, he was a writer perfectly primed for me.

Then the unthinkable happened, in the sense that it happened and I thought about it: I heard something else about Nicholson Baker. Something downright troubling. It was a couple months later,

and I was back in Philadelphia, at another bar, having another beer
with another friend, a writer friend. For a good twenty minutes I had
been musing openly about Nicholson Baker, musing about all the
things that I'd been musing about to Catherine for months now. I
wanted to write about Nicholson Baker, and what needed to be done,
I'd been saying, what no one had ever done, was tell the story of a literary relationship from its moment of conception, from that moment
when you realize that there are writers out there in the world you
need to read, so you read them. My friend was an excellent audience
for all this because he'd heard of Nicholson Baker too, but hadn't read
him either. Perfect! He couldn't tell me anything at all about Nicholson Baker apart from his private store of cocktail party trivia. Which
included the troubling tidbit. My friend made preparations to reveal
what he knew, leaning forward and glancing from side to side at a
jolly team of barhoppers that had taken tables all around us. He sized
them up for threats—you never know. Then he spoke in a sort of dis-
creet whisper-scream, so I could hear him over the hammering per-
cussion of the bar's eighties dance music. Some time ago, my friend
said—a book or two ago, say—Nicholson Baker had plopped himself
in literary hot water by writing something that seemed to deny or
apologize for the Holocaust. An infernal electric scrape surged along
my spine at this news. My torso shivered and jiggled in a way that
might have appeared elegant had it been set to any other kind of
music. The Holocaust! No wonder Nicholson Baker had been hiding
behind the bars of his book covers—hiding so well I couldn't seem to
avoid him. My friend sat back in his chair with an expression of sickly
glee. He had no further details. It was a cruel rumor, pure and simple.
My eyes twitched, following a whole new round of mad inner musings. Did Nicholson Baker have a dark side, as is sometimes found in
writers on the canonical brink? Or was this nasty rumor an expression
of some kind of collective pent-up resistance to Nicholson Baker?

It didn't matter. Something cleared in that moment, and the rough outline of my inner musings instantly became a trajectory, a mystery—a story. Even though the marketing whisper campaign had come to seem more like war drums echoing deep in the jungle, and even though I had begun to worry that I would wind up smothered under an avalanche of Nicholson Baker appearances in my life, there had arrived a kind of literary "tipping point," and all at once I could feel myself tipping. I was hanging off the cliff of Nicholson Baker, I'd grabbed the last sapling trunk growing out of the cliff wall above the *falls* of Nicholson Baker, and I was staring down into the abyss of Nicholson Baker, into the spray and the mists, ready for the release, the plunge. Who is Nicholson Baker? At that moment, I had only a few scant facts, some ads and rumors. But I was ready to begin my long journey, my boomerang quest. And isn't that the only way a literary study ought to begin? Isn't that—honestly, now—the only way to begin a study of how studies of literature ought to begin?

8

APPARENTLY NOT, BECAUSE NOTHING HAPPENED. WHAT WAS I doing all the while my plan for a Baker study threatened to take shape? I was sitting in our dinky apartment, not reading Nicholson Baker. A tipping point wasn't enough to make me tip.

That said, my collection of Baker books grew rather dramatically in the coming months. I found a number of first editions (*The Fermata, The Everlasting Story of Nory,* and *Checkpoint*) at a used bookstore. I didn't read any of them. I came close to reading them, I had scrapes, but I never succumbed. For example, I picked up

The Mezzanine, which Catherine had sweetly given to me for my birthday (now so long ago that its cover had begun to curl too), and I read its first sentence:

> At almost one o'clock I entered the lobby of the building where I worked and turned toward the escalators, carrying a black Penguin paperback and a small white CVS bag, its receipt stapled over the top.

I enjoyed this sentence because it was one o'clock when I read it and because I was reading the book in paperback (a gold-colored Vintage edition, from 1990), even though *The Mezzanine* had first been published in hardcover (in 1988, by Weidenfeld & Nicolson, which must have seemed wonderfully fortuitous). I had to believe that in writing this sentence Nicholson Baker had specifically hoped that a reader would one day do what I'd done: sit down at about one o'clock and read it in paperback. So my reading felt fateful, foreseen. And I felt no pent-up resistance. But I stopped anyway. What happened this time was that even before I got to the book's first footnote, Catherine stepped into the room. She shouldered the doorjamb, cocked her hip, and looked at me in a particular way. I did not return to *The Mezzanine.*

On another occasion I glanced at *The Fermata.* I'd been nursing a hunch about this one. By now I had access to multiple author's notes from a whole range of Nicholson Baker books—notes that were surprisingly redundant in their caginess—and from them I learned two enticing things: one, Nicholson Baker was a musician (he didn't list his instrument, but he studied at the Eastman School of Music); and two, he attended Haverford College. The latter caught my attention because Haverford College was the alma mater of Frank Conroy, my most beloved teacher when I was in graduate school. That was the first clue: Conroy, who died in 2005, was also a musician. Conroy's canonical autobiography, *Stop-Time,* tells the story of his hardscrabble childhood and the initial steps he took toward becoming a semi-professional jazz pianist. So not only had Conroy and Baker both attended Haverford College (they both went to experimental high schools, too), they were both *musicians who launched significant literary careers at Haverford.*

My hunch was that *The Fermata* and *Stop-Time* had something to do with each other, and because I was a musician too—more on that later—I was able to recognize that "stop-time" and "fermata" were both musical terms. They were different kinds of pauses. A stop-time is an illusion of a rest, a break in a piece's time signature, and a fermata indicates that a note should be held longer than its written value. By itself that might still be happenstance. But what clinched a connection for me was that *The Fermata,* like *Stop-Time,* was an autobiography. Or rather, its first sentence, which is what I glanced at, reveals that it's a novel about a young man struggling to write his autobiography. More pointedly—and you can infer this from the first paragraph—it's about a young man telling the fantastic story of his having somehow developed the ability to *stop time.*

There's more! A little flipping and scanning through *The Fermata* revealed that it is largely about sex and masturbation. *Ah,* I thought, fingering the book's peach-fuzzy deckled page edges, *I see you, Nicholson Baker! You got that from Conroy, too!* In the most charming and famous chapter of *Stop-Time*—a scene in which the young Conroy masters the yo-yo—the older Conroy speculates on the toy's likely psychological analog:

> That it was vaguely masturbatory seems inescapable. I doubt that half the pubescent boys in America could have been captured by any other means, as, in the heat of the fad, half of them were. A

single Loop-the-Loop might represent, in some mysterious way, the act of masturbation, but to break down the entire repertoire into the three stages of throw, trick, and return representing erection, climax, and detumescence seems immoderate.

Not to Nicholson Baker. And not, it should be clear by now, to me.

So what can be made of a connection between *The Fermata* and *Stop-Time*? Admittedly, not much. It was interesting that Nicholson Baker might in some way be responding to Frank Conroy, and it was interesting that Baker and I, each in our own way, followed in the footsteps of a canonical author: Baker by studying where Conroy studied, me by studying *with* Conroy. But it didn't explain everything. It did absolutely nothing to explain why I now owned half of Nicholson Baker's books but couldn't read any of them.

That's how life remained for a while. Nicholson Baker books lay scattered all over our dinky apartment, effectively in lockdown, and I found myself dodging them as they strived for my attention, which I wanted to give them, but couldn't, just couldn't. Worst of all was my copy of *U and I*. It was inescapable. With its now spookily twisted cover, my copy of *U and I* was forever creeping into my peripheral vision, mysteriously migrating from the nightstand, to the coffee table, to the radiator next to the toilet. I entertained the possibility that Catherine had been moving the book around, trying to entice me to read it, but that was pure fantasy. The truth was that my interest in Nicholson Baker, my resistance to him, represented dual pathologies resulting from publishing and teaching, and I had been moving the book around all on my own. Calm in the face of crisis, Catherine had given me *A Book of Books* and *The Mezzanine* to yank me out of the whirlpool of negativity that had already began to eat at our love. But that's not what I saw. Rather, it seemed to me that Catherine had grown secretly jealous of the potentially

all-consuming relationship I might wind up having with Nicholson
Baker, and she was planning to lure me away with sex. Madness!
My copy of *U and I* wouldn't allow it. I continued on unconsciously
picking the book up and putting it down in places where I might
find it again, and then forgetting that I had picked it up and put it
down. As a result I began to fear the book, as a soldier fears ambush
on poor ground. Our entire apartment was poor ground. My copy
of *U and I* was an unrelenting guerrilla warrior.

And that's when it happened. That's when I learned why I'd
been experiencing an endless rush of Nicholson Baker appearances
in my life, and the reason made all the difference. He was promoting a book. I was surprised at this, but I shouldn't have been. Of
course he was promoting a book. He was a writer. He was on an impossibly long promotional tour, first for the book's hardcover, then
for the paperback, and what had happened was that while I'd managed to remain ignorant of the nature of his newest production, I'd
been unable to avoid hearing his name almost everywhere I went.
Then, only months after I published my anthology of "creative criticism," I learned the title of the book that Nicholson Baker had been
vaulting around the country promoting. *The Anthologist*. It's about a
teacher of undergraduate literature and writing who edits an anthology in response to a series of crises in his life.

I felt no click or seizure at this, no queasy sense of tipping. I
simply flushed with awe, and felt a painful passion, a passion that
was passion*ate*. Yet I couldn't reach for *The Anthologist* because I
didn't own it. I did own a copy of *U and I*. I finally sat down to read
U and I.

Or I lay down. It was 4:12 in the afternoon on May 27, 2010,
and I lay down on the small couch in my small office, one edge of
it beginning to fray from the claws of the cat that climbed onto my
chest to sleep while I read. The room smelled fresh. I could hear the

complicated business of birds in the trees outside, and beyond them
the sounds of lawn mowers and occasionally obnoxious interstate
traffic. There was music and sizzling in the kitchen, where Catherine, ever patient, was making us a rice and zucchini dish.

I opened the book to the epigraph. I almost never read epigraphs, even though I sometimes use epigraphs. Who has time for
epigraphs when there's a whole canon of books you haven't read?
But this time I did. *U and I* begins with a quote from Cyril Con-
nolly: "It may be *us* they wish to meet but it's themselves they want
to talk about."

Precisely, I thought. I was in love.

9

U AND I BEGINS AT 9:46 AM ON AUGUST 6, 1989—IT'S IN THE FIRST
line—and that's important. Nicholson Baker settles into a comfy
chair with his keyboard on his lap, trying to ride the momentum of
the book he just finished—*Room Temperature,* which I hadn't read
and didn't own—but he doesn't have any idea of what he wants to
write now. He's following his gut. What he winds up typing, he
writes, something about the pleasure of writing in the morning
(I write in the morning too, but find it hair-pullingly torturous),
reminds him at once of something from Updike. He got it from
Updike, he realizes. It's not original. He abandons the line, but his
plan basically works, because what he realizes is that for some time
he'd been thinking of writing something about Updike.

Something else worked too. A few minutes before I had been
anxious and agonizingly impassioned, and I'd reached for *U and
I,* oddly near at hand, with all the deadly import of a legionnaire

lunging for his gladius. I had lain in the calm room with the calm cat on top of me, but inside I was boiling away. That all began to dissipate as soon as I started reading. Now I was still in the first paragraph, but already I could feel something happening. To be sure, I was acting on the book—I was reading it—but it was acting on me too, making something happen, the beginning of a convulsion. Finally, I couldn't hold it back any longer: I laughed, slobbered a bit. It was a funny book. Not guffaw funny, but giggle funny, which maybe just means it was a human book.

More important, I suddenly knew why I'd been unable to read *U and I* until now.

Many years before, I'd been thrown for a loop when my canon-dabbling brought me around to Henry James's famous ghost story *The Turn of the Screw*. I loved this book. But I was equally troubled by it because there turned out to be a wide discrepancy between what I read and what I'd expected to read. I hadn't ever read anything at all about *The Turn of the Screw*, but I had an expectation of the book—repressed spinster driven mad by class angst—because some of the scholarly theories about it had crept out of their academic tomes and clawed their way into my mind. This troubled me greatly. I wound up producing a small study of *The Turn of the Screw* lamenting the fact that a far more commonsense read of the book, indicated by James himself, had been quashed: It is an allegory of how literature works, a depiction of powerful literary relationships in which the minds of writers and readers commingle, à la Emerson, to create a story.

James would have been stunned, as I was, that his view of his story went almost completely ignored. "What we call criticism," he once wrote, "its curiosity never emerging from the limp state, is apt to stand off from the intended sense of things, from such finely-attested matters, on the artist's part, as a spirit and a form, a bias and a logic, of his own." It's only gotten worse since then. These days, not only is it permissible for academic critics to "stand off from the intended sense of things," they're more or less required to consider stories from the perspective of someone else, someone not themselves, someone whose views could not possibly have anticipated the work under consideration because those views had been formed only after the work was produced. The cart before the horse, in other words. That's what institutional literary criticism tends to be these days, a whole caravan of carts before horses, all lined up but not going anywhere because putting the cart before the horse renders the cart useless and confuses the horse.

Clearly, criticism had gotten under my skin—like ringworms. The weirdest part was that it meant *The Turn of the Screw* had been canonized for all the wrong reasons. And what if it wasn't alone? Or worse, what if there were other really good books out there that had not only been misread, but had simply disappeared? This marked the beginning of my crisis—but also my mission. I began canvassing all the serious writers and readers I knew for a *better* writing about reading. There turned out to be a whole range of such work, a covert tradition, and almost every serious reader I knew had some book, or some essay, that wasn't criticism in the traditional sense but had cemented their view of how literature ought to work in the world. Almost all of this work emphasized that the most important "context" in whatever we read was us, the self that literature was supposed to help us fathom.

And that's why I'd been unable to read *U and I*. *U and I* was firmly planted in the tradition I had studied. What I now recognized, even as I happily read through the first few pages, building up a head of steam, was that on first appearing in 1991 *U and I* had been the first book-length contribution to the covert tradition of creative criticism to have been published in quite some time. So not only should I have read *U and I,* I should have anthologized it.

That's when life intruded—for both me and Nicholson Baker. Before Baker can decide what to write about Updike, Donald Barthelme dies, and Baker has to take his young family to the zoo. He's about nine pages in, and the book's plot, such as it is, pauses. On my end of things, Catherine's rice and zucchini dish was ready, and I sprinkled on a whole bunch of shredded Parmesan and scarfed away while Catherine noted without comment the open, facedown copy of *U and I* next to my plate, its now-doubly twisted covers giving it the aspect of a bird taking flight.

After dinner I returned to my reading to find Baker returned from the zoo, back at work, but paralyzed, unsure how to proceed. Barthelme's death has thrown him for a loop. Nicholson Baker had studied with Donald Barthelme for a time—a two-week course, I read somewhere; it was the closest he'd ever come to academic instruction in creative writing—but he makes no mention of it here. His ego intrudes. That is, his initial thoughts, on hearing of the death, are of himself: first, no one from the literary world had called him with the unhappy news, so he feels remote; and second, how can he use the death to his advantage? What's interesting here, beyond it being already clear that Nicholson Baker is going to be one of those writers who draws you in by fessing up to uncomfortable facts about himself, is that the self-promoting uses of Barthelme's death he then comes up with—one, writing a fiction about the passing of an important literary figure; and two, writing a commemorative essay—both derive from Henry James. Baker's idea for a "neo-Jamesian story" is clearly a reference to "The Figure in the Carpet" or *The Aspern Papers*, both of which had been critical to my small study of *The Turn of the Screw*, and I'd also read a number of the commemorative essays that Henry James had produced and that Baker thinks to use as a model.

But both ideas trigger shame, and before long Baker abandons his plan to write about Barthelme's death. "I abandoned Barthelme completely," he writes. It's at this moment, in its abandon, that the basic conceit of *U and I* becomes clear: Not only is it the story of an underappreciated writer attempting to appreciate a more appreciated writer, it also chronicles a writer trying to decide what to write. He has an inkling that he might like to write about literature in some way, perhaps to acknowledge his debts, reaffirm his mission, and chart a literary future for himself. But how should he do that? It's a conundrum. On the one hand, he admits that writing a fiction about Barthelme would be "crudely opportunist." On the other, a commemorative essay would not be *enough* like fiction, would not do what fiction does. Not plot-driven fiction, he specifies, not fiction whose only suspense is "first-order plot anxiety," but fiction that "capture[s] pieces of mental life as truly as possible as they unfold." The intended effect of these lines is that you realize that this is exactly what you've been doing since the morning of August 6, 1989: watching a mind unfold.

And this, to my mind, was the more or less foundational characteristic of creative criticism: writers depicting their minds, their consciousnesses, as they think about literature. So when Baker returns to the reflexive inspiration of his unfolding mind—Updike—I was right there with him, in the sense that he was right there with me, agreeing with everything I'd been saying for years. But that made no sense. *U and I* had appeared long before many of the writings about literature I had anthologized: Nicholson Baker wasn't agreeing with me, I was agreeing with him. "We read, really," V. S. Naipaul wrote in an essay about his literary relationship with Joseph Conrad, "to find out what we already know." Quite right—and that's one of the more underappreciated pleasures of reading. Reading may sail us into terra incognita, but it's also a means of exploring and fathoming where we've come from. *U and I* was an influential book, and a steady stream of creative criticism had followed after it, the very stream I'd panned for lustrous nuggets. It confirmed what I already knew. It *shaped* me without my even having read it.

Which made me anxious. Not first-order plot anxiety, but an anxiety that approximated the anxiety that Baker himself begins to feel in regard to his subject matter: he's immediately convinced that Updike could have done better at age twenty-five what Baker is attempting at thirty-two. And here I was, at forty-three, looking laterally to the Baker of right then, fifty-three, but also backward to the much younger Baker who had helped shape my worldview. This shouldn't have bothered me. We're always reading important books from the distant past written by long-dead writers who produced what they produced when they were younger than we are. But it did bother me—it *did*. Oh, if Nicholson Baker had only been a dead writer! That would have solved everything. You cannot slander the dead; you don't have to worry about hurting the feelings of the dead; you cannot be jealous of the dead. You've always got that on them, as it were. But Nicholson Baker was not dead, and neither was Updike, at least when Baker was writing about him. We both had the same problem, Baker and me. Our egos were in the way. Maybe that's why we traditionally wait until writers die to write about them. The dead are older than we are even if they died young. And the not-dead younger writer—even when they're *now* older than we are—presents the greatest problem of all.

This was illustrated perfectly in the months after my tipless tipping point, when I found an essay about Nicholson Baker written by Martin Amis. I was reading Amis (rather than studiously avoiding him) because I'd started thinking about editing another anthology. I'd found a remaindered copy of some of Amis's literary writings, *Visiting Mrs. Nabokov,* but there wasn't much in it I could use—perhaps a piece about Philip Larkin, in which Amis relinquished a bit more of his Amis*ness* than was generally the case. That was the problem with him. Martin Amis had an ego, a self, but he wasn't at all interested in plumbing it, or unfolding it, and that's why he was one of those writers often described with crass synonyms for male genitals. In his essay "Nicholson Baker"—I almost didn't read it—Amis is a total dick to Nicholson Baker. He's even, preemptively, a dick to me. The piece is mostly the story of Amis pitching a fit over having been asked to interview a "literary junior." Baker is "inadmissibly young" (thirty-six at the time), and Amis makes a point of taking him down a peg by pointing out that a neologism that Baker had coined in the then newly published *Vox*—"strum," a synonym for masturbation—had been, Amis wrote, "casually tossed out by [Amis] two novels ago." What a prick! Furthermore, Amis characterizes his need to charge Baker with petty plagiarism as "get[ting] the B-and-Me stuff at least partly out of the way." Cocksucker! That's exactly why I hated Amis and all the English writers like him. He was far less interested in ideas than he was in making sure you knew *he* was more interesting than his subject. This was true throughout *Visiting Mrs. Nabokov.* His commemorative essays all commemorated himself.

In fact, he wrote exactly the kind of essays Nicholson Baker explicitly worries about writing at the beginning of *U and I*—immature, indulgent—and rather than depicting his unfolding mind, Amis tended to depict his mind folding itself farther and farther in, in a kind of horrid origami. I realized that maybe I'd thought Nicholson Baker was English not because of his name, but because I'd stumbled across this awful essay years before and had associated Baker with Amis's Englishness and dickishness. Of course there was also the fact that Baker had lived in England for a year—I'd read that too, by this point—and perhaps he had done so, I thought now, because Henry James was a role model. Henry James mistook *himself* for an English writer. "I aspire to write in such a way," he once wrote to his brother, William, "that it wd. be impossible to an outsider to say whether I am, at a given moment, an American writing about England or an Englishman writing about America."

10

NICHOLSON BAKER ISN'T THINKING ABOUT ANY OF THIS IN *U AND I*—he couldn't be, he hadn't granted the interview yet—but he does fret for a while over how to proceed once he decides that writers writing about literature must depict their unfolding minds. That's what he's trying to get at, I think, when he admits that he has never "successfully masturbated" to any image or scene from John Updike. I loved the fact that he revealed this. The image of a grown man failing to arouse himself with a book is funny, sure, but more important, it underscores that the common denominator of good writing is passionate incursions into those regions of human experience we refuse to discuss in any other precinct of human discourse. The subject matter changes, but the basic task is always the same: careful attention given to that which is mostly left folded, creased, hidden. That might mean anything from the slums of London, to the frustrating abstractions of cosmology, to the uncertain mind of a fretful critic.

But how do you be fretful and critical at the same time? Nicholson Baker's unfolding mind has no idea, at first. Throughout the first part of *U and I*—fifty pages, a full quarter of it—he struggles to invent what he thinks criticism ought to be. He starts out trying to remember a line, any line, from Updike. "Vast, dying sea" is what comes to him: Updike's sad description of one's leaky inner reservoir of remembered literature. From there Baker goes on to produce a list, a "train" of images from his internal Updike reservoir. The list doesn't help. It's fading and dying. So he produces another list, a more Thoreauvian accounting of what Updike he's read, but that's not particularly helpful either. Nor is it vast. Still he sticks to this idea of remembered literature. Henry James, he tells himself, hadn't reread every dead writer's work he commemorated, had he? Of course not. And this is pivotal, because it's now that Baker turns away from Henry James to consider his brother, William.

By this point I'd gotten used to the idea that in executing my Baker study I was going to be encountering a range of points of contact between his life and my own. After all, it had been an accumulation of such points that finally got me to sit down and start reading him, now about an hour ago. So this time I was ready for it. Long before Baker turned away from Henry James to consider his brother—or rather, after it, but before I read it—I had turned away from my short study of *The Turn of the Screw* and written an entire book about William James.

This profoundly affected my read of *U and I*'s most pivotal passage. Rather than the usual, pleasing trance state of reading, a heightened state in which an arbitrary activity triggers flurried consciousness, this was more like a prolonged period of déjà vu. Because I had just then been saying to myself, as I read—had just then been conducting a separate, internal dialogue as I mindlessly stroked the warm cat on my chest and absently registered Catherine doing something in the bathroom (she was always doing mad scientist stuff in the bathroom, mixing dangerous chemicals for her ancient photographic processes, though what I was hearing was some kind of buzzing noise . . .)—I had just then been saying to myself, *Poor Nicholson Baker, he wouldn't be struggling to figure out how to proceed if only he'd read a little William James!* And that's exactly what happens in the book. Baker applies his what-do-I-remember routine to William James ("'Hey, what about Henry's brother, old William James—what do I think of him?'"), and after he gets past the impulse to reduce writers to lists of quotations spooned out of the tureen of his failing memory, he remembers a scene instead.

It's New York, 1981, a McDonald's on the Upper East Side. He'd gone in to collect a free Big Mac, some kind of promotion, and he'd taken along a little William James to read while he ate. He got embarrassed while he was there—McDonald's *is* an embarrassing place—and he tried to hide his shame in the book. He opened it to a random diagram. Reading this, I thought I knew exactly what diagram it would be once he described it. Indeed, his description felt like the description I would have written, the description I am writing. It was the diagram, I thought, that William James had used to illustrate his theory of consciousness, each thought depicted with a graphy wave like a story arc: the work of the mind was best illustrated with overlapping story arcs. Nicholson Baker wrote that the diagram he flipped to was a "glorious sight" when he saw it, and it was a glorious read when I read it. *U and I* doesn't reprint the diagram Baker was looking at, but here is the diagram I was certain he meant:

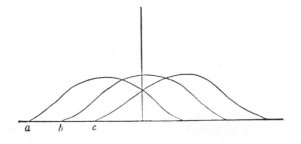

And now there's a slightly weird part, because Baker calls his diagram a picture of the "recently christened, pre-Joycean 'stream of thought.'" Well it's certainly pre-Joycean because William James contracted to write *The Principles of Psychology*, in which the diagram appears, in 1878, and James Joyce wasn't born until 1882. But when Baker says "recently christened," it's a bit misleading because he means *really* recently—like, a few pages ago. In my copy of William James's collected works, one of those Modern Library editions with ultrathin onion skin pages, the diagram above appears on page 165, and "stream of consciousness" is christened on page 159. It's William James's phrase. I wondered, even as I happily felt found in Nicholson Baker, why "stream of consciousness" had not popped up on Baker's shorthand list of remembered James phrases. More important, it was here that William James insisted that "such words as 'chain' or 'train' . . . do not describe [consciousness] fitly." Of course this made me think back on Baker's "train" of Updike quotes. James would have disapproved. Rather, James wrote, we should go to metaphors like "river" or "stream" to convey the action of the mind. *"In talking of it hereafter, let us call it the stream of thought, of consciousness, or of subjective life."*

Here I had to stop reading. Catherine called my name. I snapped myself out of my déjà vu and recognized the sound from the bathroom: the electric razor. I felt a deep testicular stir at this. She needed my help. I still had Nicholson Baker's naked ego throbbing in my mind when I got to the bathroom. Or maybe it was me throbbing. I loved the quiet intimacy of grooming Catherine. It was evening in our dinky apartment now, a nice spring evening with a faint chill and the air's invisible impregnation of pollen, an atmosphere of things coming alive. Catherine handed me the razor, and we did the necessary contorting.

"You won't believe who just popped up in *U and I*," I said.

"Barthes?"

"William James."

This was an old game. Whenever I'm working on a subject, I'm always looking for ways to introduce it into conversations, probably because I'm no good at small talk. I did this all the time with William James. Know who first introduced student evaluations to university courses? William James. Know who invented those frog-ear stickers to cure seasickness? William James. Know who woke Gertrude Stein up to the occult possibilities of mangled prose? William James. Catherine only nodded. She was probably thinking whole estuaries of other things as she reared her head, adjusting her stance and swinging her great chunk of hair out of the way like a puma twitching its tail. I started thinking about other things too. For example, I came to appreciate Baker's sly stream of consciousness realization that stream of consciousness was the answer to his dilemma, his stuckness. A whole theory, an equation of Nicholson Baker, suddenly flooded into my mind:

 +  =

As well, I was thinking about the work that I wanted to do on Nicholson Baker, how rather than getting the B-and-Me stuff out of the way, as Martin Amis had prescribed, I wanted to put it *in* the way, I wanted it to become the way. But if I did that, or if it occurred to me to do that while Catherine and I stood awkwardly posed in the bathroom and I was feeling a sense of having gotten past at least some of my confounding negativity, then probably even an oblique reference to the highly intimate and often unremarked-upon activity in which we were now engaged would seem irrelevant to some, maybe even immature and indulgent, even as it seemed absolutely essential to me. And that was sort of the whole point. We never read outside the context of ourselves—we're forever finding our reading interrupted by dinners and phone calls and requests to assist with delicate hygienic tasks—yet the exploration of ourselves as we read is somehow off limits: You can't talk about that when you write about books. This was so wrong that even a writer fated for canonization could find himself unsure how to proceed after he'd decided to go ahead and do it. But it's not wrong. And the fact that some people think it's wrong is exactly why it's right. Literature must do whatever it's not supposed to do, and literature *about* literature must do the same. Of course it mattered that Nicholson Baker sat down to start writing *U and I* on August 6, 1989, and of course it mattered that Catherine had not been trying to distract me with sex. Rather, she'd midwifed my rebirth from a crisis of faith. She hadn't been moving *U and I* around our apartment, but she had identified my dilemma before I even knew I was in one, and it was she who had recognized that my glimmerings of familiarity with Nicholson Baker might well be my salvation.

11

BEFORE I BOUGHT *U AND I*, I HAD ORDERED AND STARTED READING Martin Buber's *I and Thou* on another hunch I'd had that Baker had referenced it in the same way *The Fermata* seemed to reference *Stop-Time*. I didn't finish it because I didn't see a connection at first, but on continuing *U and I* the next day, at a park a couple blocks from our apartment, my head resting in the socket just above Catherine's hip bone, the connections appeared and multiplied. Baker's folded-mind metaphor is anticipated by Buber's first line: "The world is twofold for man in accordance with his twofold attitude."

Buber sees the world as falsely dual, which means it is in a state of crisis. We all begin with a literal, umbilical, "I-You" relationship, but before long an accumulation of clutter—knowledge—transforms all our "Yous" into "Its." Once we've shifted to "I-It" we've fallen into "modern man's lack of relation." Our goal should be to return to the "real duality," the "I and You," which, for me, was only a tiny step from *U and I*.

A short time before, Catherine and I had been lying on our sides, executing a groggy spoon position that enabled me to secretly but publicly massage one of her breasts. So I was feeling pretty "I-You." It was a sunny day, and I had a good book in mind and a good breast in hand. Then we shifted positions so that my head could rest in her hip socket and I could read Nicholson Baker. Catherine wasn't reading in the park, she was just napping and *being,* and the new position enabled her to run her hand over my chest, slipping her fingers between the button gaps of my shirt and lightly strumming my chest hair. This was the background of my reading for some time.

I didn't care if others in the park saw this. I wanted them to, in fact. I had a strong desire to share my true relation with the neighborhood. I was already beginning to make the connection to writing about books, to criticism—that's exactly what criticism should be, a public display of affection—but I was also thinking about how our neighborhood was the only neighborhood in which I'd ever witnessed someone draw a gun and discharge it, so maybe it could use a frank demonstration of good relations. Not that our neighborhood was awful. It wasn't. It was a nice neighborhood, with tree-lined streets and a pleasing blend of early twentieth-century architecture, and it was even a literary neighborhood. Fitzgerald had spent time here. The bar where he used to get drunk was just down the street, though now it was open only once a month, a kind of monument to binge behavior. There were other bars in the neighborhood too—wine bars, vodka bars, and neighborhood bars—and Catherine and I frequented all of these, which I note because I'd heard that Nicholson Baker was a nondrinker, a complete teetotaler, didn't take a drop. We did. We took drops.

When I said that Catherine moved into my dinky apartment, what I really should have said was that Catherine *and her books* moved in. Immediately after her arrival we had to go shopping for shelves to hold her tidy archive of literature, criticism, and art books. I had my own library, of course, the many bookcases of my canon-dabbling, yet Catherine's modest holdings intimidated me. Open any book of hers—and I did when she went for power walks—and you found practically as many annotations as words, important passages marked and prioritized, in light pencil, with a charming system of stars, one to four. Each book contained a galaxy of stars. Her bookshelf was a tightly packed universe of literary exchange.

While globe-trotting between India, Paris, Berlin, and home, Catherine had sojourned intellectually from art history to high theory. She was no canon-dabbler. There were a number of authors she absolutely loved—Duras, Barthes, Didi-Huberman, Benjamin, Kristeva—and she had read not only their representative work, but most everything they had produced. I was proud of this in her, but I was also mortified. Catherine loved Henry James too. How could that be? *I* loved Henry James. It made me jealous of James because Catherine was supposed to love me, and yet here they were, the two of them, seeming to love each other, and in addition she loved all these other writers as well. She was downright promiscuous with literary relationships! Not that they had interfered with our relationship. As one might expect, the first few months after Catherine moved in were an unadulterated period of adulterating each other in all the ways we could think of.

Which isn't to say it was a perfect time, because we were also in the process of verifying that we were both certifiable. That's what happens when you fall in love. Your sanity falls in love with your beloved's sanity, and you adulterate each other. Then you move in together and realize there's this whole other side to them—their Mr. Hyde, their *in*sanity. My insanity was, as I've already suggested, a deep-rooted negativity that manifested as a tendency to do a whole lot of talking when there wasn't anyone around to listen. I didn't *hear* voices, I spoke them, revising conversations I'd already had, or preparing for conversations I'd not yet had, or, as during a particularly dark time in my life, repeating over and over the absurd phrase "I would like to be assassinated in a violent coup d'état!" The extent of this quirk—I sometimes turned off talk radio so it wouldn't interrupt—didn't become clear until Catherine moved in and I had to start whispering.

Catherine's insanity was intimidatingly literary. Like Madame Psychosis (Joelle Van Dyne) from *Infinite Jest,* which I read shortly after she moved in, Catherine was from Kentucky and had been a beauty queen and a cheerleader—and she was *totally* crazy. She had a perfect storm of perfectionism and workaholism and cockiness and insecurity that left her endlessly busy and productive but perpetually convinced that she wasn't doing enough and wasn't good enough. So as we wandered nights from the wine bar to the vodka bar, it became easy to think of Catherine as my Zelda as well, the neighborhood a kind of miniature Paris, ours less a moveable feast than a stumbling one. When we once watched a Dylan Thomas bi-opic in our dinky apartment—specifically, a scene in which Thomas and his wife, both certifiable, stumble through their front door drunk and laughing—we cried out because *there we were,* the scene could have been filmed a few feet from the television on which we watched it.

But for the most part my read of *U and I* came during good times—there was spring, there was love—and the times were good *because* I was reading *U and I.* That being the case, I rather selfishly ignored the fact that my rebirth came at Nicholson Baker's expense. "This essay is the test of whether I should bother being a writer or not," he wrote, hinting at some deep-rooted malaise of his own.

I finished the book in another day or so. It confirmed a host of suspicions: he *was* Barthelme's student briefly; he *did* go by "Nick"; and he *did* attend Haverford College because of Frank Conroy. Several times I experienced the rare, out-of-time pleasure a reader can feel on glimpsing career-spanning themes that for the writer are just beginning to emerge. For example, when *U and I* fesses up to the young writer's fetish of attempting to elegantly employ ob-scure words, it was, for me, like looking simultaneously through a telescope and a microscope. Baker resurrects "florilegia," a medieval synonym for anthology (though he gets it slightly wrong: "florile-gia" is the plural form, "florilegium" the singular), and in reading the passage in which the word occurs multiple times I thought I could spot *The Anthologist* on the distant horizon while at the same time peering in at minuscule spermlings of influence wriggling a beeline toward me. And even though I hadn't read any of Baker's "sex books" (as I'd heard them described by Baker readers)—*Vox, The Fermata,* and *House of Holes* (which wouldn't appear until

August 2011 but was already getting mentioned on websites for publishing insiders)—I thought I could see them beginning to take shape as *U and I* described the thinking of writers who incorporated sex into their work: "'My overemphasis on sex is leading me back toward subtler revelations in the novel's traditional arena of social behavior, by jingo!'" *U and I* references a canonical bevy of influences (e.g., Pater, Proust, Nabokov, Murdoch, Trollope, Arnold, etc.), but apart from the suggestive title it never even mentions Martin Buber. Nevertheless, I stand by my assertion. If Nicholson Baker hadn't read *I and Thou*, then he'd been remotely influenced by it in the same way I'd been remotely influenced by *U and I.*

The book's pleasures aside, a couple things did bother me about *U and I,* and it was just when Baker turned to James's water metaphor to guide his own meandering course—"the trembly idiosyncratic paths each of us may trace in the wake of the route that the idea of Updike takes . . ."—that I felt myself nudge up against a pair of logs jamming my own stream of Baker thought. First, his mother. *U and I* is as much about Baker's mother as it is about Updike. It's dedicated to her (*"For My Mother"*), and some of Baker's earliest memories of Updike are of his mother laughing uproariously at Updike passages that the young Nicholson can't yet appreciate. In fact, Updike becomes the apparatus that Baker's mother uses to figuratively wean her son from the maternal bosom. Yet many years later, when Baker tells his mother that he's going to write a book about Updike, he ignores her advice. She says that in order to do a respectable job of it, he would need to go back and reread all of Updike. Baker shrinks at this and claims that what "comes to mind" when he thinks of Updike is of more value than what he might "summon to mind."

That was log one. Log two was structure. Early in the book, Baker claims that he already thinks of Updike as an imaginary friend ("I *am* friends with Updike"), but that doesn't stop him from structuring the rest of the book, everything after the stream of consciousness revelation, around three attempts to actually befriend Updike. None of these encounters is particularly satisfying, not even one late in the book that finds the charmingly boyish Baker at tending an Updike book signing with his sweet mother on his arm. *U and I* ends with a suggestion that Updike based a fictional character on one of these clumsy Baker self-introductions. "And that's all the imaginary friendship I need." The end.

Not for me. My gentle feeling of logjam eventually morphed into an impulse to level a criticism or two. And that, perhaps not coincidentally, is what *U and I* tends to do whenever Baker isn't plotting to make sure that Updike knows that he and Baker are "fellow contributors" to *The New Yorker*. Indeed, what mostly "comes" to Baker about Updike is things that annoy him. For example, he has little affection for Updike's "queasy adolescent heroes," nor is he taken with Updike's having signed on to the self-flattering notion that writers have a heightened "capacity to lie." Baker forgives a palpable mean streak in Updike, but feels indicted when Updike complains that literary streams of thought are too often "clogged" with asides and diversions. "The only thing I *like* are the clogs," Baker writes. He describes *The Mezzanine* as having been "a veritable infarct of narrative cloggers."

But most important is that the thing that comes to Baker's mind most *naturally* when he thinks of Updike is not Updike's fiction at all, but his writing about literature. And Baker does not laud Updike's writing about literature. Quite the opposite. Even though it was Updike who offered the now-canonical advice that all prose should be written "ecstatically," Updike's writing about literature was anything but. "This pronouncement," Baker writes, "ought to hold good for critical prose as well—and yet if I can force myself to utter a fixed doubt about Updike, it is paradoxically that he isn't ecstatic and immoderate enough about the writers he loves."

U and I takes the Updike advice that Updike ignored. It's an ecstatic, immoderate, even inebriated book. But in the end, I was left less drunk than clogged. Like me, Baker feels "scorn" for traditional literary criticism, and he feels compelled to chart a new course. He names his new critical method—the method of no method—*memory criticism,* and after his initial lists of partly recalled quotations he tries to remember a whole bunch more Updike passages. Once he finished the book, he looked up all the actual quotations and inserted the correct quotes, bracketed, in the text. So what you wind up reading, really, is Nicholson Baker discovering again and again that memory criticism fails. He flubs quotations, overlooks vast stretches of the oeuvre, and by the end he's awash in bracketed self-doubt:

[. . . What is wrong with me?]

Good question! That might have made a good book.

It's probably clear by now that I was no longer playfully bumping up against the logs that clogged my Baker stream. No—I was maniacally pounding against them. "That's insane," I said to myself, out loud, every time Baker tried and failed to remember another Updike passage. I was just as annoyed by the try-to-meet-Updike tactic. True, I had met Salter, and I was happy to have done so because of his saintly off-page presence. But that was luck. My long-held suspicion is that ever since Dickens came to America for his groundbreaking reading tour in 1867, literature has been on a steady slouch away from actual reading. If the point of books is only to befriend authors, then why read them when you can just walk down the street and meet them? Baker was right to say that books offered imaginary friendships, but don't they need to *remain* imaginary? Just go to the reading! Just get the book signed! This was pretty much directly related to my crisis: Books, it seems to me, are inching closer and closer to ontological obsolescence, to *not needing to be.* The "best" books these days—from a publishing perspective—are not books that need to be books, books that require the passion of a serious reader to complete them. They are books that transmute seamlessly to film. The impulse to meet an author before you've read their work is a close relative of the dreaded phrase "I'll wait for the movie," and these days it's perfectly reasonable to speculate that the book, the codex, might prove in the end to have been little more than a deceleration in storytelling's fall from epic poem to Hollywood epic.

Of course, I was thinking all this because I'd begun to wonder whether embarking on my Nicholson Baker project meant that I should try to meet him. Of course not. We're already in love, goddammit! What could I possibly hope to consummate with a live meeting that couldn't be consummated with a good book fuck? I was glad I'd been out of town when Nicholson Baker was creeping around our city, peddling his wares. That would have ruined everything, because there was no way Nicholson Baker could have successfully followed onto the stage a sparkling off-page presence like James Salter. I would have seen him, and thought, "What a chump! I'll never read *that* book." And I never would have lunged for *U and I* and been saved as a result. It was then that I resolved to never sully my deep-felt unconditional passion for Nicholson Baker by actually encountering him.

Having made this ironclad resolution, I calmed down enough to recognize that my public display of affection for a beloved writer had twisted into a public display of annoyance. I'd prematurely come full circle. I'd once been annoyed by what Nicholson Baker seemed to be hiding, and now I was annoyed by what he'd revealed. How did Nicholson Baker and I suddenly become that couple who snarl and spit at each other in public, in full view of strangers? *"Quit whining, Nicholson Baker!"* I whispered, when Catherine was nearby and might hear me. *"Everything you write should be a test of whether you should be a writer!"* Maybe it was the hubris that got to me. I mean, Baker was all of thirty-two years of age and he had the gall to imagine what attending Updike's funeral would be like, and then to speculate on what he might say when *The Paris Review* got around to interviewing him. And it all happened! Even before I read *U and I,* Baker spoke at Updike's funeral—became his actual friend, in the end—and I'd heard that there was a *Paris Review* interview in the works, too. I was actually grateful for the interview, because it meant I'd soon have access to the "interview of record," but was that really all you had to do to get interviewed by *The Paris Review*? Say they should interview you? Well, me too!

That was actually my greatest fear, assuming that my Nicholson Baker project was on its way to becoming a book about Nicholson Baker: it would be dismissed as a *me too* book. For what it's worth, Baker fears the same thing in *U and I*: he reminds himself that he can't do only what Frederick Exley did in *Pages from a Cold Island.* Baker must "take the next step." Taking the next step was even harder for me, though, because I had already anthologized some of the writers who had taken the next step on Baker. I had to take the next step on them, too.

All this annoyance wound up being tempered by a single redemptive thought. No one was sitting around trying to figure out how to turn *U and I* into a movie. Evaluated with that rubric, *U and I* is a terrible book. But it was just this kind of book, I reminded myself, a naked, throbbing-ego book that drives insane your own throbbing ego—outrage is a *form* of arousal—that absolutely needs to be a book. Or to put it slightly differently, if we really mean *love* when we say that we love an author, then the story that we tell of that love cannot limit itself to the erotic first flush of the relationship, to simple lust, it must include too that which it might be uncomfortable to consider, the spats, the snarling, and the spitting. What did I have to tell Nicholson Baker? We can't just remember books. No, memory criticism overlooks the fact that the innovation of the book was the invention of the ability to reread, to research. Reading becomes a craft and an art only as a function of our ability to look things up—again. If all anyone were ever to do was remember books, then that's what we would all wind up doing, remembering the once important tool of human thought, the book.

12

IT WAS THEN THAT MY STUDY OF NICHOLSON BAKER LOLLED into a state of hibernation, a painful period of waiting that lasted almost a year. I taught a lot and wrote a little, and Catherine made many photographs in our bathroom and left the book-editing business where she'd worked for six years and launched her own even more successful business, and we waited without knowing we were waiting. It was during this time that I finally read *A Lover's Discourse,* which is about waiting.

A Lover's Discourse is a quicker, sexier version of *I and Thou.* It reads less like Buber's sullen theologian gravely sermonizing from the ship-prow pulpit of his mind than like a series of absinthe-soaked aphorisms sorrowfully blurted by a hip scholar out drinking way too late with his students. Both books boil away at love, and both attempt to brew a medicine up to the task of curing the

alienation of modern civilization. What's Barthes's solution? Waiting. Waiting, he writes, is a delicious suspension between "languor"
and "satyr."

Didn't I know it. It was only a short time after Catherine moved
in that a peculiar dynamic of waiting evolved between us. Whenever
we decided to go someplace—for oysters, say—we each embarked
on separate sets of prejourney preparations and rituals that had initially formed before we were together. In performing these, neither
of us wanted to finish first, to be the one "ready to go." There were
two reasons for this: one, once we were ready to go we would have
nothing left to do but sit there and wait; and two, once we were left
sitting and waiting, all we would be able to do was sigh heavily and
fidget so that our partner would feel rushed and pressured through
their prejaunt ablutions. Our solution to this caused only deeper
problems. Rather than sit and wait, whenever one of us broke down
and was ready to go, we would embark on a time-killing activity
of some kind that looked exactly like an essential procedure. For
example, if Catherine needed to pee before we walked out the door,
I would sit down and begin playing a game of chess on my laptop.
When she was done peeing, Catherine would see me stuck deep in
thought and begin futzing with her Mamiya, looking quite intent.
Game completed and not wanting to interrupt her photographic
work, I would find a news story that would hold my interest well
past the moment when she was finished futzing. And so on.

Finally, one of us would say, "Are you ready?"

"Yes, I've been waiting for you."

"No, you haven't. You were doing something, you looked busy."

"I was killing time."

"So was I."

"You always do that."

"*You* always do that."

Waiting, in other words, was the way in which our relative insanities stood in wary regard of each other. When these scenes did not descend into battles that caused us to abandon our plans completely, Barthes helped to explain them. He explained our orgasms too. He had a lot to say about gifts and giving—"The amorous gift is sought out, selected, and purchased in the greatest excitement—the kind of excitement which seems to be of the order of orgasm"—and by the time of our year of waiting, Catherine had thoughtfully given me so many Nicholson Baker books I'd become multiply orgasmic. Catherine was not so lucky. It was during this time of waiting that her orgasms began to trouble her. One day we sat down to talk about them. It wasn't that they were either absent or unsatisfying. Quite the opposite. As we'd gone about adulterating each other, Catherine's orgasms had become more and more intense, had grown by orders of magnitude, and now, seismically speaking, they were eruptive, volcanic orgasms, orgasms in which every one of her pores seemed to open up and ejaculate. They were less screaming orgasms than *streaming* orgasms, orgasms of roof joist–shattering intensity, orgasms that did, in fact—because we traveled a fair bit during the year of waiting—damage the structural integrity of an untold number of bed and breakfasts all across the Midwest, and at least one in New Hampshire, all of them classic robber baron–style mansions, some made of stone, and each needing to be reassessed for insurance purposes after we left. These were the orgasms causing her stress. The stress was this: What if she stopped having them?

I spied the literary analogy in this at once. That was the problem with reading, one of the many problems of life as a serious reader. Literature tends to excite as a function of driving the imagination forward, consistently getting better and better. But what happens when you read a book that produces a heretofore-unimaginable spew of ego-escaping thrill? These books, *great* books, cause as much stress as they relieve because they raise the bar for every book that follows them, and once you've read a really great book, you naturally start to worry that you've peaked. It will never again be quite so good. Of course, I didn't mention this to Catherine as we imagined the end of her orgasms. Instead, I called on Barthes. "'I perceive *an infatuation of being,*'" I quoted, "'which is not so far from what Sade would have called *an effervescence of countenance* ("I saw the sperm shooting from his eyes"). . . . '" Or maybe I only poorly summarized this, because for Catherine it sounded way too much like something we'd glimpsed while watching pornography together: men masturbating themselves and ejaculating on women's faces. Catherine always flinched and turned away at this, and in my sessions of prescreenings of *possible* porn for us to watch, I'd had to enforce a deal-breaker rule on this particular encounter-ending trope. That was fine with me as I'd much rather watch people kiss and embrace as they come, or maybe occasionally watch a man spill onto a woman's stomach or breasts. Catherine seemed to agree on this point, though it didn't prevent her, whenever we mistakenly glimpsed a so-called "glazed" face, from shooting her Sade-like gaze directly at me, as though my simply being male made me an accomplice to the crime and perhaps an adequate scapegoat for whatever Hammurabi-style punishment might restore justice to an unfair universe. But thankfully, and generously, Catherine said nothing in reply to my stray Barthes summary. Perhaps she could tell I already regretted it, and I'm sure she knew that I, more than anyone, hoped her orgasms would continue indefinitely.

In all this I could sniff a coming storm. The storm that would arrive when the year of waiting was over. It was during this time that I did a little online searching to see whether Updike had ever responded to having been the subject of *U and I*. He had, in an awkward interview. Updike praised *U and I* (he had anonymously reviewed it too on its release, though I didn't learn this until much later) and he recognized that it was "not exactly about [him]." But he took a swipe at Baker anyway: "The nerds of the world buy Baker." His most curious reaction came in response to *The Fermata*. "It was pretty fierce," he said, "fiercer than anything you'll find in any of my fictions. Some of those sex scenes (laughs)   wiping your sperm out of a woman's eyelashes is kind of . . . new."

This infuriated me. Wasn't that what writers were supposed to do? Make it new? And was it really new to Updike, or was he chuckling ("(laughs)") because he suspected that Nicholson Baker had only ever imagined wiping sperm from women's eyelashes while Updike himself had been glazing housewives for decades? I doubted it. It was new to Updike either because he'd never had a good Internet connection, or because he was unable to recognize how Baker was taking the next step on *him*. I was happy that my subject, Nicholson Baker, was quite possibly the only writer to have ever made John Updike blanch. Yet as thrilled as I was, I was fearful of what might happen to Catherine and me when I finally read *The Fermata*.

13

IN *U AND I,* WHEN BAKER SETTLES IN TO HIS PLAN TO WRITE something about Updike, his first order of business is to phone a magazine editor and pitch an idea for a longish article to be called "U and I." The editor worries that that "U and I" sounds a little creepy. Baker muscles out a contract anyway. He produced the piece, but it was too long—it was destined to become *U and I*— and the magazine wound up publishing only a fifteen-hundred-word excerpt, the scene that concludes with Baker's streaming William James revelation.

Similarly, it was during the year of waiting that I decided I was writing *B & Me,* and that I'd been writing it for some time. But I didn't call an editor—I called my agent instead. I liked my agent. He was a good guy, and we had done some excellent things together. And I liked calling him, because he generally answered his phone—which is rare for agents these days. Oddly, my agent did not answer his phone on this occasion, even though I took care to call during regular business hours. Generally, my agent picked up shortly after the second ring, as though his phone sat near at hand, but he wished neither to appear too eager by picking up after the first ring, nor risk a hang-up by waiting for the third. But this time he didn't answer at all. I had to leave a message. In publishing jargon, this meant I had a call "in" to him. There was nothing more to be done. I had to wait.

That's what I mean about a period of waiting. These days writers must wait not only for the arrival of their fickle muse, they must wait for editors and agents to "get back" to them. Of course editors and agents are waiting too, for marketing people and publicists and the art department, and it's a practically impossible situation with everyone being so busy. A writer's only real hope is that all those he waits for, even his muse, check their voice mail regularly and that everyone's schedules are not already so clogged as to make impossible the kind of cosmic conference call that might result in something actually getting done.

When my call happened—actually an e-mail—I discovered that my muse and my agent had begun to grow apart. They'd lost that loving feeling. In all honesty, it was the agent more than the muse who had strayed. A long exchange ensued. I did more than my share of groveling on behalf of the good and wise Nicholson Baker, but I managed only a light chink in the shiny armor of the profit motive. My agent claimed that I was being difficult for suggesting that a book ostensibly about Nicholson Baker might prove to be "commercial" if it was done right. He hit a sour and slightly poignant note when he admitted that he spent his whole life watching publishing houses reject books as not commercial enough when they were a million times more commercial than a book about the state of modern literature as viewed through the lens of a "mildly successful novelist." The unavoidable conclusion was that my agent had come to believe that I should write what publishers already believed was commercial, rather than try to convince publishers of the possible commercial value of a book that needed to be written, a book that, as publishers liked to say, I was "born to write."

So I fired my agent. Which was both a relief and a delay. More waiting! After several weeks of hyperventilation and a frantic search for a new agent, I began to grow accustomed to the bizarre sensation of free fall that is agentlessness. At first the impact of rock bottom seemed only a second or two away, but then I stopped panicking and realized that I was actually in a kind of orbit: falling, yes, but happily floating, and after a time a kind of weird peace came over me, a whooshing glimmer of what it might be like to not pursue a serious literary life. Then I got an e-mail. An agent said she loved my writing. And even better, after a perfunctory courtship and the formal launch of a new agent-writer relationship, she disappeared. Perfect! Now I had a serious agent, one so busy attending conferences and nurturing professional relationships that she had no time to take my calls or work on what would become the book proposal for *B & Me: A True Story of Literary Arousal*.

Before she vanished, my agent and I agreed that our proposal—the business plan of *B & Me*—would amount to the Holy Grail of nonfiction book proposals. For the same reasons it's widely believed that teachers of literature and writing ought to be versed in their subjects before they walk in the classroom, so is it generally held that writers should acquire a significant body of foundational knowledge on the topics they propose to write books about. The proposal for *B & Me* would say little more than "I will write a book of some kind about a noncanonical author I haven't yet read." Try making that sound like a winner! I was anxious to begin—I couldn't wait, though wait was just what I was going to do—but my agent wasn't anxious in the least because she knew that if we were going to have any chance at all, we had to wait until the fall. So with my best interests at heart she ignored me for the entire summer.

14

WHICH TURNED OUT TO BE OKAY, BECAUSE CATHERINE AND I HAD to move. This had been our plan for a while now. We'd been keeping our ears to the rails, on the lookout for better working conditions (better pay and graduate students), and during the year of waiting we kept most of our belongings wrapped up in figurative kerchiefs and remained poised to break into a sprint along the tracks at the first sight of an engine that might let us hoist ourselves to a better fate. But when a locomotive came belching around the bend, we hesitated: It wasn't clear whether the train was chugging toward better pastures or purgatory. It looked like the latter. We spent dispiriting evenings soaring through low-res satellite imagery of the new land's real estate listings. Local architecture was a desiccated extrapolation of the brutal dirtscape. The new state was shaped like a butcher knife, and imagining living there was an ongoing nightmare of that fat, jagged blade chopping off our fingers, one by one. In literary terms, we would move—if we moved—from Fitzgeralds to Joads. Even the diplomatic hardship post we once contemplated pursuing to spring ourselves from academia seemed a tonic by comparison.

Then we stumbled on a buried treasure: a one-hundred-and-twenty-five-year-old farmhouse for rent a few miles south of the university that offered me a job. The place had an *actual* pasture, populated with a menagerie of retired petting zoo animals—a fleet of miniature donkeys, a duet of hypercompetitive goats, a pig obese even by the forgiving standard of "potbellied"—and beyond the rail-posted property there were rolling fields, some woods, and a lake the size of a small airport. The house itself had antique hardwood, warping pocket doors, and an extra room for what Catherine called her "chemistry," the toxic chemicals that had blinded or driven insane many early photographers. All this for a fraction of what we paid for our dinky apartment, the apartment whose heat we didn't control, whose laundry was four stories down, and whose lone bathroom sometimes, after a long drive, left us racing down the hallway, arguing over which of us had the greater need to "go." Best of all—and this sealed the deal—the farmhouse, until a year or two past, had been a functioning bed and breakfast.

We needed a bed and breakfast by then. The year of waiting had been a year of slowly growing resentments, of tensions tiny as germs slipping in through unprotected ducts. The wait for the official sanction to write about Nicholson Baker left me surly and exhausted, in as deep a state of crisis as the crisis from which it was supposed to rescue me. The anxiety of not yet being able to begin the book that would improve my negative mood left me floundering in a pessimism that caused Catherine, too, to wilt. It's possible to liken literary relationships, which are temporary in nature, to real romance because real romance—to invert the metaphor—is subject to the same sorts of fluctuations of arousal that we might feel when a book takes a wrong turn. Real passions flutter too, can even be snuffed out like the brief candle of the agent-writer relationship. That's what happened to Catherine and me: We'd begun to flicker like a flame in high winds. Where once we had slyly chuckled at other couples around bed and breakfast morning tables—couples tethered by children rather than love, couples whose only intimacy came at orchestrated annual retreats—we now found ourselves similarly blighted. One night, just before we moved, we noticed that it had not happened overnight. At first the lull had been easy to dismiss as just that: a sacrifice as I taught and dedicated reading time to Roberto Bolaño's *2666* and William Gass's *The Tunnel,* and as Catherine furiously printed images and fielded an endless influx of editing work. Initially, the nondaily couplings had a palpable upside in that there was the heightened intensity of having waited for it, the backup of fluids resulting in more satisfying discharges, just as a kink in a garden hose builds a pressure that makes for a more profound stream once the kink is removed. The problem did not make itself apparent until nondaily lagged into weekly, and weekly frittered away into biweekly, and when I say problem what I really mean is that the body is smarter than a garden hose, which under pressure finds its weakest spot and dumbly bulges there until it ruptures. Rather than this, rather than burst, what the body does is recognize that something has interrupted the flow of supply and demand, business is down, and what do you do when business is down? You slow production, cut a shift, and lay off the part-time help. *We* slowed production.

The correlate to reading here is only too familiar. Irrepressibly hectic modern life, the multitasking that makes us feel efficient even as studies indicate compromised performance, the resulting exhaustion that is the by-product of modernity and that is colored with the paints of an ever-expanding palette of diagnoses (e.g., hysteria, neuralgia, melancholia, anhedonia, repression, depression,

ADHD, chronic fatigue, etc.)—who in the face of all this would
think to invest in the slow-growth stock of reading? Why read when
you can buy short and day-trade? And reading was something else
Catherine and I had sacrificed. When she first moved in we read
together often; it was practically foreplay. We read all of *The Lover*
to each other, which is a less sexy book than you'd think but which
is still quite wonderful, and we read portions of Grégoire Bouillier
and *Bonjour Tristesse,* and I read to her sections from Gass ("Books
made me masturbate!"—exclamation mine), and the part of *2666*
in which two men in Dracula's castle masturbate to the peephole
view of the coupling of Baroness Von Zumpe and General En-
trescu, whose foot-long cock is the pride of the Romanian army. We
stopped doing that, we stopped reading together—and just as with
our coupling, it was less guillotined than trailed off. At first, we had
traded reading back and forth, but after some months it became
clear that Catherine enjoyed being read to more than she enjoyed
reading, which was fine because I enjoyed reading. It was similar to
talking to myself. But what I was probably doing was staving off the
pain of not reading Nicholson Baker by making Catherine listen
to works that gave full-throated voice to my poisonous negativity.
So of course she began to lose interest, and soon enough our sessions became less and less frequent. When I would tentatively ask
whether Catherine might like to read together this evening, when
I made a "pass" at her in this way, her face would droop and her
shoulders would collapse as though constricted by a straitjacket.
No, tonight she just wanted to shut down, turn *off.* Couldn't we
just watch a movie or something? Of course we can, my sweet, my
love. We snuggled before the screen of my laptop. I told myself
that we'd never be one of those couples who took up sentry posts
on either end of oversized sofas, but even though we twined our
limbs together there grew a film—*film*—between us, and this film

instructed our bodies to hold their horses, stop the presses. We traded streaming orgasms for streaming video. Instead of porn that inspired us to coupling, we watched movie stars who coupled *for* us. Catherine's secretions, which had come from her like the full-body poisons of jungle frogs, stopped entirely, and I shut down too, and started to worry that my cock was the pride of no army, nor a battalion, nor a platoon, nor even some lowly private.

So the former bed and breakfast offered the promise of renewal. It also enabled us to commit to Paris for the holidays, which would give me a chance to settle an old score with myself and give Catherine a chance to relive the days when she had been serially engaged to enough Frenchmen that conversations about them required the plural form: "the fiancés." Actually, Catherine had begun saving money for the trip months before she agreed to chase me into the waste, and what the waste really enabled was my tagging along, which I was thrilled to do because by then I knew—from his *Paris Review* interview, which was published during the year of waiting— that Nicholson Baker had spent time in Paris too. I planned to read his sex books there.

15

WASTE IT SURELY SEEMED WHEN IN A FLASH OUR MOVE WAS OVER. I'd visited the new land in January, when the place was merely postapocalyptic; by July it was the circle of hell reserved for conservative politicians and armadillos. Driving south we marveled when the car's thermometer ticked past one hundred degrees—in a month it would twitch up to one hundred and seventeen. We drifted through an endless diorama of garbage and roadkill, streaking past bloody visions of skunks, turtles, and domestic cats caught midstride and dissected on the highway as though truckers swerved their rigs at night for sport. The Junkyard of America, Catherine called it, there being so much space here that when something was used up or broken— a car, a barn—the best option was to leave it there and plow around it. There were actual junkyards too, as common as diners in New Jersey, great mountains of rusting metal fed upon by Jurassic cranes, and it was all oil land, the country's pipeline crossroads meeting just a few miles east, the hard earth seemingly pounded to its rocky crust by the mallet heads of seesawing derricks erected on every spare plot. It all would have been wonderful for Catherine's photography if only she didn't rightly worry that images of the poor and forlorn were a form of victim exploitation. Anyway, we were the victims.

The former bed and breakfast *was* a buried treasure in that after we arrived we had to dig it up. Everything was caked with a century's worth of petrified earth. Okay, that's going a bit too far—but what doesn't go too far is that the former bed and breakfast turned out to be a nexus of plagues. The first was simply heat, July setting a record for the hottest month of any state in recorded history. Next were slugs, phalanxes of gummy, thumb-sized worms with prehensile eyestalks that happily breached the century-old floor and fanned out across the kitchen. Then there were tornadoes, a mile off, pruning forests and swiping away the roofs of houses. Flash fires hopscotched the nearby countryside, and forty yards from the kitchen window a bolt of lightning etched a self-portrait along the trunk of a weary old oak. Fracking earthquakes, the result of chthonic greed, concussed the land from below and cracked the farmhouse drywall. It's clear, I hope, that I'm collapsing weeks and months here, but I don't really have to: in October, we crouched together behind the sofa during a tornado watch until the greenish eye-of-the-storm stillness was broken not by gentle rain, but by aftershocks cast down by an angry god, doubly jealous.

We tried bucking our spirits with humor. Where once, back in our dinky apartment, we had made serene proclamations like "How about we visit the local internationally renowned museum of modern art!" and "Let's grab a gourmet beer at our walkable neighborhood's friendly pub!" we now pushed through our teeth halfhearted one-liners like "Honey, I'm taking the trash to the burn pit!" and "Let's brave the blistering heat to hand-feed the llamas!" I've probably made the former bed and breakfast sound remote, but a recently expanded four-lane highway with a national reputation for vehicular death lay only seventy yards from the porch, and just a quarter-mile off stood a forward operating base of the imperial army of sprawl. I took most of this in stride—I had to, it was my job and my idea—but for Catherine it wasn't so easy. In August I seized on a stray remark she made about Cole Porter and ordered a sampler collection so that I could woo her with "Too Darn Hot." But not only was it too darn hot for such a wooing, I played the song too darn loud while Catherine was trying to get some work done. Anyway, she meant Nat King Cole. Catherine was left stricken, splattered with the many colors of sadness, a regular Pollock of modernity by-products, and all that dried paint, fired to a crust in the kiln of our new home, left her paralyzed, *clogged.*

Our landlord, a gentle Vietnam vet who told us stories of close combat with pythons (and who, in teaching me the operation of the farm's riding mower, admitted that its controls reminded him of the tank he had steered over the bodies of Viet Cong soldiers), gambled that a pair of kittens recruited as mousers for the farm might salve our general sense of trauma. The kittens charmed us but had to contend with their own lineup of plagues: the heat, a different species of worm, and coyotes that put me in mind of the allegorical dog packs that wander the plague summer of Kenneth Patchen's *The Journal of Albion Moonlight*. Jackals in all but name, the coyotes swarmed the hills around the farm, their howls like the battle cries of some lunatic clan. They did not descend to the former bed and breakfast until one night when the power failed. They took one kitten with them, and the other climbed onto the roof and stayed there for months.

That's when Nicholson Baker's *House of Holes* was released in hardcover.

16

HOUSE OF HOLES BEGINS WITH A HOLE AND ENDS WITH ONE, A grave and a womb respectively. Or more accurately, it begins with a disembodied arm disinterring itself at a site where granite is quarried for tombstones, and it ends with two miniature people completing a gestation inside a magical egg. In saying this I am breaking the implied pact of this book, which is that in really reading a writer what you should do is start with their earliest work and move through their career, as they did. But of course that's not always possible. Most of the time, it's safe to say, we land at a midpoint in a writer's career, and that's no more a sin than flipping to the end of a book to see how it all turns out. Indeed it's only in books—actual printed books—that you can easily start and stop your reading, that you can preread and reread, and, these days, as the book itself suffers from a cluster of plagues, it seems only right to pause and assert that the books that ought to be rescued these days are not the books that require a "spoiler alert"—such books are already spoiled—but books that aren't spoiled even if you know what's going to happen, even if you peek at the end, even if you're reading them for a second, or fifth, or dozenth time.

Of course, I had practical reasons for reading out of order. I was writing a book proposal. Even as I was striving to maintain my Nicholson Baker innocence, I had to figure out how to appeal to an audience of editors who, due to the thigh-high stacks of other book proposals beside their desks, all equally deserving of attention, were likely cynical. So, first, I skimmed *The Anthologist* on our porch swing. The heat was terribly fierce, average daytime temperatures were hovering around one hundred and nine degrees, and a great orchestra of insects lurked in the grass and shade trees, sawing their bowlegs. It wasn't all that long before I spotted William James peeking out from Nicholson Baker yet again. The narrator of *The Anthologist,* Paul Chowder, says, "The thing about life is that life is an infinite subject matter. At any one moment you can say only what's before your mind just then." This is a slightly diluted version of another quotable James moment, when James refutes Herbert Spencer and insists that thought is not only reflexive, but subject to will: "My experience is what I agree to attend to. Only those items which I notice shape my mind—without selective interest, experience is an utter chaos." I closed *The Anthologist* at once.

Next I read *House of Holes,* under quite different circumstances. I had been following the press coverage of the release—the "splash"—for a while, and when fall rolled around my agent insisted that our proposal should at least touch on what I might say about the book. So one day I drove to a bookstore and bought a first edition. When I got home I found Catherine crammed in on one end of the sofa, studying scanned negatives on her computer. I sat at the other end and started reading, silently. *House of Holes* is a series of improbable erotic scenes that play out at a slightly fantastic commune called the House of Holes. Thinly drawn characters from regular life find themselves magically atomized and sucked down into everyday sorts of holes—pen tips, straws, pepper grinders—and then they are reconstituted on the campus of what the book's reviewers called a "sexual utopia," though none of them mentioned the fact that Baker had grown up in Rochester, New York, just a stone's throw from Oneida, the *real* sexual utopia. Quite obviously, I thought, the book continued *The Anthologist*'s interest in the work of the mind: To get to the House of Holes, characters have to transcend rigid mental states, "fwoosh" to "off-limits" "mind-zones" where they can express true consciousness.

But it's also a book about come faces. Baker had come a long way since *The Fermata.* An alarming number of scenes in *House of Holes* end in come faces, or with women shrieking to be soaked in come. Critically speaking, this was both exciting and troubling. Might Baker be rubbing Updike's face in it, as it were? One of the very first characters in *House of Holes* is an Updikian golfer-type who gets sucked down through the pin of a golf course's seventh hole. This character is not named Rabbit, nor is he given features that resemble Updike's, but the link was there to be made, I thought. This was troubling because I made the link while sitting directly opposite Catherine, whose distaste for the whole come-face idea made her quite possibly the worst potential reader for *House of Holes.* So I said nothing of it. But soon enough that was a problem too, because *House of Holes,* like *U and I* and all good literature, understood that its job was to trigger physiological change in its readers. It might have been any of a whole clutch of chuckles, groans, and strategic leg shiftings to disguise arousal that left me needing to offer Catherine an explanation with a quote from the book.

"'All you need for good porn is a pretty smiley woman who's having fun, and a dude with a hard dick who isn't fat.'"

I didn't look at Catherine as I recited this line. What if she didn't find it funny? What if it didn't plunge her out of her cloggedness? It was a moment that could go either way, when the struggling ember of our love might vanish into a wispy tendril of smoke.

"That's so . . . perfect!" she said.

I kept reading and twisting in my seat and shrugging my shoulders until she couldn't really concentrate on her work.

"Well, are you going to share?"

"'She sat splaylegged on the blanket, and Dave brought out his massive, porn-maddened spunk-spewer.'"

Before describing Catherine's reaction to this, I should make the argument that even though *House of Holes* is mostly pornographic—in his splash of interviews Baker insisted that he didn't mind it being labeled such—it does concern itself with a higher set of ideas. But even saying this in this way causes problems. Modern literature lacks a decent metaphor to describe works of ambition. "Higher purpose" smacks of elitism, and "deeper meaning" sounds about as thrilling as embalming a puppy. Other metaphors are contradictory. A work that "makes you think" forbids you the comfortable state of not thinking, just as a book you "can't put down" denies free will. "Heavy-handed" prose annoys us even as we long for that which is "heavy" in significance. Even pornography turns you "on" to get you "off." So what to do with a work subtitled "a book of raunch" that takes pains to align itself with the history of utopian thought? Baker himself called on Henry James—of course!—to describe the writing of the book. In his *Paris Review* interview, he claimed that certain scenes required the same gender-swapping talent James mastered in writing from the perspective of women. And it's women, actually, who give voice to what wisdom *House of Holes* has to offer. Around page twenty or so, Lila, the House of Holes's colorful madam (the Margaret Fuller of Brook Farm, the Zenobia of Hawthorne's *The Blithedale Romance*), warns a resident-applicant to "Be honest. So few people are able to tell the truth." The book, then, and perhaps all works of ambition, may be said to be about the difficulty of telling the truth. I'll go a step farther. These days, few people are able to *hear* the truth. That's why sometimes we react to truth with both awe and disbelief, as though this true thing we've just heard is something we've long known but failed to recognize until now. The joy literature provides is the joy of discovering what was always inside us, à la Naipaul, a joy tempered by regret that we've lived this long denying it, just waiting for someone with the spirit and industry to say it. That pretty much describes Catherine's reaction to Baker's spunk-spewer. She laughed a laugh that slowly slackened to a look of fragile illness. She smiled involuntarily. Her eyes assented while her head wagged slowly back and forth. She turned back to her computer, but her attention was now divided. She was of more than one mind.

That was just the beginning, the beginning that started when I brought home the Holy Grail of nonfiction book proposals and could no longer be said to be preoccupied with Nicholson Baker because now I was *occupied* with him. Catherine was too, in a way. One afternoon she gave me her particular look and said, "How about you read me a little Nicholson Baker?"

Hallelujah! We'd weathered all the plagues and bad weather. "Sure, I'll give you a little Nicholson Baker," I said, which caused her only to stiffen and insist that we were not going to start referring to my cock as Nicholson Baker.

Fair enough. The important thing was that we were reading together again. Which was itself a little dangerous, because was it wise, really, to share your literary arousal with an intimate partner? Buber would have been suspicious; Barthes would have said go for it. In any event, that was not my main concern once we climbed up to the bedroom. I hurriedly leafed through *House of Holes,* searching for a non-come-face scene. No easy task. It wasn't like I'd been annotating for that the first time around. It didn't matter, though, because we didn't get to the end of the scene I chose before Catherine said okay, that's enough, and got up to put on some nice music. And, in fact, the way we wound up reading *House of Holes* was not so terribly different from how Baker once said *he* reads: "I'm fickle; I don't finish books I start; I put a book aside for five, ten years and then take it up again."

17

BUT THAT'S NOT WHAT I'M GOING TO DO WITH NICHOLSON BAKER. Or at least I intend to do something more than use *House of Holes* as a healing sex manual. That said, it was a direct result of Catherine and me being in bed together that I started reading *The Mezzanine*.

There's a long-standing link between beds and storytelling—the bedtime story—and, at first glance, it might not seem particularly fruitful to ask how or why storytelling first came to be used as a sleep aid for children. Yet at the same time, we've all heard that the most familiar of bedtime stories, fairy tales, weren't originally meant for children at all, and the dubious claim that most fairy tales are really about sex is practically a fairy tale itself. Reading bedtime stories to children is a curious practice in general, because stories require conflict, there needs to be something happening, and presumably this is the kind of thing you'd rather stick around and see resolved than nod off and miss. The mother of all fairy tales makes the point: Good stories kiss us awake. It would seem then that the art of the modern children's story would be to produce a story that has a recognizable conflict but that does not risk being so arousing that a child would prefer listening to it to zonking out.

Once we grow up we reject this completely. As adults, the worst thing we can say of a book is that it put us to sleep. But where do we keep books when they're in queue to be read or consulted? On the nightstand—just as I'd done with my copy of *U and I*. Trained from youth to associate books with bed, even serious readers read with the hope that stories will ferry them from consciousness to unconsciousness. We thus stack the deck against books' success. We're ready for bed, we've called it a day, but heaven forfend a book should actually put us to sleep.

Before I read *The Mezzanine*—and I should stipulate that it wasn't when I was trying to go to sleep that I began reading it, it was in the middle of the night after I'd woken up and could not *return* to sleep—I'd already come to realize that sleep, children's stories, and zipping in and out of consciousness were repeating themes in Nicholson Baker's career. Beginning right around the time of his William James revelation, Baker had a period of working short, as they say. In the early eighties, he published a handful of stories and essays. This neat batch of work, which I've now read, wholly supports my thesis about Baker and the James brothers. For example Henry James's early stories, which mine his era's new thinking on thinking, display inordinate interest in altered consciousness and frequently depict characters moving in and out of ordinary consciousness—waking and falling asleep. Similarly, Baker's early stories, one each printed in *The New Yorker* and *The Atlantic* (he received both acceptance letters on the same day, lucky duck), and one in a now defunct journal called *The Little Magazine*, kick-start his own interest in sleep and children's stories. Most relevant to the moment when I was about to begin reading *The Mezzanine*, a moment in which I was lying with my head propped on a pillow, desperately not sleeping, is "Snorkeling," which appeared in *The New Yorker* in 1981 and begins like this: "Royal woke up feeling expansive, his head comfortably stabilized between two pillows."

Happenstance? No way, because the whole story, even the title, is about sleep. "Snorkeling" is a fabulist tale about a man who stumbles onto a bizarre corporation that facilitates sleep outsourcing by way of some arcane technology. Royal contracts to have "drones" do his sleeping for him, and this enables a Walter Mitty–like fable in which a working stiff with barely enough time to live his life suddenly has the extra hours he needs to approach greatness. As it happens, Royal had been an insomniac as a child. But how did his mother, in a flashback to all those years ago, encourage him to sleep? With a bed-time story. Or rather, with a peculiar form of bedtime story. Royal's mother burbled out a description of an underwater scene intended to plunge her son in the depths of unconsciousness. Sleepy sharks and groggy rainbow fish tumble sonorously through a hydrorama whose only noise Royal's mother rendered as "Fwoosh, fwoosh, fwoosh . . ." The trick doesn't work, but "fwoosh" reappears in the present mo-ment of "Snorkeling," when Royal, having discovered the downside of artificial sleep deprivation (he will become a "drone"), mesmerizes his girlfriend with a similar bedtime lull: "fwoosh . . . fwoosh."

Hence the first shaky claim of my study of Nicholson Baker: These fwooshes, the verbal equivalent of an attempt to stream some-one else's consciousness, are echoed by the "fwoosh" that thirty years later flushed characters to new "mind-zones" in *House of Holes*. A thematic hint planted three decades apart confirmed my suspicion that Baker was a writer of significant ambition, and the nature of that hint proved that *U and I* was not the only time Baker recognized that consciousness was better served by liquid, rather than mechani-cal, metaphors. (Incidentally, "Snorkeling" has an enticing typo: an open parenthesis that never closes. Given *The New Yorker*'s attention to detail and the fact that "Snorkeling" has never been reprinted, it's tempting to wonder whether it's actually *not* a typo, whether Baker is suggesting that we think of the rest of the story, the rest of his career, as contained within a parenthetical statement that will never end.)

Baker's early essays confirm all this. "Changes of Mind," "The Size of Thoughts," and "Rarity" all appeared in *The Atlantic*—the James brothers, too, published early work in *The Atlantic*—and they resemble William James's essays in at least three ways: one, they each assume, as James always did, that introspection can lead to universal truth: "If your life is like my life . . ."; two, Baker borrows James's tactic of italicizing entire phrases at pivotal moments: "*. . . as irrevocably as the bus driver tossed out the strange sad man's right shoe*"; and three, he outright lifts James's strategy of organizing arguments into numbered subsections: "(1) *All large thoughts are reluctant*"; "(2) *Large thoughts are creatures of the shade*"; "(3) *Large thoughts depend more heavily on small thoughts than you might think*."

It's possible that it was these essays Baker was referring to when he told his *Paris Review* interviewer that he had written "a couple pieces" on an Olivetti electric typewriter in Paris (both Jameses spent formative early years in Paris, too), but frankly it's hard to imagine these essays as the work of even a precocious twenty-year-old (he'd spent his junior year in college abroad), and the first of them wasn't published until Baker was twenty-five. But regardless, it's clear that Baker was already thinking a lot of the thoughts that would sneak in the back door of *House of Holes*. "Pursue truth, not rarity," he writes, autodidactically. "(All that is untrue is small)," he self-advises. And less aphoristically, he screeches out a Jamesian aria:

> A thought that can tear phone books in half, and rap on the iron nodes of experience until every blue girder rings; a thought that may one day pack everything noble and good into its briefcase, elbow past the curators of purposelessness, travel overnight toward Truth, and shake it by the indifferent marble shoulders until it finally whispers its cool assent—this is the size of thought worth thinking about.

Where do you find such thoughts? Henry James. Henry James appears either directly or indirectly in each of these William James–like essays. "I decided to think about Henry James's sentence: 'What is morality but high intelligence?'" Baker wrote. And in "The Size of Thoughts," he claims that off the top of his head he can count only ninety-one people who have had large, original thoughts. Henry James is first on the list. William goes unmentioned, but he's there too, percolating.

18

AS BAKER HAD, I'D BEEN KEEPING ALL THIS IN MIND AS I WENDED my way toward what for any critic is a crucial transition: reading his or her subject's first book. It was a lot to keep straight, and maybe that was why it had been almost a five-year stretch from the appearance of the last of Baker's early essays to the publication of *The Mezzanine*. Biographically speaking, Baker was juggling many balls during this stretch of his life. He himself was a working stiff, having resisted the academic writer career path, and his wife had given birth to their first child, a girl named Alice. (A couple references seem plausible here: All Alices measure themselves against precocious blond underworld travelers, surely, particularly when they are the daughter of a writer whose subsurface fascination with children's stories is not hard to palpate; but William James is another possibility: both his famous sister and his wife were Alices.) Baker has spoken of a season of trouble, the spring of 1982, when he received a piece of "unwelcome news" that resulted in his smoking "nearly a hundred dollars' worth of marijuana" at his portable typewriter (William James once famously took mescaline and stumbled through Harvard Square mumbling to himself). The results of this debauch, chronicled in "The Northern Pedestal," printed in *Esquire* a decade later, "analyze his interior state" but offer no clue as to the bad news. Had a book proposal not sold? Was it his parents' divorce, or somehow related to what he called his "growing paranoia about liquor"? In *U and I,* Baker's mother encourages him to write a tell-all drama about their family, but Baker finds the material wanting: "'But there is nothing to tell! Some money squabbles—so what!'" Sounds like the James family. In any event something troubled him during these years, something that delayed for almost half a decade the production of *The Mezzanine,* which tops out at a mere one hundred and thirty-five pages.

But whatever bothered Baker didn't bother me at all. I was thrilled because I could see what was coming. In "Rarity," Baker writes of the "ecstasy of arriving at something underappreciated at the end of a briareous ramification of footnotes." So Baker's crisis, whatever it was, was not keeping me up nights. And it wasn't why I was up in the middle of the night now, trying to imagine some way of making the time pass more quickly. That was Catherine's fault.

19

LET ME EXPLAIN.

Having used, at least once, *House of Holes* to relight the dual stovetop burners of our reading and intimate lives did not succeed in completely reheating the leftovers of our passion. It wasn't going to be that easy. Metaphorical flames, like actual flames, do not always catch. Matches sputter before they touch the wick, campfire kindling proves too damp to ignite. Our predicament, marooned in the butcher-knife purgatory, left us struggling like primitive man to invent fire, and it's no accident that the repetitive, friction-inducing strummings and strokings one might experiment with so as to generate the heat that might combust a knot of dried moss resemble the furious activities people engage in to bring themselves, and others, to a boil. The difficulty, of course, is that while the climax of a body must be followed by a period of repose, a fire will not tolerate rest. Flames need to be nursed, tended. Without careful attention, the result will be a cold smolder.

Which is what happened to us. A glorious group encounter with Nicholson Baker took us temporarily to the House of Holes, but we fwooshed home again as soon as the chapter ended. And rather than the sustained tumescence of our love, we experienced a metastasizing growth of a territorial instinct that we each came to feel in regard to the total surface area of our mattress.

To back up a smidge. Early in our relationship we had been quite insistent that we never go a moment, in bed, when we were not wrapped up in each other. But as time had gone on we began to unconsciously negotiate a sleep treaty that drifted us farther and farther apart, and divvied up our sleep paraphernalia into distinct stashes. I got three of the five pillows, Catherine got the side of the bed closer to the box fan. Because she was closer to the fan she tended to be colder at night, and what that meant was that her half of the bed required more covers. So each night before lights out she would spend several minutes piling and arranging a stack of extra blankets—a whole *bolt* of valuable Indian textiles accumulated during her yearlong study of sari production in rural India—for her side of the bed alone. This had the effect of creating a line down the middle of the bed, and, of course, before long, this line was no longer a mere line but a boundary. We had transmuted from sleeping like identical twins gestating in neonatal embrace to fraternal siblings cordoned off by a tough partition of tissue.

The history of nation-states proves that once a line in the sand is drawn, it's only a matter of time before battles over resources begin, before cultural identity becomes intertwined with irrational nostalgia for useless tracts of land, before annoying but harmless political saber rattlings become provocative and dangerous trans-border excursions. So it became with us. Sometimes when Catherine thought I was asleep, I would feel her sit up in bed and lean over—violating my airspace—to gather intelligence as to whether I'd crossed the border illegally. In addition to being a light snorer, I sometimes fidget and kick at night, and so occasionally she was right, I'd not managed to remain on my side of the bed. And to be fully truthful, I did, once or twice, intentionally burrow an arm or leg under that warm frontier and take a trespasser's pleasure in occupying space that did not "belong" to me. Other times, however, Catherine was completely out of her mind about all this, and I had remained entirely on my side of the bed, was *falling off* my side of the bed, even as she accused me of having punctured the citadel in which she slept less like a princess atop a pea than like the pea itself, smooshed beneath forty or fifty pounds of fragile Indian textiles.

Once at a bar, when I thought we might be able to laugh off such moments, I joked that if Catherine didn't watch it she might soon find herself not stopping at the get-up-and-lean strategy for measuring relative percentages of mattress occupation, but actually climbing out of bed and walking around to my side to assay the situation. I delivered this line fully believing it to be humorous as a function of crossing another line, the one between reality and fantasy. It wasn't. Catherine sipped her lager and said, "I do that all the time, honey."

That's what happened on the night I began reading *The Mezzanine*. I was lying there, scrunched over on my side of the bed, contorted into some strangled-by-the-cord position, desperately

resisting the impulse to move and relieve the pain the position created in my lower back, and finally unable to resist this motion, a
shift that resulted not in any real penetration of Catherine's side of
the bed, though my arm did, unintentionally, push one of my three
pillows into the delicate pea who had been, until then, peacefully
asleep under a fat mound of fabric.

The alarms sounded! Drowsy Princess Pea bounded from the
bed! I remained frozen, but my skin sizzled head to toe as the floor-
boards creaked, tracking Catherine's progress around the room.
She approached crouched, her long, wild, wriggling hair coiling
around her face in crazed slitherings. I dared not view her directly,
but peered at her warped moonlit reflection in the shiny body of a
bedside lamp. *It was her Mr. Hyde.*

The only monster in Nicholson Baker I knew of then—a
"pornmonster" in *House of Holes*—didn't seem particularly relevant at the current moment, but appropriate baddies fairly
seethed through my recollections of Buber and Barthes. For Buber
any institution was an It, and therefore a golem, and for Barthes
silence itself was the beast, and the moment to fear was the moment in which "the loved being becomes a leaden figure, a dream
creature *who does not speak.*" I squinted at Catherine's twisted
reflection as she hovered over me. At this my own inner demon
began to rumble to life. I fought against my own reflexive rage!
With love! *This*, I thought, *this is the monster I must love. I love you,
my troll, my bogeywoman.* I did not move. Catherine completed
her assessment, the conclusion of which could only be that I was
not on her side of the bed.

"Goddammit," she muttered, and stumbled off to pee.

It was in the aftermath of this, after she had crawled back under
the covers and I was too anxious to sleep, that I went downstairs
and fumbled about in the dark for my copy of *The Mezzanine*.

20

ACTUALLY I HAD TWO COPIES. I HAD THE GOLD-COLORED COPY
Catherine had given me, the first sentence of which I had read and
enjoyed, and I had a slightly dinged-up first edition ("light shelf
wear") that I acquired after I sold my proposal and ordered first editions of every one of Nicholson Baker's books. It was this copy that
I found on a shelf and carried through the dark rooms.

The blinking green power light on the tower of my computer
and the steady LED charge indicator bulb, also green, of a sonic
toothbrush in its pod in the bathroom gave the sleeping house a
close to extraterrestrial feel. It's this color of green that back in
the eighties—when *The Mezzanine* was being written—came to
be synonymous with the digital revolution. It was then a green
associated with night-vision technology and the mysterious inner
workings of escalators (I was fully expecting to see this described
in *The Mezzanine*), but starting in the eighties, this alien green,
like the black of Model-Ts, was the sole color of personal computer screens, of ominously blinking cursors, of letters themselves. It was a green that spoke to the future—a little-green-men
Martian green in a we-are-the-Martians-now sense—and it was
a full decade before better screen technology came along. Now
it's a color reserved for tiny beads embedded in small electron-
ics. And it's only when it's particularly dark that we notice how
bright these lights still are, how in a pinch they can still show us
the way, and how they burn in the background of our lives, like
memories.

I peed and rinsed my mouth simultaneously, the weird pleasure of urination combined with masochistic mouthwash pain,

and then I nestled in on the sofa. As I often do with books, I took
a good look at *The Mezzanine* before I opened it. The first edition

has an oddly elongated trim size. Books generally have the rough proportions of a pool table, and deviations tend to signal the kind of book you're picking up. Squatter books—closer to the size of a greeting card—may suggest that a book is either treatise-like or philosophical if the binding is cloth, or pulpy if the paperback cover feels like a cereal box. Squish down farther until a book is wider than it is tall and it's probably a children's book, art book, or coffee-table book, all of which rely on images that don't reproduce well in trim sizes designed for text. The first edition of *The Mezzanine* is just the opposite of this, taller than it is wide and stretched even beyond the cost-cutting elongation of academic books, and it must have occurred to Nicholson Baker that the trim size of his first book embodied his body: every feature story I'd read about Baker emphasized his extreme height, which was one of the things, along with psoriasis, that he had in common with Updike. (I'm short and my skin is just fine.) The title of the book is oddly placed too, printed vertically down the right-hand side of the cover like Chinese characters, and both this and the trim size conspire with the cover art: a cartoonish rising escalator scene. We see the back of a somewhat bulbous man holding the small white bag (but not the paperback) from the book's first sentence, and though the man is unaccompanied in a crowd, he holds aloft the index finger of his free hand, what could possibly be a call for a restaurant check or an auction bid, but which, given that he is alone on an escalator (and given the empty thought balloons rising from his head, just as he is rising), can be only a kind of aha gesture, the phalangeal equivalent of an exclamation point. The cover depicts a moment of insight so surprising it is adorned with body-language punctuation. In this, the image faintly echoes Renaissance art in which distorted pinkie fingers indicate status.

Contrast that with the picture of Nicholson Baker on the back of the book: Baker as a young man with his hands hidden behind him as though each holds a pawn and you're about to play chess with him. He looks like a chess player, actually: practically bald at thirty-one, his shirt button line poorly aligned with his belt buckle, and wearing a smug grin as though he's got some hustler's opening trap waiting for you. Oddly, it's a full-bleed jacket shot, the kind of author photo you'd expect from a romance publisher that hopes their author's raw attractiveness will translate to sales. Why else forgo blurbs? I asked myself: Was Nicholson Baker an attractive man? He'd since gone the way of prophets (I'd first pictured him as a hobbit, but truth be told he looked more like Gandalf than any wee halfling), but as a young man he looked destined to become a CPA, and he did work briefly in business, in finance, and *The Mezzanine* draws on this time in his life. I opened the book—it felt like a restaurant menu—and found the photo credit on the back flap: "Abe Morell." Aha! I thrust my finger into the air. That was photographer Abelardo Morell of *A Book of Books,* produced almost two decades later (and with a rare square trim size). Baker and Morell had been friends for many years, it seemed. First author photos are an important moment in a writer's life (Catherine took my first author photo: Years before we were involved romantically, she came to my house for a three-hour photo shoot sodden with sexual tension that, looking back, we both wish we'd had the guts to act upon), and that Baker chose Morell for his photographer would have indicated a fondness even if I hadn't known they later did a book together. Recognizing this made me quite happy, as though I'd entered the two men's community. I got an additional shot of community when I turned back to the start of the book and found this:

This was totally charming, and it was a reminder that I was not only about to read *The Mezzanine,* I was about to enter the community of everyone who had ever read *The Mezzanine.* Who was Eileen Dobrin? I had no idea, but she had lovely handwriting and she cared enough about her books to stamp and sign every copy. Had Eileen Dobrin sold her copy of *The Mezzanine,* or had the book remained in her library until she died and it wound up in the used bookstore that advertised it online? I didn't know, but I could probably find out. Did I really want to? I *did* want to, but I was already second-guessing that impulse, just as I was now second-guessing the impulse to feel anything like friendship toward Baker and Morell. Maybe I was second-guessing what I'd already thought about imaginary friendships needing to remain imaginary—because writers are real people, and the community that literature generates is real. Yet I don't think I'll ever feel closer to Nicholson Baker than when I read his work, or to Eileen Dobrin than when I hold her book. If literature is humanity at its absolute best, striving after the hard truths, straining to shed the egos that cripple nonliterary relationships, then books, the actual objects of books, are the physical expressions of the struggle to craft a better humanity. Entering the *culture* of books, even the culture of a single book—and every book is the culture of its audience—makes the world feel a little better, a little more true and welcoming. What follows logically from this is that every step that cheapens the object of the book—from the paperback to the e-book—is a stride in which the literary world marches in lockstep with modernity's relentless procession toward convenience. So I was right, I thought, to have convinced myself that augmenting my reading experience with actual human presences would be a kind of backsliding. Books are not the introduction to a human relationship; they constitute one.

This got a little tricky once I began reading *The Mezzanine,* as I presently did, flipping past the dedication ("For Margaret," Baker's wife) and rereading the sentence I'd already read and moving forward, because reading a certain kind of book is a whole lot like meeting its author, is virtually indistinguishable from it, in fact, and what I felt invited to do by the first edition of *The Mezzanine* was hold that full-bleed photo of Baker in mind as I tracked the action of the first paragraph, which follows a very Baker-like figure walking across the lobby of the building where he works, and flows along with his mind as he makes a mental association from a pair of freestanding escalators to a shaft of sunlight cutting down from a high window, such that we already know that the escalator is a stairway to heaven and that we will not merely ride it, but *ascend* on it. And then I ran smack dab into the book's first lengthy footnote at the end of the paragraph, a passage that describes an illusion of light or shine in the moving, now close-at-hand escalator handrail, which is quickly compared to the edge of an LP record.

Now, I knew this was coming. Long before *U and I* compared *The Mezzanine* to an infarction resulting from clogged arteries, Baker established a goal: "I want each sequential change of mind in its true, knotted, clotted, viny multifariousness," he wrote in "Changes of Mind," "with all the colorful streamers of intelligence still taped on and flapping in the wind." Sounds nice. Less so in practice. Because my first thought was annoyance—again. I mean, I'd come downstairs to read a book about going upstairs, and I'd left behind a stressful raising-a-demon kind of moment, hoping to get at something better, some truer human feeling and maybe a twang of companionship. And just when I began my own little escalator ride through the text, it broke down. That's exactly how the book *feels*, like you're on an escalator or some other type of what the Baker-figure soon calls "systems of local transport," gliding along, and then suddenly it stops, but you keep going because you have inertia and you have to catch yourself with a foot—otherwise you'll fall flat on your face. So you do that, and the energy is absorbed in your ankle and seeps up into your knee and hip, feeling like a stress test performed on a cracked piece of metal. You wince, sigh, and then dutifully scan down the page and read the footnote and sigh a little more over whether that really needed to be a footnote, and then collect yourself and brace for the reverse jarring as the machine starts up once more. And what happens then? Another footnote. And another, and another—until Nicholson Baker is absolutely right, you're going to have a fucking heart attack if you read even one more footnote.

The truth was, I *loathed* footnotes. That's what I realized when I started reading *The Mezzanine*. Footnotes, to my mind, were exactly the thing that distinguished literature from scholarly writing. And scholarly writers not only lacked elegance and good humor, they relied heavily on awkward intrusions because the value of their work was never measured by how well they'd said what they'd said. By the end of chapter one of *The Mezzanine*, it's clear that shoelaces are pivotal to the story—that's what's inside the little white bag on the cover—but footnotes are not actually like shoelaces at all, I decided. I'd been wrong about that. Rather they are like shoehorns, and even though *The Mezzanine* describes the pleasant feeling of a snug-fitting shoe, what I felt as a result of all those footnotes was more like the feeling of having tied one of your shoes too tightly, when you can feel the laces digging into the surprisingly nerve-rich skin on the top of your foot, and of course when that happens in your actual shoe, you just stop and retie it. But when it happened in *The Mezzanine*, all I could do was ask myself a question: Why was Nicholson Baker causing me pain over a simple pair of shoelaces, a trifle, an insignificance?

For me the answer was in the past.

21

AFTER GRADUATE SCHOOL, INSTEAD OF MOVING TO PARIS, I moved to a beach community on a small island in New Jersey. I lived alone, which enabled me to concentrate on reading. What I mostly discovered was that I wasn't a particularly good concentrator.

I noticed that I had a tendency to drift while reading, that as I read, my consciousness would chop itself up such that one part of me would go on reading, while a higher, "governor" part of me would wander off into daydream. This was wholly involuntary. I would sit down fully intending to dedicate myself to the sacred task of reading, and it would happen anyway. I would be reading along, and then suddenly I would discover that I was not reading, had not been reading for some time. My mind was elsewhere. Or, I might have asked myself the question that the Baker-figure, not far into *The Mezzanine*, attributes to the absent-minded: "Where was my head?"

Reading, I came to realize, *real reading*, is an act of strenuous will, like running a marathon or climbing a mountain, or upholding a commitment or keeping a promise. I decided that what I needed to do, if I expected to be able to truly concentrate on words, was read *out loud*, not, as poets say, so I could hear the sound of the language, but simply so I could comprehend it at all. So that's what I did. That year's canon-dabbling included a couple of the longer Dostoevskys, the essential Kafka, the obligatory Hemingway and Faulkner, some Woolf and Welty and Paley, and a bunch of newer folks—Stone, Atwood, McCarthy, DeLillo. By winter I had canon-dabbled my way to Conrad, and I spent great swaths of time walking up and down the island's mostly abandoned shoreline, strolling past slimy slinkies of whelk eggs and monstrous, gangly horseshoe crabs, not always watching where I was stepping because I was barking *Heart of Darkness* and *Lord Jim* into a stiff wind that seemed intent on stuffing all those words back into my mouth.

I felt like the island's lonely lighthouse keeper, though the island's only lighthouse was a two-story decoration that stood in the middle of a traffic rotary. Plus I wasn't alone, even in winter. I was renting the front half of a small cottage from a very old woman named Emma Praul who lived in back and was terribly lonely and afraid of dying. Only a thin door separated our apartments. It locked from Emma's side, and sometimes she opened it without knocking to ask me to play cards with her. Once she caught me peeking at a scrambled adult channel on television—the scrambling ruined the picture, but the sound was crystal clear. More often she caught me reading to myself when it was too cold for the beach. It was the reading that bothered Emma more. Of the television she merely noted my peculiar viewing habits and waved me into her dim rooms, where a tattered deck of cards waited beside a score pad and a teapot. Emma was ninety-two. She had skin like baked phyllo. "I don't want to die!" Emma said, as though it were a line necessary to the game we played, like "Go fish!" or "Gin!" Sometimes she cried, and I reached over to squeeze her skeleton hand. Emma asked me why I read so much. Crazy Eights with a man one-quarter your age seemed a perfect way to count down the seconds to a dreaded death—but reading? Why read when you could just watch your stories on unscrambled television?

This is a fair question, and I may not have had a particularly good answer for it until something seemingly minor happened that winter. One day it was warm enough to walk and read on the beach, but cold enough to require the use of a cheap ski mask I'd bought for just that purpose. On the way out the door I discovered that I had misplaced my ski mask. I couldn't find it anywhere. I became distressed—unduly distressed—and this became a mystery layered atop the mystery of the missing ski mask. Why was I so upset about it? Surely it's a comfort to discover that a thing you require is inexpensive—it restores your faith that a society based on money and private property can provide for basic needs—and what losing such a thing might suggest to an already frustrated mind is that one's trust in the system has been misplaced. Yet even though I was fairly poor at the time, I could have afforded a new ski mask. But that wasn't good enough. I kept looking for *my* ski mask, and I began to panic when all my efforts to find it—you know you're in a panic when you start looking under sofa cushions—failed. I doubled-checked the cottage, then triple-checked it. The ski mask could not possibly have been anywhere else. I kept careful track of it and was quite sure it was in the house. Eventually the missing ski mask took on the quality of an emblem—it stood for my basic inability to grasp how the world worked: elementary physics, the universe. This led to a thought I had no desire to think: there was something wrong with my life. Instead of living in some bohemian flat in Paris preparing for a literary life, I was living in a shack in New Jersey watching scrambled porn. My whole *life* was scrambled, it seemed. What did I do about all this? I just kept looking for my two-dollar ski mask, becoming more and more distraught. It wasn't mixed in with any of the laundry I'd not done in more than a month, and it wasn't hidden beneath any of Emma's vintage furniture, none of which I'd ever moved. Finally, having slogged my way through the last few stages of grief, I ended the search, called off the rescue, and broke down sobbing for my precious ski mask. A short while later I went to the beach anyway and found the ski mask on the path from the road to the shore, having dropped it there on my way home the day before.

The story of my ski mask is not interesting—the ski mask itself is insignificant—*unless* the real subject of the story is what was happening in my mind, unless the ski mask was a symbol of my mind. A symbol of what? Of fooling myself. I was getting a lot of reading done in New Jersey, true, but I was also disguising myself by living there rather than in Paris. In losing my ski mask, I was unmasked. I was forced to confront my mistakes. That this was even possible, that some part of me would tell me to go to New Jersey instead of Paris, would foil my ambition and stand in the way of what I truly wanted, was surprising and frightening. Looking back, I realize that it's similar to what Nicholson Baker was getting at in his early essays: A brain can be "shrunken from neglect" and will find that "its hum of fineness will necessarily be delayed, baffled, and drawn out with numerous interstitial timidities." That was me again, years later, in the middle of the night, looking up baffled from *The Mezzanine,* waiting.

Baker was right about something else too: large thoughts depend on small thoughts. How? Symbolism. A small thought (my ski mask) leads to a large thought (there was something wrong with my life) by finding itself suddenly invested with inordinate significance. These days one rarely hears symbolism discussed in any context other than books, and only then with the dread we associate with high school and undergraduate English courses. But what the story of my insignificant ski mask reveals is that symbols are not reserved for literature. Quite the opposite. Symbols are what transport us from ordinary experience to general truth and monumental decision making. Symbols appear in books only because they first appear in life (and later, books themselves become a symbol of how hard we're willing to work to understand ourselves). That's how our brains process experience. Insignificant objects playing an important role in our growth and thought is how we naturally, even biologically, organize experience into memory, into a life narrative.

That's why Emma was more disturbed by my reading than my porn. She preferred a story on a screen to a story on a page because she had forgotten how to recognize the inestimable value of insignificant things.

22

HOW DOES THIS HAPPEN? IN A SPAN OF ABOUT A HUNDRED YEARS—the period of Emma's life, roughly—we've all become quite comfortable with the idea that what a writer writes might first appear on paper, but if all goes well will eventually wind up on a screen: a movie screen in the first part of the twentieth century, a television screen midcentury, a computer screen at the turn of the millennium. Just as written storytelling began to emerge as a true art form—some argue for Flaubert on this point, but I hold with those who favor Henry James—a whole new medium for stories was born with moving pictures. Many have expressed concern over the paper-to-screen trend, but the more prevalent view is to see it as an advance. Why not watch a story on a screen? It's spectacular. It's easier. Ever since, those who have found themselves drawn to telling stories have been forced to choose: on the one hand, you can be solely responsible for a book that will reach an audience dwarfed by the audience for film (and you may hope it winds up on a screen anyway); on the other, you can write a screenplay that might eventually reach a huge audience, but by the time it does it probably won't resemble your work much and you'll receive little credit for it (beyond handsome remuneration).

All pretty familiar, I'm sure. But what about the reader-to-watcher trend that follows the paper-to-screen trend? How does the watcher of a film differ from the reader of a book? I don't want to launch an attack on film—I like film—but I do want to resist the prevailing opinion that books and films are largely equivalent, that not much gets lost as we happily traipse from one to the other. Moving picture storytelling will never completely displace written storytelling, but even very artful filmmaking threatens books in at least two important ways.

First, while the viewers of a film may be very active as inter-
preters of the characters and images they are presented with, those
characters and images *must actually have existed in order to have been
filmed.* That is, they were created by vast teams of set designers, ward-
robe specialists, graphic designers, actors, location scouts, animators,
and makeup technicians (to say nothing of writers, directors, and
producers), and each of these are artists and craftsmen in their own
right. The work that is performed by the reader of a book, visualizing
figures and places based on verbal descriptions, slopping together
images from the wet goo of words, is, in a film, done literally behind
the scenes, by that scrolling battalion of names that most people can't
be bothered to sit through at the end of a movie. No matter how
exciting or touching a film may be, it's impersonal in this way, and if
we do wind up feeling roused to a sensation of intimacy with a direc-
tor or an actor, it's probably an illusion, we're probably giving them
too much credit, credit that rightly belongs to individuals whose
names, finally in lights, illuminate only empty theater seats.

Reading, by contrast, is the product of exactly *two* conspiring
intellects. A reader first decodes chunky, arbitrarily shaped letters
and punctuation into words and sentences, and then employs these
as props to invent, to produce, the story. As a reader you know that
editors and book designers pitch in with the creation of a book, but
the sensation you feel if you're really reading—not just thinking this
would be a whole lot more fun on a screen—is terribly personal, like
gentle ticklings of silk straps tethering you to a singular, authorial vision. Disembodied, the author directs the book, but it's readers who
act out the story in the feathery nether region of their imaginations.
Most simply put, film is a visual art, a book is not, and an essential
intimacy is lost when we move from the latter to the former.

The second threat is threats. The advent of screens and moving pictures has been profitable in many ways, but a plot-anxiety

inflation crisis looms. As film has compiled its own canon, film-makers striving to make it new have generally attempted to do so less with innovative techniques and inventive stories than with simple raisings of the stakes. Once upon a time it was enough for the thieves of a heist film to snatch a jewel that postfence would let them retire comfortably; now, no caper-flick satisfies unless its bandits pocket billions and are chauffeured to Cannes in denouement. Action films used to please with a threat to a small town and a climactic fistfight; now, heroes dispatch hundreds of interchangeable foes to stave off the end of the world. Monster films once thrilled with man-sized beasts, lagoon creatures, and the like, but the mutants have grown steadily larger, creeping first to titan-height such that a single mammoth might topple a city, and evolving from there to leviathans the *size* of cities. Digital special effects enabled a quantum leap in stakes inflation. Before the early nineties, say, a film viewer might at least have been called upon to cooperate with effects less immersive than suggestive. But these days it's practically a rite of spring to go to the movies and learn via coming attractions that the summer will be interrupted at regular intervals by visually convincing global threats, extinction-level events, and sundry judgment days. This is mostly Hollywood, but even independent films have been flooded with a trickle-down effect of serial killers, regime-ending political crises, and time travel–unravelings of the multiverse.

That literature has suffered collateral damage from this onslaught can be inferred from the fact that *The Mezzanine* was initially met (the original reviews were mostly positive) with accusations of being "experimental" and "avant garde" simply because it was about a regular guy on an ordinary lunch break thinking about everyday objects whose significance, like my ski mask, was that they were emblematic of something larger than themselves. That's the problem of cinematic stakes inflation: It makes ordinary life seem tedious and difficult.

Up to this point in my study, I'd been thinking that Nicholson Baker and myself, ten years apart, were not really of the same generation, but actually it's been decades since the advent of screens dumped everyone from Emma Praul on forward into the same generational boat. We don't all bunk in the same berth (and the crossing of some meridian midcentury meant that children from that point forward would have to learn that stories came from books only after having been introduced to them with moving pictures), but these days pretty much everyone alive is screen-compromised. That's why Emma, even as her life seemed unfulfilled, righteously clung to her belief that her TV was better than a book. Reading was an act of strenuous will long before it had screens to compete with, and now books must contend with the fact that we have evolved an instinct to leave the work of the imagination to others. Great thoughts are not only reluctant and shy; a part of us actively resists their discovery.

Whatever the effect of screens, it's hard to argue that the situation has not grown steadily worse with the rapid growth of their kind and function. But even those who feel no listing of the great vessel in which we all cruise, no teeter as it stuffs its hold with ever-expanding multiplexes and issues handheld electronic devices to each and every mate, must acknowledge an even more profound flop. These days, despite cherished claims, most writers no longer write directly onto paper. Rather, they type onto screens, and if they're lucky what they write makes a reverse trek to become a book.

Nicholson Baker, as it happens, took early note of the fact that his was the first generation of writers to have the option of writing directly onto a screen. That's how he works, in fact. It now seems ho-hum that *U and I* begins with Baker sitting down to write on a "keyboard," but it would have read nearly as science fiction when it first appeared in 1991. Even earlier, too. Baker has claimed that he wrote *The Mezzanine* in a furious three-and-a-half-month stretch—from August 1 to November 17, 1987 (he really means a draft, as excerpts had already appeared in *The New Yorker*)—on a Kaypro portable computer that he purchased in 1985. His shift from writing short stories and brief essays to a book-length manuscript coincides with his having traded the hair trigger keys of his Olivetti electric typewriter for the flatter array of springy ergonomic buttons and the pulsing light of slightly blurry green letters. If Mark Twain gets credit for having submitted the first typewritten manuscript, then *The Mezzanine* should perhaps be regarded as the first literary novel of note to have been composed entirely on a screen.

23

BUT WAIT. ISN'T A LIGHT-*EMITTING* COMPUTER MORE LIKE A movie projector? Baker may have had just such a thought, as not long after he finished *U and I* he wrote an essay about the history of movie projectors.

"The Projector" begins with a detailed analysis of a projector-room scene in Chuck Russell's 1988 remake of *The Blob*. A small-town projectionist is among the Blob's early victims (a hobo, several teenagers, and a lonely dishwasher get it first), and actually it's a metascene in that it comes at a similarly plot-heavy moment in the projected film within the film. Baker performs various nifty hermeneutic tricks here—in keeping with the theory of stakes inflation, he notes that while the 1958 Blob was a "giant protean douche bag," the upgrade was "far peppier and more enterprising"—but what truly piques his interest is the scene's glaring omission: The projectionist projects the film within the film not with the huge, flat projection platters that even by 1988 were multiplex SOP, but with an ordinary upright-spool projector of the kind most would associate with late-evening holidays, when the family has grown tired of bickering and someone breaks out the shoebox of eight-millimeter reels. Or scratch that. Because Baker's interest is not piqued by this at all. Rather, he finds it "terrifying."

What's he afraid of? Even if a certain fondness for schlocky movies is apparent from the care with which Baker surveys projector-room scenes in "The Projector," Nicholson Baker actually couldn't care less about films and screens. Or rather, he cares a great deal. "I've always tried to write unfilmable books," Baker told his *Paris Review* interviewer, "starting with *The Mezzanine.* Maybe this little black-and-white word mound can still be imposing in a world in which we have macro lenses and all kinds of lush cinematography. Maybe prose can be more visual than film." In other words, even though the ostensible subject of "The Projector" is film, it's really about something else, and a whole worldview slips out neatly from Baker's observation that the remake of *The Blob* "brings every detail, or almost every detail of the first film up to date." That's how the world works, even literature, and that's actually what *The Mezzanine* is about. The problem with *The Blob*, however, the "terrifying reality" of it, is what it *didn't* update, what it couldn't bring itself to update, because the truth is that platter projection systems damage film, threaten the medium. It's odd that Baker notes this, because if you tug almost any thread hanging loose from the tapestry of his early career, what comes gushing out along with the string is the belief that progress is possible and measurable in insignificant things. The point he makes here, however, is that sometimes the world makes changes that seem like advances, but really aren't. And when that's the case, when we've mucked something up that was perfectly good to begin with, we're reluctant to admit it and so we disguise ourselves to ourselves instead. "The Projector" is Baker's first faint note of complaint, and just as his own writing moves from the page to the screen, the real object of his growing concern is not projectors but paper.

24

BUT THAT'S GETTING A LITTLE AHEAD OF THINGS. BAKER started to worry; I started to grow comfortable. I grew comfortable as a function of a disturbing middle-of-the-night realization: My struggles with Baker's footnotes said a whole lot more about me as a reader than they did about *The Mezzanine* as a novel.

In chapter two, you realize that the book has begun in medias res, at its moment of greatest action. That's a plot-anxiety joke. You sense from the beginning that the journey, such as it is, will end at the top of the escalator, and though there's no moment when the Baker-figure says "Then I stepped on the escalator . . ." or "Then I felt myself tugged up to speed with the escalator's hidden conveyor . . . ," or whatever—the story sort of hiccups forward—you realize pretty early on that the bulk of the book will be made up of midride musings about events stretching back to a few minutes before lunch. So, total elapsed time: a little more than an hour for lunch, plus the walk from the door to the escalator, then the odd jump to the protracted ride. The period of greatest action, then, the book's most plotful stretch, is over before you even start to look for such a thing. This insight into how the book worked cracked the barrier of frustration I threw up at having been slowed down by the footnotes. Sometime during chapter two I began to understand that *The Mezzanine* is *about* how hard it is for a modern reader to read it. That is, it's a book that demands that if you're going to follow it then you'll have to climb to another level in your own mind, ascend to your own personal mezzanine, return from the lunch hour of regular life, and get back to the work of sustaining attention to what and how you think. The book has many footnotes, sure, but even the nonfootnote sections have the *tone* of a footnote, a tone that assumes that you're reading because you want to be reading, that you're reading something that you could have skipped, but didn't. That's modern literature. You can choose to skip it—many people do.

Which sounds direr than the book itself. Baker's earliest reviewers remarked that *The Mezzanine* is a notably happy book: the Baker-figure is largely conflict-free, even as he attests to intense internal dramas ("incredulousness and resignation") that result from the malfunction of insignificant objects, bandage wrappers, staplers, tape dispensers, etc. Even more important, *The Mezzanine* appears happy to be a book and not a movie; it is *enthusiastically* a book, and what that means—even the early reviewers noted this—is that it doesn't resemble many other books.

So I stopped my midnight reading. It wasn't a good idea to have tried to use *The Mezzanine* to fulcrum myself out of stress-induced insomnia. The next day I hopped on our landlord's four-wheeler and motored out past our small lake to a stand of trees that Catherine and I had discovered once the heat broke and we started taking walks through the woods. I hung a hammock between two conveniently spaced elms, and read the rest of *The Mezzanine* swaying in a breeze that approximated the book's contented mood. The Baker-figure, who grows only more Baker-like as the story proceeds, tall, bearded at twenty-three, with a mother "interested in materialist analogies for cognition," has a youthful exuberance that is contagious even as you know, as I did, that his faith in progress won't last. It's another of the book's jokes that you don't learn the Baker-figure's name until four-fifths of the way through, "Howie," which I leave in quotation marks because you don't hear the name unless others address him (no word as to whether "Howie" thinks of himself in the diminutive, though he doesn't protest).

None of the early reviewers I read linked "Howie" to *The Mezzanine*'s most prominent feature—meditations on *how* everyday devices work. Most prominent among these is shoes, which pop up three times on a list that "Howie," early on, makes of connections between insignificant objects and crucial moments in his development as a person. Shoes are critical to *The Mezzanine* because it's a broken shoelace that sends "Howie" off on his lunchtime jaunt in the first place, but shoes in general are "the first adult machines we are given to master," and "Howie" reports that he had gained valuable intellectual confidence when sometime before he had managed to "personalize an already adult procedure" by working out a better shoe-tying methodology for himself. In short, *The Mezzanine* uses insignificant objects to tell the story of "Howie"'s mechanical coming of age.

It's a little unfortunate that the critical enthusiasm for "Howie"'s attraction to "the often undocumented daily texture of our lives" wound up pigeonholing Baker as a guru of minutiae. That's another problem with the state of modern literature. A writer's initial success becomes the name of his or her pigeonhole, and what's to blame, probably, is a cultural pandemic of repetition addiction, palpable in everything from repeating soundtrack loops, to suburban architecture, to automobile design. Baker warned himself of the dangers of early success—he chided "writers [who] curtail their finer efforts because the merest suggestion of expertise is enough to coast on for a decade"—and admirably he scolded himself before anyone else did: *U and I* denigrates Baker's own 1989 essay "Model Airplanes," and he worries that in the piece's wake he would "seem to be obsessed with model airplanes." Pretty much. Because there was no one around to point out that what "Model Airplanes" really did was explain why it was okay to write short, model-like novels: it was an embodiment of an axiom from one of Baker's earliest essays: "We must refine all epics into epigrams!"

That kind of discovery of buried, causal connections between disparate works in Baker's career made me feel as though I had begun to cut out from a tangled, overgrown hedge a trailhead of sorts, and looking down the path I grew as excited as the nameless fictional critic set to the scent of an overlooked meaning in Henry James's "The Figure in the Carpet." Incidentally, Henry James makes an appearance in *The Mezzanine,* too, inside a protracted footnote near the end of the book that tells a quick history of footnotes. William James is in the book too, though hidden. "Howie" credits his girlfriend, "L" (not "M," though Margaret Brentano was Baker's college sweetheart), with a thought similar to the James-Lange theory of emotion. And, more broadly, *The Mezzanine* may be said to embody what William James claimed of objects and symbolism in *The Principles of Psychology,* just a few pages *after* his stream of consciousness diagram: "Any natural subject will do, if the artist has wit enough to pounce upon some feature of it as characteristic."

25

THESE FIRST FAINT OUTLINES OF WHAT I HAD ALREADY BEGUN TO think of as the real figure in Nicholson Baker's carpet sent me scurrying back to the beginning of *The Mezzanine.* About ten pages in, Baker uncorks the first fifty-cent word of his career: "vibratiuncles." Initially, still reading in the middle of the night, I was annoyed by this word because it meant I had to find a dictionary. That's a little easier today than it used to be, and the online *OED* is a wonderful resource to have at one's fingertips, but it wasn't actually at my fingertips because I didn't have my laptop nearby. I sighed miserably and unnestled myself from the sofa, and when I found my laptop

I discovered our Wi-Fi wasn't working. Of course. So I reset the Wi-Fi and had to sit there and wait for it to fix itself. I'll resist the impulse to go on at length about how it's the nature of our times that we waste a lot of time sitting and waiting for our things to fix themselves: I'll simply note that it leaves us characterized by inactivity. Waiting for electronic devices to fix themselves is the modern equivalent of watching water boil. Just when I thought the Wi-Fi was never going to fix itself, it fixed itself. I gave another sigh, this one of relief. And what did I find when I looked up "vibratiuncles"? They're small vibrations. Importantly—because the sentence that uses "vibratiuncles" could just as easily have used "small vibrations"—"vibratiuncles" first appears in the work of eighteenth-century philosopher David Hartley's theory of mind. It's an explanation for how sensations link to memory.

Now we're getting somewhere. Because even though "vibratiuncles" are, by definition, "diminutive" or "miniature," the use of the word in *The Mezzanine* is a clear indication that Nicholson Baker's interest in the impossibly small and insignificant does not mean he's obsessed with minutiae. The small is of interest only to the extent that it hints at the large; an active reader infers the epic journey from the epigram. What's the journey? "Howie" likens his own passage into adulthood to the travels of Balboa, the work of Copernicus. This is similar to science fiction writer L. Ron Hubbard's having once likened his Scientology-founding *Dianetics* to "a voyage of discovery . . . an exploration into new and nearly uncharted realms" of the human mind. Wacko that he was, Hubbard is relevant to *The Mezzanine* because "Howie" casually tosses out "engram" as synonymous with "memory." True, "engram" traces back to the mneme traces of early-twentieth-century zoologist Richard Semon, but the word reached public consciousness only by having been adopted by Scientology in the sixties and seventies as a term for unhealthy memories. And Hubbard died just a year before *The Mezzanine* was published. (For the record, both Baker and Hubbard were probably thinking of William James, whom John Dewey once praised as "almost a Columbus of the inner world.")

All these links and connections were thrilling as I was thinking back on them, because by the end of *The Mezzanine* you realize that it's links and connections that amount to the book's own theory of mind. The common denominator of the many "systems of public transport" described in *The Mezzanine* is the chain or the train that drives them, which is the book's metaphor for the work of the brain. Baker hasn't yet discovered, or he's forgotten, the limitation of chains and trains as thought metaphors. At this point he's still on the prowl for his mother's materialist analogies, and his tragic, boyish faith in progress tells him that as our machines have improved, so has our understanding of how we think what we think.

It's common to forgive young writers the naïveté that is so often coupled with enthusiasm. And I did—I did. I forgave Baker as I approached the end of *The Mezzanine* out in the hammock, Catherine now with me. It was several days after the clash of our hidden titans, and we never did speak of it, though the hammock offered its own commentary in that it was impossible to divide its elastic rope bed into distinct sides, and the only comfortable position trapped my shin beneath Catherine's backbone and lodged her ankle under my jaw. She had her laptop screen; I had my book. We lightly swayed. I generally read faster as I approach the end of books, *The Mezzanine* particularly so. The book was about almost nothing, but it aspired to updating the entirety of literature. When "Howie" worries that newer styles of doorknob don't really amount to better door-opening devices—"What is this static modernism that architects of the second tier have imposed on us?"—he might as well be speaking of books, of the modernism that Baker might have seen as a chapter better excised from the story of literature. How else to explain the shift from his early tales, dabbling in the fantastic and absurd, seemingly all but disavowed, to this act of what might be called remodernism, which shapes a philosopher's theory of mind from an archaeological passion for the shallowest strata of contemporary life. And that, rather than the thrill of exploration, is what I'd really begun to feel on having returned to the start of Nicholson Baker's career: the wonder of an archaeologist sifting through the hard clods of the past and stumbling on a picture petrified in the dirt, a form that sharpens as the millennia are chipped away with dental tools, horsehair brushes, and gentle puffs of breath. This is the feeling you never get as a canon-dabbler, the feeling you can't share even with those closest to you, even when their limbs are all tangled up with yours.

I turned to the final chapter of *The Mezzanine,* and what I saw there made me secretly tachycardic, my heart plucking the hammock ropes like lute strings. It was a very short chapter, just a paragraph, a single brick of text on a single page. But before I began reading it, my eyes flitted over something near the very bottom, three capitalized words. I resisted actually looking at them; I *read* them, but I saw them only peripherally: "Hallman's! Hallman's! Hallman's!" I'd come to appreciate *The Mezzanine,* come to feel that it was almost talking to me. Now it actually *was* talking to me. I began the paragraph. "Howie" is at the top of the escalator, looking back at a cigarette butt trapped and tumbling—clogged—at the spot where the escalator steps disappear into the machine's inner works. "Howie"'s train of thought chugs out an analogy: it's like a jar caught on the conveyor at the end of a supermarket checkout line.

It's not "Hallman's," but "Hellmann's"; it's not me, but mayon-naise.

26

IT'S THIS JAR THAT FORMS A SUBTLE BRIDGE TO NICHOLSON Baker's second novel, *Room Temperature*, which begins with a cryptic epigraph from Wallace Stevens: "I placed a jar in Tennessee . . ." But even having happily noticed this, I worried over three things the next day, as I finger-pried *Room Temperature* down from a shelf and motored out to the hammock.

First, the jacket: The swoopy teal and peach cover of this one, like pastel swirls on the box of a cheap brand of laundry detergent (designed by the same artist who produced the clever cover of *The Mezzanine*), is so disgusting I refuse to discuss it any further. The publisher (sometime between *The Mezzanine* and *Room Temperature*, Weidenfeld & Nicolson became Grove Weidenfeld; Baker

must have been loyal to George Weidenfeld, a British baron: he had published *Lolita* with Nigel Nicolson, who left the firm in 1992) was likely aiming for book-to-book continuity, a common practice, though it was this same continuity Baker knew he should resist. Similarly the author photo is again credited to Abe Morell (he would do the photo for *U and I* as well, after Baker moved to Random House), yet the picture this time around struck me as strange because while Baker is interestingly lit, he appears unusually severe. It's odd, in general, to see a man in a suit on the floor: He looks as though he's just fallen and isn't at all keen on being photographed.

Second, cosmetic similarity: The title of *Room Temperature*, like *The Mezzanine*, promises no thrills—it synonymously flirts with that damning critique, *tepid*—and a quick flip through revealed that *The Mezzanine* and *Room Temperature* each had fifteen chapters and were roughly the same length. Baker, however, had my thought long before I did. He records it as *U and I* opens:

> A week or so earlier I had finished and sent off a novel, my second, and I was still full of the misleading momentum that, while it makes the completion of novels possible, also generally imparts a disappointingly thin and rushed feeling to their second halves or final thirds, as the writer's growing certainty that he is finally a pro, finally getting the hang of it, coincides exactly with that unpleasant fidgety sensation on the reader's part that he is locked into a set of characters and surroundings he knows a bit too well by now to enjoy.

Not exactly glowing self-endorsement.

Third, the problem of direct correspondence: The book appeared to be about fatherhood (I picked this up from interviews—Baker claimed to have finished it on Father's Day, 1989, but once again he probably meant a draft, as Father's Day, 1989, came a month and a half before *U and I*'s claim that Baker's second novel was completed "a week or so" before August 6, 1989), and while as a very young man I had played with the idea of adopting a baby girl as a "single father" (it seemed a strange plan only when

I revealed it to others), I eventually left behind the whole idea of parenthood, surrogate or otherwise. The various concordances between my literary life and Nicholson Baker's had made it clear that I should read him, but what would happen when he tackled a subject that held no interest for me? Catherine, either. She had decided against children very early, when she was barely more than a child herself, and it wasn't until she was thirty-six that she was able to find a doctor willing to clog and laser-weld her fallopian tubes. That delay may account for why she now seemed less disinterested in children than peeved that scientists hadn't yet found a way to completely eliminate that period of life, youth, that tends to be romanticized and artificially prolonged even as it is only ever recalled with mixed feelings. "I *never* want children," I'd known Catherine to say. *"Never!"* Nevertheless, once fall settled in she began to grow worried for the remaining farm kitten, still living on the farmhouse roof. Adopting the kitten was out of the question, hissingly rejected by our own imperious feline, but Catherine often wandered outside to coax the little girl down from her coyoteproof roost with infant coo calls of "Baaa-by! Where's the Baaa-by?" Both purred through mutually comforting periods of cradling and nuzzling before retiring to a room and a roof of their own, respectively.

All these worries more or less evaporated as soon as I climbed into the cradle of the hammock and nuzzled up to *Room Temperature*, which opens with a cradling scene: "I was in the rocking chair giving our six-month-old Bug her late afternoon bottle." Actually, "scene" overstates it, as *Room Temperature* is characterized by compressed time. "It was three-fifteen on a Wednesday" begins chapter two, and just a few lines later the narrator, a new Baker-figure ("Mike" this time around, a reviewer of television commercials) offers up his "theory of knowledge":

. . . with a little concentration one's whole life could be reconstructed from any single twenty-minute period randomly or almost randomly selected.

So the total elapsed time of *Room Temperature*, shrink-wrapped into the time it takes to bottle-feed an infant, is even shorter than the lunch-and-escalate elapsed time period of *The Mezzanine*. I cheered inwardly at this. Even as Nicholson Baker was conscientiously monitoring the rising index of stakes inflation in the screen-compromised world, he was actively reducing the stakes in his own work. Like *The Mezzanine*, *Room Temperature* is made up of Mike's benign musings, but while "Howie"'s corporate bildungsroman is systematic and workmanlike—bullet-pointed, at times—Mike's strings of images and memories, coming seemingly randomly, are triggered by the objects he chooses to attend to from his seat in the nursing room. "Howie" is in motion, surveying conveyors as he is conveyed. Mike is static, but rocking the Bug is "like riding a slow train."

The title of the book describes the implied milk of the feeding (*Our Bodies, Ourselves*: "Formula or breast milk should be warmed to room temperature . . ."), but it also characterizes the quiet story itself with the faintest of Goldilocks references: not too hot, not too cold—just right. That's mostly in the background, a fairytale allusion shifting and darting behind painted philodendrons at the rear of the stage. Even a drive-by "Princess and the Pea" reference gets more play. But what's in the foreground—Bug—points to an even more archetypal children's story. Who's the Bug? Baker's daughter, Alice. *Room Temperature* is dedicated to Alice (*"For Alice"*), and we're already in Wonderland when we turn the page and recognize Wallace Stevens's cryptic jar in Tennessee as a flask placed in Alice's path. *Read me*. I was still on page one when I stumbled across the first of the book's several Carrollian-sounding names, "Dr. Momtaz," "Grevel Lindop," and "Neimtzov" (Baker has cited the other famous anagrammist, Nabokov, as an even more crucial influence than Updike), all of which suspiciously appear within twenty pages or so. I paused for a time and did some eager tinkering in the margins. "Grevel Lindop" comes close to "developing," and "Neimtzov" looks briefly like "time zone," but none of the names in the book actually anagram into anything. Momtaz and Neimtzov are real surnames, and Grevel Lindop is a real British literary critic (the *Times Literary Supplement* is draped over Mike's knee for most of the twenty-minute feed). So was I not then peering through some kind of looking glass? I *was*. A quarter of the way in, just as I was about to give up on the Alice reference, Mike tells a story of discovering a bouquet of inspection slips tucked into the various pockets of a recently purchased sport coat: the color of the ARMHOLE PRESSING slip is described as "Alice blue."

Something odd happened when I read this line: I looked up from the book and saw Alice blue. Or rather, satisfied at having spied a subtle association camouflaged behind a scrim of plot, I paused my reading midsentence and laid the book down onto my chest and looked off into the distance. And there was Alice blue, neither the deep ocean navy at the top of the sky, nor the blurry perfect white along the jagged horizon, but between, a faint Eastery pastel just a few degrees up that even without prompt I might have likened to the color of Alice's dress. (For the record, *Alice's Adventures in Wonderland* describes absolutely nothing as "blue," and includes a reference only to Alice's "skirt" in chapter twelve.)

Room Temperature invites these sorts of intricate associations— from *"For Alice"* to "Alice blue"—as Mike, like "Howie," is a voice whose main purpose is to claim that a book's real adventure is the inward journey, to express a preference for the mind's reflexive associations over selective memory. My jump from the book to the sky may itself have been a reflex triggered by an association Mike makes, a few pages in, from the flapping wings of several birds he can see out a window, to the imagined image of a dog's floppy ears as it runs "excited zigzags across a field." Even more than "Howie," Mike is keenly interested in these sorts of thoughts, in the similes and metaphors that fwoosh us from one concrete thought to the next (he recalls his father encouraging him to nurse an instinct to attend to "transitions" between subjects of conversation), and his general contentedness during this randomly selected twenty-minute period is a function not only of nursing the Bug but of the outside world looking "unusually good and deserving of similes today." Deserving? Precisely.

On falling into the routine of afternoon reading in my hammock—I was now writing the early parts of *B & Me* in the mornings—I'd had my own run of outside-world associations. At one moment my reading was punctuated with the calls of a pair of hawks, and a lengthy aside Mike delivers on the history of punctuation, specifically a discussion of obsolete parentheses, caused me to see the swooping, veering birds as a set of brackets—{ {—loosed from the page and hunting in tandem for something to splice. More consistently I listened behind my reading to the farty noises of a species of insect that, once I had settled into the hammock and remained still for a time, would continue their periodic bursts of happy flatulent propulsion. These inspired—and for this I hold responsible both *Room Temperature*'s Virgin-and-Bug milieu and the fact that a local insect, the Jerusalem cricket, was named for its peculiar resemblance to a tiny baby—a brief and perverse vision of the adjacent fields populated with thousands of miniature constipated six-month-olds, all perched on methane-powered jet scooters and all looking like gleeful little Nicholson Bakers.

Now these are robust, fanciful associations, and my question is this: Would I have been having thoughts so layered and textured had I not been reading, had I just been lying there instead? I don't think so. Emerson once optimistically noted that civilization and nature can make for perfect harmony, as when you stumble across Beethoven emanating from a deep woods cabin. And perhaps Whitman was trying to take the next step from there when he advised readers of his poetry: "I am nearly always successful with the reader in the open air." Reading a book that is enthusiastically a book is a concentrated form of thinking, and when we read out of doors, when we put a book down and look up and see its image hovering before our paler reality like the phantom residue of a bright light or optical illusion, we are reminded of the most fundamental of associations: a book is like the world in which it is read. There is no Alice blue without the sky lurking behind the words. In this way reading, like sex and eating, is better al fresco: Literature is an airing out, and a story that dries on the line feels fresher and cleaner and paves the way for the associations that all Baker's early works link to the raw intelligence that good books nurture.

27

AND WHERE DOES THAT IDEA COME FROM, THAT ASSOCIATIONS are a sign of intelligence? William James! It was James, of course, who suggested that the ability to form complicated analogies was what separated man from brute. His description of the process is as evocative of Wonderland as *Room Temperature*:

But turn to the highest order of minds, and what a change! Instead of thoughts of concrete things patiently following one another in a beaten track of habitual suggestion, we have the most abrupt cross-cuts and transitions from one idea to another, the most rarefied abstractions and discriminations, the most unheard-of combinations of elements, the subtlest associations of analogy; in a word, we seem suddenly introduced into a seething caldron of ideas, where everything is fizzling and bobbing about in a state of bewildering activity, where partnerships can be joined in an instant, treadmill routine is unknown, and the unexpected seems the only law.

Given this, it should be no surprise that William James makes his first overt appearance in Nicholson Baker's work about a quarter of the way into *Room Temperature,* in chapter three, in a passage in which Mike describes how he came to appreciate silence and negative space. Chapter three is an excellent example of a fizzling and bobbing consciousness: It skips from the mobile that Mike's wife, Patty, had constructed from those colored inspection slips (turning in the room's barely perceptible breeze, it's the Alice blue–colored slip that "c[omes] into view" and gets the chapter rolling), to a recalled exchange in which Mike encourages Patty to write down her ideas for a mail-order business of finely crafted paper art, to Mike lying in bed trying to decode what Patty writes of their lives in a notebook by carefully listening to the "sniffing" sounds of her felt-tip pen, to a protracted meditation on just how much of our thinking ought to remain private, and then finally back to Patty's writing in bed and Mike's realization that what's even more revealing than the sound of her pen is the hesitation between the noises, the pauses, the rests: it's "more truthful to downplay the scribble and focus on the hand-slide in my own wife's record of our life."

Of course all this fizzling and bobbing is only an illusion of the real thing. But chapter three is notable too, given both my incorrect belief that Baker was British and my newfound awareness that his first publisher *was* British, for its sustained note of Anglophilia. Mike suggests that the use of the subjunctive is an echo of British tyranny; he describes at length an obscure television show about a British spy; and he quotes one British poet, "Always true is always new," commenting on another British poet. When Mike finally quotes a fellow American, William James, he does so merely to point out that James had failed to teach him what Patty's pen noises have succeeded in teaching him, and what was notable about this moment, to me, was that the line of James he quotes, "James's 'intention of saying a thing,'" comes once again from *The Principles of Psychology,* this time a page and a half *before* James's glorious stream of consciousness diagram. And given the fact that Mike spends a great deal of time describing his tenure as a "French horn major at the Eastman School of Music," it's worth observing that James, immediately after the diagram, likens its overlapping arcs to

> "overtones" in music: they are not separately heard by the ear; they blend with the fundamental note, and suffuse it, and alter it; and even so do the waxing and waning brain-processes at every moment blend with and suffuse and alter the psychic effect of the processes which are at their culminating point.

In taking note of the fact that both Mike and Baker are Eastman students with an interest in William James, I'm coming very close to doing what I don't think critics should do: infer a writer's life from their work, mistake fiction for autobiography. The problem is, Mike calls his own book an "autobiography," just as "Howie" calls his escalator the "vehicle of this memoir." Does Nicholson Baker even write fiction?

His early stories feel fictional enough, but *The Mezzanine* and

Room Temperature so mock the line between fiction and nonfiction that even referring to Baker-figures or Mike or "Howie," as I've been doing, makes me feel like the butt of a private joke. (*Paris Review* interview: "I felt I had to be someone who would leap in from outside and do some nutty thing and then run away cackling.") *The Mezzanine* and *Room Temperature* were each excerpted twice in *The New Yorker*, but that was in the eighties, when creative essays and short stories were printed side by side with no distinction drawn between them (the change came in 1992). As I read *Room Temperature*, Baker's one-time self-description as a "pretty autobiographical" writer began to seem like a wild understatement. I found myself combing through the book for autobiographical hints:

Room Temperature	Nicholson Baker
Mike's birthday: January 5, 1957	Baker's birthday: January 7, 1957
Mike has an infant daughter, nicknamed Bug (no given name supplied), presumably born late eighties.	A 1993 Baker article describes his daughter, Alice, as a "barely literate five-year-old."
Mike transfers from the Eastman School of Music to Swarthmore College.	Baker transferred from the Eastman School of Music to Haverford College.
Mike once hoped to become a composer, and played the French horn.	Baker once hoped to become a composer, and played the bassoon (more on this shortly).
Mike suggests that Patty launch a mail-order business for finely crafted paper art.	Margaret Brentano has a mail-order business for finely crafted paper art.
Mike recalls meticulously constructing model airplanes as a child and describes the process of model construction at considerable length.	Baker's "Model Airplanes," published in *Esquire* a year before *Room Temperature* appeared, describes the process of model construction at considerable length and refers obliquely to Baker's youth in that he admits to having "never liked building

model cars as much as building model airplanes." (The notorious pot-smoking incident reappears here: Baker reports that his interest in model building flared anew after "a time of professional disappointment," and the goal was to use the construction of a model to "pull [him]self together.")

Mike confesses an ambition to write "some sort of concentrated history of the comma" featuring the thesis that the "comma, in short, was alone responsible for the passage of civilization north from the ancient world into the modern."

Baker's "The History of Punctuation," published in *The New York Review of Books,* in 1993, is ostensibly an overview of several grammar histories, most prominently Dr. Malcolm Parkes's *Pause and Effect,* and while Baker is a generally kind reviewer, he admits to being puzzled as to "how casual Parkes is . . . about his commas." The discussion of commas that follows appears informed by long-standing interest and copious research.

Mike notes several times—it's one of *Room Temperature*'s few recurring motifs—that he, Patty, and the Bug had recently attended his sister's wedding. His sister requests that Mike "read a little biblical something at the ceremony."

Baker attended the wedding of his sister, Rachel, on July 11, 1987. The date is included in "Wedding," the otherwise unpublished remarks he delivered on the occasion. We can infer that July 11, 1987, precedes the period in which Baker composed *Room Temperature* from the already cited claim that *The Mezzanine* was being written after this time.

Noteworthy: When I read "Wedding," I suspected at once that Baker included it in *The Size of Thoughts,* his 1996 essay collection, as a kind of homage to "A Wedding Sermon from a Prison Cell," which Lutheran pastor Dietrich Bonhoeffer wrote in 1943 while awaiting execution for having participated in a plot to murder Hitler. Baker doesn't cite Bonhoeffer directly, but I think a similarity in tone is unmistakable:

Bonhoeffer: It is right and proper for a bride and bridegroom to welcome and celebrate their wedding day with a unique sense of triumph.

Baker: In a few minutes, Rachel and Bob are going to be pronounced husband and wife. These are excellent words, husband and wife—they lean toward each other, they exist in reference to each other, they link arms.

What to make of this? I wasn't sure yet. In noting a link between Baker and Bonhoeffer, I'm doing what I'm doing a lot of in these pages, compiling notes upon notes, waiting for themes or melodies to emerge (consider the faint notes of "Ode to Joy" that an attentive listener hears in the first movement of Beethoven's Ninth Symphony), planning the echoes for both *Checkpoint,* which I'd learned was about the attempted assassination of President George W. Bush, and *Human Smoke,* Baker's book about World War II. Even without "Wedding," it would be hard to believe that a writer of Baker's caliber could produce these books without Bonhoeffer in mind, and all together it added up to the first hints that spoke to the malicious rumor I'd heard that Baker had somehow denied the Holocaust.

28

AND WHAT TO MAKE, IN TURN, OF ALL THIS? I WASN'T SURE ABOUT
that either, except to say that I didn't think *The Mezzanine* and
Room Temperature were simple romans-à-clef using a façade of invention as inoculation against scandal and liability. What they made
me think of, what my reflexive association was, was James Agee's *A
Death in the Family*, a book also ostensibly about fatherhood that
won Agee a Pulitzer Prize for fiction in 1958, even though he died
before it was published and there's really no way of telling whether
he would have ultimately labeled the book fiction or nonfiction
(while he was alive he called it an "autobiographical novel"). Even
more problematic is "Knoxville: Summer, 1915," the short Agee
piece that editors slapped onto the front of *A Death in the Family*,
as prologue, in preparing the book for posthumous publication.
"Knoxville: Summer, 1915" is a brief, lyric portrait of middle-class
idyll famous for its protracted description of the hiss of garden
hoses that "fathers of families" use to water lawns in the evenings.
The hose sound is joined by other like noises—children pissing,
locusts—so that for a time "Knoxville: Summer, 1915" becomes an
orchestral arrangement of hissings, and it's the only piece of writing
I'm aware of that has been alternately labeled fiction, nonfiction,
and poetry. Once, it was even set to music by Samuel Barber.

Given Mike's and Baker's backgrounds as would-be composers,
I probably would have needed only this last to start thinking that
it might be a good idea to keep James Agee in mind while reading
Room Temperature. And sure enough, about halfway through, Mike
fizzles out a suggestive association of an airplane air-conditioning
vent with a garden hose:

I wondered for the first time whether the shape of the nozzle's inner cone was in fact more than decorative, whether it functioned aerodynamically . . . even at the hissiest stage near shutoff, to offer a palpable incumbency of coolness—unlike the gun-sprayers on garden hoses, which just before the flow of water was completely cut off created instead a Panamanian circular fan of mist [*Agee: ". . . the water was just a wide bell of film"*] on a plane perpendicular to the direction you were pointing the hose.

Classic early Baker, I saw now. Sly acknowledgment of a canonical predecessor, and an extension of the literary line with an even more exhaustive description of a recent advance in mechanical engineering. Plus Baker helped me understand the first line of "Knoxville: Summer, 1915," which I'd never quite fully grasped: "We are talking now of summer evenings in Knoxville, Tennessee, in the time that I lived there so successfully disguised to myself as a child." The line reflected back to Baker in that the descriptions we get of the Baker-figures encourage us not only to picture the Baker of his jacket photos, but to imagine a precocious and prematurely aged Baker. Mike of *Room Temperature* goes out of his way to describe an early loss of hair on his head and the early appearance of hair on his cheeks, as though, despite the pleasure he takes in the Bug, he too had only ever been disguised as a child. That led to another question: Why all these allusions to children's stories in books so clearly intended for adults, in books chock-full of references to philosophy, poetry, and the social sciences?

In Baker and Agee both, I came to think, there was a defiance of categories, a defiance of the modern library and bookstore practice of dividing books up by age (children's, young adult, adult) or genre (fiction, nonfiction, poetry). Of fiction and nonfiction, Baker once said that "one kind of writing feeds your head and one empties it," though he didn't specify which was which and his early "novels" pretty clearly aspire to both. Agee argued that "a certain kind of artist, [could be] distinguish[ed] from others as a poet rather than a prose writer," but he did so only after "Knoxville: Summer, 1915" proved even that to be an artificial division. The ever-expanding project of literary taxonomy (e.g., language poetry, historical fiction, literary journalism, etc.) is a gauge that measures an erosion of modern literature: modernity's lurch toward hyperspecification has fractured even the literary arts, and terms of fusion like "autobiographical novel" now seem problematic. Classification by age is even more insidious. The effect of categorizing some literature as "children's literature"—as books that children can use to prolong their childhood, as opposed to books that children can use to introduce themselves to the adult world—is that books wind up as little more than toys: writers become birthday clowns, and readers, after finally escaping artificially extended youths, become brats only disguised as adults. As I passed the midway point of *Room Temperature*, I began to see how it acted as a logical extension of *The Mezzanine*. *The Mezzanine* is the story of Nicholson Baker cracking open his egg from the inside, climbing out full of enthusiastic chirps. *Room Temperature* is a missive from the other end of the same gestation, in which Baker, holding the Bug, acts as incubator and nest. To be sure, there are moments when *Room Temperature* risks reading like Daddy porn ("She was a remarkable, remarkable daughter"; or, less innocently, "her captivating little coffee bean of a pudendum . . ."), but I needn't have worried over whether the book would apply to me, whether I could find myself in it. The real infant of the book is neither Baker nor the Bug—it's *us,* the reader. The book swaddled me just as I swaddled it two-handed in my lap, slowly rocking in my hammock. Those who lead a literary life seem old when they're young and young when they're old, but they're never actually either. Like a good book, they are bound by neither category nor time.

29

FOR AN AUTOBIOGRAPHER, IF THAT'S WHAT HE IS, NICHOLSON Baker had a pretty boring life to draw upon, unlike those writers who seemed important to him—Frank Conroy, Dietrich Bonhoeffer, and James Agee—each of whom, for a variety of reasons, had spectacular lives, perfect for literary renderings. *Room Temperature* acknowledges as much when a real jar appears in the book, on page five. Mike notices that the Bug's milk bottle has raised measurement marks molded along its flanks, and he associates this with glass peanut butter jars that were once manufactured with similar markings so that they could be used as measuring cups once the peanut butter was all gone. These older jars he associates with his mother, who once told him stories of eating peanut butter "straight from the jar" while she was pregnant. As a boy, Mike performed an act of radical empathy:

> Perhaps because of her own maternal craving she didn't mind later when I took a full jar and a silver spoon upstairs with me while building my plastic models.

Hence, by association, Nicholson Baker was born with a "silver spoon" in his mouth. And "silver spoon" reappears in its more common figurative usage three pages from the end of *Room Temperature*.

Peanut butter jars go on to play a crucial role in the book. Late in the action, Mike recalls having once imagined composing an experimental symphony that would begin with the puffy, vacuum-suck sound of a peanut butter jar being opened for the first time. That he didn't compose the symphony, that instead he gave up music to become a reviewer of television commercials who dreams of one day writing a book about commas, perhaps begins to hint at why Baker left music for a writing career.

When Baker told the *Paris Review*, "I'd exhausted the whole musical side of myself with the trombone story," or, to be more accurate, when I read this line in the interview before reading any of Baker's early stories, I had two simultaneous thoughts. First, I thought, "Well, that's patently false." I hadn't even read Nicholson Baker yet and I knew it wasn't true. *The Mezzanine* begins with a musical simile. *The Fermata* is titled after a symbol of musical notation. *The Anthologist* includes actual printed bars of music. Not only had Nicholson Baker not exhausted his musical side with the "trombone story," music might be the only note that echoes throughout his entire career.

Second, I thought, "Trombone story? *I* play the trombone."

To back up a bit. I don't recall exactly when I learned that Baker's instrument was the bassoon, but I do know that I laughed when I heard it. Why? Musical instruments, as everyone knows, form a sort of hierarchy of sexiness, with strings at the top (guitars and violins), assorted combinations in the middle (Miles Davis on trumpet, pursed-lip girls playing flute, breathy jazz ballads on tenor sax), and double reeds firmly and inexorably on the bottom (oboe, bassoon). The bassoon, sort of a piccolo didgeridoo, is quite simply the most preposterous of orchestral instruments. Despite a late twentieth-century surge in sonatas written for the instrument, its history is almost like its sound, a background buzz, a bit harsh, forgettable. The bassoon is exactly what you'd choose if you'd been drawn to music but hoped to project an air of ironic tragicomedy, and it's tempting to speculate that the young Nicholson Baker's choice of instrument demonstrated the same sort of raise-the-bar chutzpah that would later compel him to try launching a literary career with plotless novels. A careful read of *Room Temperature,* however, suggests something even more revealing.

Chapter eight begins with quick, capsule descriptions of the sleeping habits of the Bug, of Mike's father, and of Mike himself, and before long the stream of thought curls back to Patty writing in bed. For a moment, Mike thinks he can make out the quick, swishy sound of a comma dicing up her thoughts. This immediately puts him in mind of the oversized commas ("enormous, elaborately typographical") of one of his professors at Eastman. In music a comma is a breath mark, but breaths are not indicated by composers, as not everyone has the same lung capacity. Rather, individual musicians (and their professors) punctuate their own music. Mike proceeds to tell a lengthy story—the longest continuous narrative in *Room Temperature*—about his professor erasing a comma breath mark that Mike had carefully inserted in a "Flight of the Bumblebee"–style étude, and then demanding that within a week Mike master the play of the piece using only a single breath. Harrowed, Mike employs his preternatural ability with similes to grow his lungs, filling his mind during practice sessions with

> images of bullfrog pouches, bagpipes, dolphin blowholes, the surplus neoprene meteorological balloons that were advertised in the back of *Popular Science,* the floating spheres in toilet tanks, and the children's book about the Chinese kid who inhaled the sea.

It's the second of these, "bagpipes," that stood out to me because in the long aside that follows—before we learn how Mike's étude assignment turns out—we hear how he came to be interested in music in the first place: via an impressive performance of a bagpiper at a party thrown by Mike's parents when he was in the fourth grade.

What's so hot about bagpipes? To be honest, bagpipes (also a

double-reed instrument) make a fairly grating noise, like a motor running at dangerously high revolutions per minute. Still, they tend to be
associated with occasions of great solemnity, even grief. By contrast,
the bassoon is associated with no occasions at all, yet its alien sound
is similar enough to a bagpipe that it would be entirely reasonable for
a child drawn to music by a rousing bagpipe performance to choose
the bassoon as its orchestral equivalent. But that's not what happened.
"The next day I told my father that I had to learn the bagpipe," Mike
recalls, and it's his father who steered him to the French horn instead.

Regardless of whether the bagpipe story is true, why not the
bassoon here? Why fiction *now*, when the bassoon would have been
the more logical choice? Could it be a holdover of Baker worrying
over his image, as all writers do? Baker's early author notes omit the
bassoon detail, but the cat had actually been out of the bag since at
least 1982, when the *New York Times* cited Baker's "trombone story"
(published in the March 1982 issue of the *Atlantic*: his contributor's note specified that he had "played bassoon with the Rochester
Philharmonic Orchestra") in an article about musical composition
and the creative process. What that meant, because there were
likely far more readers of the article than readers of the story, is that
at the very dawn of Nicholson Baker's career, more people came
to know him as the "bassoon writer" than as the precocious and
talented author of a "trombone story." It didn't stop there, either.
Most feature articles about Baker that have appeared in the years
since have gone out of their way to make hay of what was really
a brief, inconsequential career as a fourth-chair bassoonist. Even
though Baker appears to have resigned himself to a quirky, schticky
persona—Hemingway has rifles; Baker has a long, unwieldy tube of
an instrument—early on it must have been terribly frustrating for a
writer of significant ambition to have let slip such fodder for light,
comic interview questions.

Or maybe it's even more interesting than that, as the word "bassoon" (the near-homonym "buffoon" is practically unavoidable) appears in exactly none of the books that Baker had published when I began reading him. (I know because I'd also downloaded searchable versions of all of them.) Music is everywhere in the books, as is an interest in the action of the brain, and I find it very unlikely that a writer who thinks often of music and who closely attends to the mind's reflexive associations would have never, while writing, reflexively thought of the instrument to which he dedicated a formative decade. He must be *avoiding* writing about bassoons. In contrast, bagpipes appear in Baker's work regularly. In *The Everlasting Story of Nory,* which I hadn't yet read, but which is about a young girl and is again dedicated to his daughter, Alice (*"For my dear daughter Alice, the informant"*), a peculiarly loud microwave oven sounds "like the humming note of a bagpipe." More recently, an article that Baker published about violent video games noted that one game's virtual deaths were attended to by "a tactful moment of funereal bagpipery." And more fancifully, but also more suggestively, the pornmonster of *House of Holes,* a creature that "masturbates constantly" and is the living embodiment of bad pornography, looks like "a bizarre bagpipe."

Does all this bagpipe imagery speak to residual feelings Baker had about his bassoonist career and the world of professional music? Does it explain the absence of bassoons in his work? If so, then it's worth noting that the bassoon-to-French-horn shift in *Room Temperature* was not the first time that Baker, in writing about music, scuttled his own instrument for one slightly higher on the sexy instrument scale. The first time, of course, was the uncollected "trombone story," which is unimaginatively titled "Playing Trombone," but which is actually a quite wonderful story—and one that does, in fact, make a glancing reference to a bassoon.

30

WHICH BRINGS ME BACK TO ME.

In 1978, the same year that Nicholson Baker has claimed to have finally sold his bassoon, I was in the sixth grade, entering my first music classroom. When the time came to choose instruments I picked the flute because I'd noticed the pursed lips of girls taking their first crack at the instrument and I wanted to radically empathize with them. But I couldn't do it—no matter how much lip pursing I did, I couldn't make a flute make a noise. This being an obstacle to a musical career, I had to choose another instrument, and this time I went with something that looked easy: the trombone. The trombone has only one moving part, but this fact alone meant it wasn't easy. The "slide" is effectively an elongated tuning slide, and what this means is that in order to be a good trombonist you need an ear capable of distinguishing variations of sound resulting from even minuscule movements of the slide. I did not have a good ear.

There were other problems as well. I couldn't triple-tongue to save my life. I understood in the abstract that triple-tonguing was a tongue-twisting trick that trained your tongue to trickle out trills of notes, but that taught me nothing at all about how people actually managed to triple-tongue, and triple-tonguing turned out to be a terribly important trombone talent. Also, I panicked whenever I was expected to improvise in afterschool jazz band. I froze. I improvised silence. Worst of all was sight-reading, playing music without ever having practiced it or studied it beforehand. Then I *did* improvise. I gave up the trombone at twenty, having played for most of the previous summer with a youth orchestra and having, as a result, a simultaneously horrifying and triumphant experience that now stands for my entire tenure as a trombonist.

I was the orchestra's ringer, but only for my age. At nineteen, I was five or six years older and far less talented than most of that ensemble's near prodigies. In the early part of the summer we played Strauss waltzes for gatherings of elderly people and rehearsed for a youth orchestra competition to be held that August in Scotland. Our program abroad included *An American in Paris,* a Sibelius violin concerto, and Shostakovich's Fifth Symphony, this last being the work that would test my mettle. The final movement of Shostakovich No. 5 calls for the principal trombone to hit a high A, along with the principal trumpet and the principal French horn. High A is close to the top of the trombone range, and in practice I hit the note badly every time, which is to say I didn't hit it at all. Our conductor, an Italian named Mr. Caniglia, who was not a particularly good communicator (conductors are notoriously language-challenged Italians), berated me mercilessly over that high A. Once, when he realized that I couldn't tell him whether I'd been sharp or flat in my most recent attempt at the note, he turned for help to the violins, a row of pompous, preadolescent girls. "He's sharp!" they shrieked in unison. Another time he instructed me to remove my mouthpiece from my instrument and place it on my music stand: this was the only way to ensure that I would not play it wrong. I didn't take this treatment lying down. I went to the library and researched Shostakovich. Yes, Stalin had claimed that the climactic high A of Shostakovich No. 5 embodied the Soviet ideal, but hadn't Shostakovich later called Stalin an oaf? He *had,* I informed our conductor. It's supposed to be out of tune, I explained. That's *irony.* Mr. Caniglia was unmoved, and he pestered me until we left the continent. My one glorious moment as a musician came at the festival's final performance, when I knew that I'd hit the note correctly only because of the expression on Mr. Caniglia's face as I played it.

I describe this scene because "Playing Trombone," a fanciful, miniature *Künstlerroman* that tracks the education of a young trombonist from the recognition of his genius to the moment when his genius has been quashed by the institutions of professional music, contains one almost exactly like it. The prodigy is assigned a solo that calls for him to hit a high E. He's singled out in rehearsals for criticism by a remarkably inarticulate conductor, and though he comes through in the clutch ("[He] reached for the note, willed it forth. In a bulb-flash of sound it lit the hall for an instant of blue perfection") what the note truly sounds is the end of his passion for music. So perhaps with Baker. "Playing Trombone" not only contained what to that point was the lone bassoon cameo in Baker's career (there's a reference to a fermata, too), it also established the children's story motif. The story begins with a fairytale lilt ("There once was a miner who lived . . ."), and soon enough the trombonist's episodic education and career approximate Alice's series of nonsensical encounters in Wonderland. The speech of a music teacher, quite mad, ensures that we make the association:

> Ah, have you ever *felt* the absolute power of, say, an A-flat major triad when it is played on a good piano in the context of absolute silence? Wait! *Felt!* 'Felt' is a partial clue. Who gave a famous tea party in a children's book? The Hatter. And why was the Hatter mad, people? Because felt was used in hat manufacture, and mercury was essential in making felt, which caused brain damage. But here's the key: felt is what tips the hammers of every good piano in the world—the felt hammer is the mediator between my hands and the piano wires—those prison bars, that slanting, silver-gray rain. Once again, mercury and the piano, the piano and mercury. Our instrument is our universe.

"Playing Trombone" is not, however, the Disneyfied Wonderland that gave us Alice blue. Rather it offers advance warning to would-be musicians, much in the same way Carroll's muted cautionary tale, a jolly dystopia, alerts children to the cruel and nonsensical world of adults that they are fated to enter,

Mike's étude assignment in chapter eight of *Room Temperature* ends much as the trombonist's career does. He succeeds in playing the étude in a single breath, but his professor only nods and says, "All right, it's physically possible." He reaches for a pencil and puts the breath mark, "a beautiful deliberate, dark comma!" back where Mike first placed it. Mike is jubilant at first, but soon recognizes the lesson to have been an exercise in empty virtuosity. Within weeks he decides to transfer to Swarthmore, "where commas could be stuck in and taken out without the risk of physical injury."

So Mike, it can be said, expresses a hope that language might succeed where music fails. *Room Temperature* presents us too with études in the form of long, billowy sentences, and Mike offers the idealistic argument that the nature of modern life reinforces the need for a virtuosity of thought, as conveyed by words and punctuation creatively combined:

> In our desire for provincial correctness and holy-sounding simplicity and the rapid teachability of intern copy editors we had illegalized all variant forms [of punctuation]—and, as with the loss of subvarieties of corn or apples, this homogenization of product was accomplished at a major unforeseen cost: our stiff-jointed prose was less able . . . to adapt itself to those very novelties of social and technological life whose careful interpretation and weighing was the principle reason for the continued indispensability of the longer sentence.

This is what Baker, abandoning one kind of comma for another, smuggled from music to literature.

A link between writing and music is of course nothing new. We compose music and prose; we read both too. But does that mean that reading a book is like listening to Mahler, or J. J. Johnson, or the Talking Heads? No. When musicians read music, they are playing it. When I started reading aloud to myself—and when, in my hammock, I found myself reading aloud Baker's étude sentences, using commas as breath marks—I recognized the sensation at once: sight-reading. Written language is like a score: Before you learn to read, it looks like gibberish, difficult and strenuous, but eventually you make a breakthrough and you can read the words and sentences without sounding out each and every letter. Many stop there, but those who don't find that after a great deal of study and practice they can sight-read even difficult books with impossibly long sentences that twist and writhe like complicated melodies. Then, and only then, do you get it: the almost occult ability to tap into an author's mind, to hear the characteristic hum of their voice whispering breathless in your ear.

31

THAT'S WHAT, IN THE DEPTH OF MY CRISIS, I'D FORGOTTEN HOW to do—take pleasure in the careful study of a challenging book. I discovered it again in Nicholson Baker, and as a result I'd grown energized. Thinking forward to all the Baker books I hadn't read, I felt like a perfect lever or a well-calibrated tool, maybe like one of those adjustable wrenches that amplify torque. Baker was in my blood now, which meant that I'd begun to dream and fantasize about him, and now that I thought about it I wondered whether my elaborate vision of the fields around my hammock teeming with joyriding

Baker-babies was not the result of actual reading, but was the even deeper product of a reading-addled brain at work in the in-between, just right, Alice blue of human consciousness.

In any event it was this sense of vigor and renewal that explains why I responded poorly when, nearly finished with *Room Temperature* (I was at a boil now, dying to get my schoolwork done so I could ride out to the hammock and finish it), I came home from school one day and found Catherine wearing *those* shoes. Those shoes were the shoes she'd worn late one night when we'd still been courting by mail and a sexy bedtime exchange compelled me to forgo sleep and complete the six-hour drive to her house in four and a half hours, and she answered the door in shoes with ribbony straps that tied around her ankles and climbed partway up her calves. I'd taken a great deal of pleasure in untying those shoes, and ever since they had served as an informal signal that we might soon be intimate. But now I was so keyed up by Nicholson Baker that I didn't even look at her shoes, even though that morning we had discussed the possibility of having sex later in the day, which is how we'd come to manage the ongoing deterioration of our intimate life. Our conversation went something like this:

"How long do you teach today?"

"'Til four, depending."

"Are you coming home right away?"

"Yes. Why?"

"What are you doing then?"

"When I come home? Reading Baker, probably."

"Maybe we can find time to—"

"Sure!"

This was quite lovely of Catherine because as I'd found a renewed sense of purpose in Nicholson Baker, she had continued feeling clogged. She watched admiringly as I scribbled wild annotations in the margins of books like an insane mathematician trying to keep up with inspired equations, and she listened dutifully whenever I stumbled across a passage that I just had to read aloud to someone beside myself. But even this was a strain. She'd had no luck making a home for herself in the former bed and breakfast, and while for me the vision of Catherine shoe-smacking her way across the kitchen floor in pursuit of a wily and ultimately evasive scorpion was the stuff of light comedy, for her it was only a detail cropped from a much larger canvas depicting the world fallen into ruin. In short, it was harder for her to muster intimate energies than it was for me, yet she had managed it. And what did I do? I walked briskly past her and stuffed *Room Temperature* into a shoulder bag.

"I'm headed to the hammock!"

"How long will you be gone?"

"Don't know! 'Til I'm done."

I left her to care for the remaining farm kitten—by now simply called Baby. More and more Baby had been venturing down from the roof, and we had started letting her sleep in the laundry room on coyote-likely evenings. Apart from planning for our Paris trip— we'd rented a charming atelier, a converted photographer's studio— Baby was Catherine's lone daily comfort. Out in the hammock, as I approached the end of *Room Temperature,* I found myself thinking of Baby and the family that Catherine and I were determined not to have. At the beginning of chapter fifteen, the Bug finally finishes her twenty-minute meal and fades off to sleep with a breath like "a sob played backward," a thought that puts Mike in mind of an old Eastman classmate, a mezzo-soprano whose laugh made him pity her. This was what life was like, he realizes, for people who were without families, without Bugs. Nicholson Baker felt sorry for us! This was perfect, because as jubilant as I had become, I'd begun to feel a little sorry for Baker. Something was missing in his life, as evidenced by the claim he would soon make: *U and I* was a test of whether he should go on being a writer. What was bugging him? I thought back on Baker's two author photos, taken not far apart in time but nevertheless charting a decline from a Cheshire grin to the flat, dumb gaze of a lizard:

I wasn't the first to have had thoughts like these. Martin Amis beat me to that too. In the years after Amis panned *Vox* ("I found I was genuinely sorry as opposed to hypocritically sorry, that the book wasn't better"), Nicholson Baker had come to Amis's mind with surprising regularity as he continued filing reports on literature. The most recent reference I'd found, in a review of someone else's book, characterized Baker's literary aloofness as leonine in nature. Amis was wrong about Baker in almost every other respect, and I may have more to say about that, but on this point he was on to something. *The Mezzanine* was reviewed quite well but did not sell particularly well. *Room Temperature* did significantly worse. Could that have been causing Baker's decline? Amis quoted an unflattering remark from Baker's editor—"Don't let Nick fool you. He wants to be rich and famous"—but I really didn't think that was it. If "Playing Trombone" documented Baker's realization that he was not a musical prodigy, then it has to be allowed that his first three books, read carefully, tell the story of his realization that he's not a literary prodigy either (*The Mezzanine*: "You realize that you are no prodigy . . .").

There were other disappointments too. *The Mezzanine* and *Room Temperature* are tiny wonderlands in which cogs in the corporate system and reviewers of television commercials can recite Pope and Hopkins from memory. But what happens when Baker tries spontaneous quotation in *U and I*? Faulty memory.

Language, too. A quick flip through the Baker books I'd not yet read turned up the occasional étude sentence, but later in his career they are far more the exception than the rule. Despite the "indispensability" of long sentences, *Room Temperature* marks the high point of Baker's punctuarial ambition.

Perhaps most important, right around this time in his career, 1991, he published a short piece in *The New Yorker* that was ostensibly about an ice storm that killed many old trees in Rochester. Really it was about two more important things. Overtly, it contained a surge of feeling wholly absent in his other work to this point, a deep abiding anger over the bombing campaign that the United States had begun in Iraq six weeks earlier: "We deserve at least this much ice after that much fire." And accidentally, because the piece was published anonymously even though Baker was already a regular contributor to the magazine, it expressed awareness that a guru of minutiae, a writer who toys with model warplanes rather than flies the real thing, like James Salter, might not be able to authoritatively address the broader strokes of history. As a writer, Baker had been typecast as a kitten in a world that was just then beginning to slouch toward lions.

Not long after I finished *Room Temperature,* something happened that made me doubt my newfound reading enthusiasm, something that made me radically empathize with Baker's own emerging doubtfulness. Catherine and I woke early on the morning of a trip. We were headed out on a ten-hour drive to one city to retrieve a series of her prints at the end of a show, and the next day we would drive them to another city for another show. As we gathered our bags in the living room, Baby hopped up onto the exterior sill of a window, mewing through the screen. "She can't come in," Catherine said, snuggling a good-bye to her own pampered kitty. "She has to learn to be a farm cat." Baby disappeared, and it was still dark a few minutes later as we packed the car. We checked our map, programmed the GPS, and departed. At the end of the driveway the car's headlights fell on something in the road. It was Baby, out in the middle of the dangerous four-laner, her body crumpled and bloody, having since the moment we'd seen her followed her curiosity as far from the house as she'd ever gone in her life. She had wandered onto the alien blacktop, into the path of a car that didn't swerve to avoid her.

"Oh, no," I said.

Catherine was reorganzing the contents of her bag. "What?"

I nodded toward Baby, and Catherine looked out the windshield, hesitated. Then she wailed, wild with sobs, a horrid unclogging. It was her fault, she cried. It wasn't, I said—it was mine for our having moved here, it was ours, it was neither. It was this plague-lousy world that punished every effort to make it bearable. More cars zoomed past Baby's body, each a wincing threat to hit her again. In the next hectic interval I dodged the traffic to scrape Baby into a cardboard coffin, and Catherine trained the car's headlights on a spot in the yard so I could dig a hole for her. We both cried a little as we finally hit the road. For me it all turned to rage a mile away when we stopped at a convenience store for coffee and a few seedy cowboys leered at Catherine as we passed.

I noted an odd device at the store's coffee station. Someone had invented a simple mechanism to solve the hassle of nested plastic coffee cup lids, the kind that once you've poured your coffee you can't just pluck single-handedly from the stack because they tend to stick to one another. Instead you have to set your coffee down and pry at them multifingeredly as though you're working out a knot in a shoelace, because that's the only way to come away with just one lid and not six or seven. The new device was an old-style knife switch, a lever that extracted the lids one at a time and practically handed them to you. Of course, I noted this because it was the kind of thing that Baker, early in his career, would have seen as a hopeful advance. *The Mezzanine* even briefly addresses coffee cup lids—"Howie" describes driving while holding "a Styrofoam cup of coffee with a special sipmaster top"—but that was decades old at this point, and no one drinks from Styrofoam anymore, and more important there never has been any kind of successful "sipmaster top." You always wind up either burning your tongue or the roof of your mouth, and the edges of the plastic holes, or the little plastic flaps that are supposed to seal the opening at not-drinking moments, always wind up cutting little surgical incisions in your lip or your tongue.

Catherine and I ran the reverse gauntlet past the sleazy cowpokes, and on the drive I let myself muse over several decades of history of disposable coffee cup lids. The evolution seemed to have drawn inspiration from everything from the Bauhaus to NASA, yet the simple truth seemed to be that no matter how complicated a lid you devise, the simple problem of drinking hot liquid while driving is insurmountable. You just can't design a good hole. No washer or gasket completely solves the problem of what's not there. Figuratively, that was maybe what was bothering Nicholson Baker. We're not all born with silver spoons in our mouths. Some of us are bombed, and some of us are born into tragic circumstances, witness brutality, and die at the hands of those who can't be bothered to swerve, perhaps because they're struggling to drink from a disposable coffee cup. Baker was years from *House of Holes,* but he already knew that some holes can't be filled, not with memories or commas or regret. A hole is negative space

32

WHEN WE DELIVERED CATHERINE'S PRINTS TO THE SECOND CITY of our trip, the curator who solicited her work decided on the spot to buy all of them, every last damn piece. We were so excited on the long drive home we stopped at a motel for a quiet, road-style tryst, in and out in four hours. It was only a temporary respite, as back at the former bed and breakfast the stain of Baby's blood and what of her I'd been unable to scoop up with my hands on a dark, busy road was still there, not yet harvested by insects. The stain remained visible for some time, and Catherine's general feeling of cloggedness did not begin to improve until a few weeks later when she left for Paris and had to contend with the mother of all clogs.

Thankfully, because our plan called for her to begin photo expeditions through the city as I finished up my last week of classes, I heard about the ordeal only via e-mail. On her first night Catherine wrote that our atelier in the sixth arrondissement was "adorable," but adorable in this context was euphemistic plumbing-speak for primitive and horrific. The former bed and breakfast was similarly charming, actually. Defying a long-standing architect's rule that the opposing ends of the human digestive tract should be structurally accommodated at as great a distance as is humanly possible, the former bed and breakfast's only fully functional bathroom sat immediately adjacent to its kitchen. True, this was a step up from our dinky apartment, which as I've said sometimes required on-the-fly calculations of deep plumbological calculus, but the bed and breakfast's practically cubist juxtaposition of intake and outflow facilities led to aerosol mixtures that were novel even to us, scents that brought me into full appreciation of Catherine's long-standing, Franco-based passion for the history and art of perfumery. To be fully honest, I failed to recognize at first that Catherine's characterization of the atelier—"downright adorable" were her exact words—was ironical, insincere. I figured it out only as her letters chronicled her crisis.

The atelier's bathroom, you see, was not adjacent to its kitchen, it was *in* it. Early French studios, it seemed, were designed to demonstrate the flexibility of staple products (e.g., brushes, baking powder, scouring pads, etc.), and the atelier's seated-shower/vanity/sink combo unit had been installed so close to the stove that the random jumblings of not-put-away items that are common in both kitchens and bathrooms overlapped such that your bread knife might wind up lying alongside your toothpaste, and your coffee cup got chummy with your deodorant. But this was mere inconvenience compared to the atelier's toilet, which was downstairs in the bedroom. Everyone knows that the maximalist history of French gastronomy is matched by its minimalist history of hygiene (e.g., peeing in sinks, Josephine's wash habits, etc.), and that the atelier even had a toilet seemed to have been an idea that came to its owners only late and when they happened to be strapped for cash for renovations. Some apartments have "half baths." The atelier had a "half toilet" that remained hidden as long as no one was sitting on it. Then it wasn't hidden at all.

Catherine's problem began, she wrote, when she pulled the chain on the wall reservoir on her first day—a Friday—and took note, thankfully before she shut the door, that what she'd been trying to flush was not, as they say, going down. There ought to be a particular word for this by-now-known-the-world-over dread, a terrible dropping sensation that flushes through you when you realize that what you've dropped and flushed might be coming back at you—*apoopalypse* comes to mind—and what Catherine did, heroically, when she recognized the severity of the tornadically swirling, ever-rising waters, was scurry up the spiral wrought-iron staircase to the other half of the atelier's bathroom, also known as the kitchen, and retrieve a set of implements that permitted her to ladle out— her phrase, *ladle out*—a generous enough helping of raw sewage such that the emergent crisis, at least, was averted.

But that was just the beginning because the toilet remained clogged, impervious to vigorous plunging, and it was right at the beginning of the weekend, and our ornery Parisian concierge, unimpressed with Catherine's atrophied French, made the assumption that the clog was the result of Catherine's having flushed something inappropriate down the toilet—an American-sized tampon probably—and so Catherine had to suffer for a couple days until a French plumber could be found, and in that period, she wrote, she wound up having to use not a formal chamber pot, but a *makeshift* chamber pot, and her e-mails did not specify which piece of the atelier's cookware she conscripted into this service. Nor did I ever ask.

On Sunday, a friendly French plumber finally arrived and took one look at Catherine's chic Parisian frame and explained to the concierge that there was no way this American caused this clog. Much more likely was that an animal of some kind, grown weary of life in Paris, had decided to end it all and in the process leave behind enough of a mess so that it could feel that its life had amounted to something. It was probably a pigeon. Everyone in Paris hates pigeons. The pigeons, in turn, hate everyone except the homeless—everyone, that is, with plumbing—and this mutually ferocious scorn keys off a kind of avian existential ennui. In some cases, near the desperate end, the birds' ennui turns aggressive and vengeful. What Catherine suffered, then, was a *suicide pigeon,* a bird that had decided to go out not with a bang but a gurgle, entombing itself in the plumbing of a youngish couple hoping to be Parisians, if only for the holidays.

From a continental remove this episode had a jaunty romance, and it went a long way toward alleviating the anxiety I'd begun to feel over visiting Paris for the first time after having years before missed an opportunity to shape my worldview there, as both Catherine and Nicholson Baker had done. I was nervous, I had some peace that needed to be made, but Catherine's expertly rendered drama kept me from brooding too long or too deep. The episode fit perfectly with my ever-growing understanding of Baker, too. If it's fair to say that a couple's history of intimacy aligns with the evolution of the plumbing with which they outfit their homes, that relationship stages ranging from the raging honeymoon of youth to the sedate partnership of old age correspond to living arrangements that initially compel attendance to body matters at close quarters but change over time with the addition of a second sink or perhaps an entire additional bathroom, each permutation alleviating certain interpersonal tensions, surely, but each also resulting in corresponding drops-off in physical familiarity and activity, then Nicholson Baker's sex books, which I'd packed in my satchel for the flight to France, were perhaps best described as an attempt to replumb the house of human intimacy, to yank out all the corroded metal and replace it with state-of-the-art piping such that we might once again become acquainted with what goes on behind closed bathroom doors. Or at least that was my suspicion before I actually read the books. Because even though it might seem strange that a writer who broke onto the literary scene with philosophical musings on escalators, fatherhood, and the mind chugging from idea to idea would suddenly start thinking a whole lot about sex and masturbation, it actually makes perfect sense, given the earlier work. On page six of *The Mezzanine,* "Howie" admits to being a "steady customer" of men's magazines and he indulges, in a footnote, in a "helpful vignette" about a convenience-store counter girl. Mike of *Room Temperature* ups the ante from there by claiming that pictures of floppy titted noble savages in *National Geographic* were his "pornography between the ages of seven and nine." And later, Mike launches into an evocative description of a fifth-grade encounter with an instructional female anatomy manikin. This scene goes on for quite some time. It's the first full-blown tongue-in-cheek sex scene in Baker's work. And it follows Mike's explanation that he and Patty had consummated their engagement not with sex (they'd been having sex for a while) but with a new way to refer to their gastrointestinal goings-on. Patty offered up "going big job" as a substitute for what polite company calls "number two" or "have a B.M." To Mike's mind, "going big job" amounts to a "further upward cranking of intimacy," and the passage, in which the engaged couple playfully conjugate their private verb, was one of those that I found so diaphragm-grindingly funny that I read it aloud to Catherine. She liked it too, and actually we did more than just read the passage. We started to employ Mike and Patty's phrase, and not just in the contexts that Mike and Patty had exhausted.

Of the many miraculous things about Catherine, the most miraculous was that she'd been a miracle baby. As an infant, she had been afflicted with a horrible illness, and it was only an experimental treatment that saved her life. The illness left no scars, but her bowels had been a problem ever since, and "going big job," for a time, gave us a way to refer to her indelicate troubles. Stuck in Paris with a malfunctioning toilet, Catherine made no mention of her bowels in her letters, but my awareness of her difficulties eventually encouraged me to read between the lines and recognize just how god-awful the adorable atelier had turned out to be.

I tried to look on the bright side—to see the toilet as half full, rather than overflowing. The atelier may have represented a step backward for us in a domestic engineering sense, but maybe *because* it was a step backward it could amount to a step forward in an intimate sense. Our intimacy had been rudely interrupted by Nicholson Baker, the former bed and breakfast, my irrepressible negativity, and the loss of Baby. Yet hope loomed in the form of lazy atelier upkeep: We would pretty much have to come to know each other in new and intimate ways. Of course, not having lived through the clog experience meant that I had a healthy critical distance on it, a distance Catherine lacked, and that's how I explained our first night in Paris, which, despite a perfect meal in a perfect French restaurant with perfect foie gras, amounted to a failure in that back at the atelier we failed to consummate France. There were other hurdles too—Catherine was menstruating, I was jet-lagged—and it was all too much, and we gave up after a short period of rolling around on the futon. Then Catherine climbed up to the kitchen so that I could try for a jet-lagged job in the half toilet before we called it a night. Ideally Catherine would have stayed downstairs so we could get right to the business of compulsory intimacy, but I didn't protest as the task I had to perform was an ugly one. My confused body was contending with a new continent and rich food, and what that meant was that my labor was conducted without proper focus. As any office manager knows, such work tends to produce sloppy results, and I was left struggling to clean up after myself with scratchy tissue paper and a toilet of suspect efficacy. Once I was finished, I flushed and gave the relevant body region a final swipe, and, as with light-colored household surfaces, it was the observed purity of the daubing mechanism that established the cleanliness of the thing daubed. What I was left with was a not exactly soiled, but decidedly not reusable, bit of wadding material. And that was my dilemma.

Should I flush again to get rid of it, risking another clog (for the duration of our stay, each yank on the chain felt like the lever pull of a demonic slot machine), or should I simply dump the tissue into the bowl to await a future flush? For safety's sake I decided on the latter course, and it was only when Catherine's own nighttime preparations took her partway into the half toilet that I got a real sense of the robustness of her post-traumatic clog mood.

"Did you use too much toilet paper?"

"No, I—"

"You *can't* use too much paper. I'm not living through that again."

"I didn't, I can—"

"You do this at home. *All* the time."

"I'm trying to—"

"You don't *know* what it was like. I know I made it sound sweet and charming in e-mails, but it was *not*. It was horrible. Horrible. And if it happens again, it's *your* problem. I'll go take photographs."

Our next day in Paris was better. An early-morning walk along the Seine became our routine for a time, and that evening we ceremonially consummated France. But this was the mood I took with me on the Métro when I headed to a brasserie in Saint-Germain-des-Prés to begin reading *Vox,* Baker's all-dialogue "phone-sex novel."

33

NOW SEEMS LIKE A GOOD TIME TO ASK AN IMPERTINENT QUESTION: What do I know about Nicholson Baker's penis? A good bit, actually:

The Mezzanine: "Howie" reveals that he had once stolen his mother's sanitary napkins, punctured them, and then "push[ed] [his] crayon-sized penis through the hole, and urinate[d] into the toilet." (An earlier footnote makes passing reference to "Howie"'s "miniature dick.")

Room Temperature: Mike excitedly tells a dorm-roomful of college girls, Patty among them, that his "genitalia were constructed on a humble scale."

U and I: Baker revels in the discovery that he has psoriasis, which links him to Updike, but he worries because his affliction is less serious: "Phase 1 involved only the scalp and penis."

It was opening *Vox* for the first time that got me thinking about all this. There was no dedication page this time around ("For M. W. B." appears in very small type in the front matter), and there was no author photo and there wouldn't be for *The Fermata*, either. What got me thinking about his penis was that for a couple books now Baker had stopped mentioning Eastman and music in his author's notes. The author's note of the first edition of *U and I* is extremely spare (year of birth, previous books, general location of residence), and *Vox*'s is about the same though it lists the magazines he'd been writing for and—here was the clue—it specifies that in addition to two novels he had produced "a work of autobiographical criticism entitled *U and I*."

Why not "memory criticism" here? It's odd because even though *U and I* toys with other names for its technique ("*phrase filtration*," "*closed book examination*") it's "memory criticism" that sticks and reappears throughout the book. "Autobiographical criticism" is a phrase never associated with Nicholson Baker before the author's note of *Vox*.

What does this have to do with his penis? Well, when I said

that *U and I* was the first book of writerly criticism to have been published in some time, that wasn't strictly true. Or at least it's debatable, as the broad range of work that fits into what is, at best, a loosely defined category makes it a difficult history to track. I'd borrowed "creative criticism" from critic J. E. Spingarn, who coined the term in a 1910 essay inspired by a remark from Goethe: "There is a destructive and a creative or constructive criticism." When Spingarn published the idea in book form—*Creative Criticism* appeared in 1917, and again in 1931—it caused enough of a stir that H. L. Mencken and T. S. Eliot weighed in, but that was about the end of it. That's why, in the 1980s, when a number of critics, mostly feminist, grown weary of sublimating their identities to masculine pronoun–rich academic prose, set out for something new, something that would let them emphasize the self rather than stifle it, they called the technique not "creative criticism" but "autobiographical criticism." ("Confessional criticism," "personal criticism," "impressionistic criticism," "sequestered criticism," "autocritography," and "plebeian autobiography" also got bandied about, but "autobiographical criticism" won the day.) This too caused a stir. Traditional critics refused to regard the work of autobiographical critics as true scholarship, and the fact that it became a debate over "scholarship" probably explains why it too petered out. What's worth considering now is the nature of the traditional critics' objections. "Naked display of one's personal feelings," one critic claimed, "more often than not falls into a complacent exhibitionism." Even that was oblique. A few years later another critic took wry note of "the recent turn toward autobiography in literary criticism and the proclivity to mention things like peeing and penises."

Actual examples of this were tame and rare. One autobiographical critic titled a chapter "My Father's Penis." Another likened his penis to a chainsaw. Particular attention was given to Jane

Tompkins's 1987 essay "Me and My Shadow," often cited as the manifesto that set the autobiographical criticism ball rolling. For one unsympathetic critic, Tompkins's brief stream of consciousness sequence culminating in a thought about "going to the bathroom" demonstrated everything that was wrong with autobiographical criticism:

> The urinary motif might appeal, I suppose, to those who are searching for a whiff of the carnivalesque within the desiccated routines of scholarly argument. But there's nothing here of the Rabelasian abandon that might fulfill such a desire. . . . The mention of going to the bathroom functions as a conventional instance of the *vraisemblable*. [But] there is no point to this, it is only mentioned to inscribe the reality of the story. . . . Or, to say it better, *this* is the kind of reality Tompkins values for herself, precisely as an avoidance of the problem of theorizing selfhood, about which going to the bathroom has absolutely nothing to say, for or against—as if one could say, for instance "I pee, therefore I am."

In other words, what one should do is ignore reality so as to understand the self that exists in reality, the self that *must* be theorized about. A general lack of enthusiasm for excretory activity perhaps explains why traditional critics often wind up just so full of shit.

Anyway, the trend line merged with Baker. Autobiographical criticism appeared in 1987, and *U and I* specifies that Baker began taking notes on perhaps writing something "vaguely autobiographical" about Updike in 1987 and 1988. Then, after *U and I,* Baker appeared to offer a retroactive nod to autobiographical critics with the author's note of *Vox,* a book that, along with *The Fermata,* which appeared two years later, outgrew the casual descriptions of Baker's penis from his early books by making the entire spectrum of taboo subjects the central focus of his first books that were *not* autobiographical in nature. The question I had, as my espresso arrived and I looked out onto the French *vraisemblable* teeming with happy little cars and impossibly well-dressed holiday shoppers– the very model of a society seething beneath with forbidden truths—was whether Baker's sex books could accurately be described as appealing only to those looking for "Rabelasian abandon."

Hardly.

34

VOX BEGINS WITH "'WHAT ARE YOU WEARING?' HE ASKED," AND from this alone we can begin to guess at the basic situation: an intimate voice exchange conducted between persons unable to view each other. That's shortly confirmed: a man and a woman, strangers, on the phone. By page nine—after the man offers a detailed description of his orgasms, which I will return to shortly—we begin to get hints as to how this conversation came about, the man and woman each describing how they stumbled across the advertisement for the phone service they have dialed. This is the only real fantasy in the book—if that can be said of a book composed almost entirely of fantasy—in that most books have settings, they are set in glorious cities, countries in turmoil, apocryphal counties, places that sometimes loom as large as the characters themselves. *Vox* has no setting at all.

Or perhaps there's an implied setting. We come to know just a few things about the world outside the spoken exchange. The man and woman call themselves Jim and Abby. Jim is from a "western city," Abby is from an "eastern city," and each had stumbled across an advertisement placed by a company called 2VOX, a seemingly automated social networking organization that the jacket copy of *Vox* calls a "party line," but which is closer to what in a few years' time would come to be known as a "chat room." When you call 2VOX you land in a virtual arena of competing voices. Male callers attempt to get themselves invited by female callers into private "rooms," and that's where Jim and Abby "are." That's where the bit of fantasy is too because even though 2VOX has monetized its product—all callers pay two dollars per minute—nothing stops a couple from simply exchanging phone numbers and conducting their business on ordinary lines. At one point, Jim and Abby contemplate this but decide against it, preferring to enthusiastically patronize a business they wish to support. But could such a company survive a real marketplace? No way. And what's the service anyway? *Vox* pretty much underscores that the only truly necessary provider of telephonic sex aid devices is AT&T. All 2VOX supplies is virtual proximity. The enterprise's success, then, suggests a kind of background dystopia in which even engaging, intelligent people like Jim and Abby, as we find them to be, have difficulty discovering each other.

But that's not the setting either. *Vox* is mostly dialogue, but it's not all dialogue. Significant hesitations in the exchange are indicated with ellipses or "There was a pause," the first of these occurring around page ten and sticking out like a comma in Gertrude Stein. Slightly more elaborate breaks, brief descriptions of the crackle of the long-distance line, or noise resulting from the shifting of a handset from one ear to the other reveal the book's point of view. *Vox* is told in the third person, but it's not omniscient: There is no nineteenth-century narrator interrupting as events proceed, nor are we attached or limited to either Jim's or Abby's sensibilities.

This makes it a kind of minimalism, and you can be forgiven, given the twentieth century's periodic obsession with literary minimalism, for at first thinking that *Vox* might align with the aesthetic trajectory that shoots through Hemingway (masculine stoicism) and Raymond Carver (lower-middle-class emotional stuntedness). But that's wrong. The setting of *Vox* does not require a reader to will belief in Spanish bullrings or dingy kitchens in rural Washington. Far more natural is the thought that came to me around page thirty or so: *We've called in too,* the price of the book was our two dollars per minute, we're there in the chat room with Jim and Abby, hearing what we'd hear if we too had struggled to find others of like mind and had simply dialed and bounced into the conversation by mistake. *Vox* is a conference call. Its setting is wherever we happen to be when we read the book.

35

WHO SHOULD *NOT* BE FORGIVEN IS MARTIN AMIS. AMIS, WHO WROTE in his pan of *Vox* that the book "asks nothing of you," and who claimed that "its slightness is inbuilt. It has no room to manoeuvre. It has *no prose.*" That's flatly and demonstrably wrong, and to ignore its prose is to pass over a critical feature of the book. But even if it weren't wrong, Martin Amis knows full well that there is a long tradition of books made up mostly or entirely of dialogue. Plato, for crying out loud. And Amis misses—or ignores—that the obvious precursor to *Vox* is not Hemingway or Carver (or even Updike or Sade). It's Henry James. Before I sat down with *Vox,* or, more specifically, after Catherine and I returned from our walk along the Seine that morning but before I headed to the Métro, I read Henry

James's preface to *The Awkward Age*, which is composed mostly of dialogue and is the work of a writer who to that point was far better known for his elaborate prose. Amis should have made this association because he quoted from *U and I*, and *U and I* quotes James's famous prefaces. (Maybe I'm being too hard on Martin Amis. After all, he didn't choose to read *Vox*, he didn't call in like I did—someone just handed him the phone. Anyway, it must be awful to be a canonical writer working in the shadow of an even more canonical father. It must be terrible to know that every time you excuse yourself from awkward cocktail party conversations, the person you've just left says to whoever remains, "Nice bloke, Martin—not his dad, though." It must be awful to know that every woman you sleep with does so because she craves the seed of the truly great, now beyond reach, but which can perhaps be reconstituted from a watered-down specimen.) And the preface to *The Awkward Age* might just as easily serve as the preface to *Vox*. James insists on the seriousness of his ambition despite the appearance of "lightest comedy," and he claims that the book draws its power from the pull of London social life. This circle

> was favourable to "real" talk, to play of mind, to an explicit interest in life, a due demonstration of the interest by persons qualified to feel it: all of which meant frankness and ease, the perfection, almost, as it were, of intercourse, and a tone as far as possible from that of the nursery and the schoolroom—as far as possible removed even, no doubt, in its appealing "modernity," from that of supposedly privileged scenes of conversation twenty years ago.

Like Emerson, James laments lost intimacy, but he believes it can be restored with "real" talk. Literature has always served this purpose: recording speech, and acting as a corrective to the tone of the schoolroom and the "supposedly privileged" conversation of previous generations. Two points are worth making here. First, it's the obligation of all writers to shoulder up against the wall of the permissible and *shove*. Writers must shove no matter how large the obstacle and without concern for the strength of those pushing back from the other side. This shoving is made more difficult by the fact that those pushing back are very often the same shovers who moved the wall to where it now stands—they nudged it forward as far as they could stomach it, and cannot tolerate a millimeter more. James did his part. He was accused of indiscretion, and he was miffed when others picked it up from there. Joyce offends James, Lawrence offends Joyce, Miller offends Lawrence, Updike offends Miller, Baker offends Updike. This or a hundred other lists, each demonstrating that literature penetrates obstacles of taboo that shift with the generations, refreshing our sense of the intimate layers of ordinary human experience.

Second, this work begins with wordplay. Does James hear the double entendre of "intercourse"? It's hard to say, but it's easy to say that "intercourse" was one of his favorite words. *The Awkward Age* uses "intercourse" nine times in contexts for which we'd now probably reserve "discourse," as Barthes did. The oeuvre is remarkably consistent on this point. *The Ambassadors* also has nine "intercourses"; *The Tragic Muse* and *The Wings of the Dove*, eight each. *The Bostonians*, thirteen. *The Golden Bowl*, fourteen. Other common Jamesian words have undergone similar transformations. In James, to "love" someone means you like them a lot. To "make love" to them means you try to get them to like you back. To be "erect" is to be righteous and upstanding. To be "vulgar" is to be simple and obvious. And to "ejaculate," for James, is to be so full of a sense of moral purpose that you simply can't help blurting out whatever it is you have to say. This last is practically cited at the beginning of *Vox*.

Before the book even really gets going, Jim ejaculates his description
of his ejaculations:

> When I'm about to come, I seem to like to rise up on the balls
> of my feet. . . . I sometimes feel like some kind of high school
> teacher, bouncing on his heels, or like some kind of demagogue,
> rising up on tiptoe and roaring out something about destiny.

To ejaculate is to passionately profess, to be a passionate professor.
Vox does ask something of you, and what it asks, even in its first
pages, is that you recognize that we should not—cannot, in any
case—divorce "peeing and penises" from having something significant to say.

36

PARIS IS A PERFECT CITY FOR LOVERS BECAUSE IT'S A PERFECT
place to fight. It's a perfect place to fight because it offers perpetual
disappointment. Paris is the only city in the world in which you
don't walk around endlessly mulling civic inadequacies, longing for
some better city, but even when you're in Paris, even as you glori-
ously recline on a wooden chaise longue inside the grounds of the
Musée Rodin or happily stroll along an angular rue in the Marais,
it's possible to feel a great anxiety over the fact that you're not in
some other, even better part of Paris.

The great Haussmann renovation of the nineteenth century is
partly to blame for this, pitting old against new, but mostly it's the
Métro's fault. As soon as Parisians no longer had to make the best of
it wherever they happened to be and could nurse a reasonable hope

that something better was just a short ride away, they climbed aboard. Of course wherever they went wasn't as perfect as it had once been because whoever was responsible for its having been pleasant and desirable in the first place had left in search of a better lot. I was thinking of all this, of the blind celebration of motion that characterizes mo dernity, as I joked to Catherine that spiral staircases seemed to have played a crucial role in the history of art and that what she should do is take an extended-exposure shot of me descending the atelier's spiral staircase and call it *Dude Descending a Staircase.* Or better, wait 'til I've just sit-down showered in the kitchen and then call it *Nude Dude Descending a Staircase.* Or better still, because our staircase was less like a staircase than a poorly designed piece of climbing apparatus, *Nude Dude Descending a Staircase and Practically Breaking His Neck.* Catherine did not find this funny and she did not take a photograph. Nor did she agree with my analysis, which she suggested was passive-aggressive criticism of art and therefore her. This much was true. I'd become annoyed and negative in Paris because she needed me to be positive and optimistic.

I discovered this on our fourth night, when I convinced her to attempt a dual reading of *Vox*: me Jim, she Abby. I'd been plotting this for a while. But we completed only a page or two before Catherine's copy of the book went limp in her lap and she couldn't proceed. "Male jerk-off fantasy," she said. This led to a far-reaching discussion of the history of our intimacy, and she needed me to be more optimistic, she said, because that's what I'd been when we began our letter-writing courtship. A *Vox*-like exchange, I wanted to scream! What she didn't realize was that I had never been an optimistic person by nature—I had grown optimistic because of *her,* first because of the promise of the wonderfully rewarding life we might have together, and then because of the reality of that life. Anyway, I *was* optimistic—optimistic that Nicholson Baker could help us return to a wonderful life! For her part, Catherine could return to a wonderful life only if things started looking up. Things could look up in two ways: one, you could either usher into reality a relationship that had so far been limited to fantasies and words; or two, you could remove yourself from the former bed and breakfast and head to Paris, which was lovely in every way, including the way that demonstrated that setting alone cannot alter a relationship that has slipped into a spiraling dynamic.

Ironically, for the entire time I was reading *Vox*—which is only one hundred and sixty-five pages long but which I had to read slowly because I couldn't read it aloud in public (though I fantasized about standing on a Parisian street corner and ejaculatedly doing so)—Catherine and I argued about all the things for which the French are famous. One day I paid eleven euros for a bottle of wine, and Catherine protested because access to modestly priced good wine was what it meant to be in France, and we should refuse to pay a centime more than seven euros per bottle. Next we raged over food, and this time I was the one complaining because I thought being in France meant that you could eat pretty much anyplace and have better food than you'd have anywhere else. My mistake. One day Catherine refused to go to the brasserie on the corner even though she was hungry (and cranky) because under no circumstances should you settle for merely good food in Paris, and we didn't find any great food until I was cranky too, which ruined our meal. Finally we went all out over sex. One afternoon Catherine came down the spiral staircase and accused me of having struck a *Dying Slave* pose on the futon (we'd just been to the Louvre). Long before, she'd claimed that I had "Michelangelo arms," but what I needed to understand, she said now, was that, arms or no, such a pose created a pressure that was not conducive to receptivity. I launched a counteroffensive at this. I said that I hadn't been striking a pose of any kind (actually I had), but if I happened to even remotely resemble the *Dying Slave,* then shouldn't she be more grateful than upset? The fight that followed left me sleepless, and I stormed out of the atelier at two-thirty AM into a Parisian storm and hiked miles through the bad weather, wandering at first but heading generally toward the Eiffel Tower, the top platform of which occasionally peeked out between buildings as I walked off my anger. After an hour I found myself entirely alone with the world's best-known monument to modernity and progress, the very progress of which Nicholson Baker had begun to grow suspicious. I made my peace with France, that wet and lonely half hour a visit to the grave of a life not lived.

The following morning when Catherine and I separated in the Métro, she headed to the Place Vendôme to take photographs, myself to the Latin Quarter to wander and read, I caught a glimpse of her through a scratched train window and felt a spidery chill at the thought that it would be the last time I would ever see her. That night I had a terrible dream about Catherine having good grinding sex with someone else—perhaps the caveau bartender to whom earlier in the week she'd murmured a coquettish *"Bonsoir . . ."*—and I woke with her stroking my sweaty forehead and saying, "What's wrong? What's wrong?" What was wrong was that I loved reading *Vox* as much as Baker loved writing it—"I like it more than any of the others—I . . . *love* it," he'd told Martin Amis—and I wanted to share it with her, because whenever we read a book that we love, our instinct is to attempt an impossible translation from private to shared experience. And the problem with that was that I couldn't share this experience with her because she'd already decided, as many had, to dislike the book in exactly the way that, to my mind, demonstrated why it was an important book: because we all live in its background dystopia.

37

THEN AGAIN, *VOX* HAS SOMETHING OF A DUBIOUS HISTORY OF people attempting to share it, a history that I was surprised, once I finally heard it, wasn't the first thing I'd heard about Nicholson Baker. For many people it may be the only thing they've heard about Baker.

For obvious reasons *Vox* was the first of Baker's books to receive a truly robust publicity campaign, and on publication it climbed to number three on the *New York Times* bestseller list and remained in the top ten for several months. This meant that many people who hadn't previously read Nicholson Baker, people perhaps looking for "Rabelasian abandon," read *Vox*. Among these, it's safe to say, was Monica Lewinsky, the onetime White House intern whose affair with President Bill Clinton led to Clinton's impeachment and tarnished the Clinton legacy such that it became one of a number of factors contributing to the outcome of the 2000 presidential election. It's not known when or how Lewinsky became aware of *Vox*, but it is known that, toward the end of her affair with Clinton—famously composed of about ten mostly oral encounters in or near the president's private study, and, notably, a number of lengthy phone calls—Lewinsky gifted Clinton her personal copy of *Vox* and quickly purchased a replacement. A few weeks later, on Valentine's Day, 1997, she placed a personal ad in the *Washington Post,* a quotation from *Romeo and Juliet* about true love overcoming impossible obstacles. She cut out and pasted the ad onto a thin piece of cardboard that she gave to Clinton as a bookmark and later testified that she saw the bookmark in Clinton's copy of *Vox* on a further visit to the private study. Clinton never admitted to having received the book, even when he was subpoenaed and pressured, and prosecutors later introduced into evidence an October 1997 inventory that listed *Vox* among the study's collection of books.

Surely it would be unfair to suggest that the so-called Lewinsky Affair, and all the history that sputtered along after it, can or should be laid at the feet of Nicholson Baker. Yet it would be just as unfair to ignore the fact that something *like* the Lewinsky Affair seems not to have been particularly far from Baker's mind as he wrote *Vox* and *The Fermata.*

That story begins about twenty pages after Jim's ejaculations, when he confesses to Abby that the initial impulse to call 2VOX traces back to a moment in a video rental store about an hour and a half before he picked up the phone. Rentals rented (pornographic, of course), Jim tells Abby, he had been exiting the store when he noticed an elaborate display for Disney's film adaptation of *Peter Pan.* A television was showing the film on continual loop, and Jim happened to glance at the screen at a moment when Tinkerbell pauses midflutter and glances down at her small-breasted, big-hipped frame in a quite womanly way, an important distinction for Jim. Abby suggests that the sequence that follows, in which Tinkerbell tries to fly through a keyhole but gets stuck because her hips are too wide, is the inspiration for a scene in *Gentlemen Prefer Blondes* in which Marilyn Monroe finds herself similarly lodged in a ship porthole. It's this sequence of *Vox,* this association—from Tinkerbell to Marilyn Monroe, from children's story to sex symbol—that serves both as the occasion of the book, the reason Jim calls 2VOX, and aligns it with Baker's broader goal of challenging the age and genre boundaries that have chopped a chaotic network of flaws into the once-pure gemstone of literature.

It's not just Tinkerbell either—it's Alice again too. Long before *House of Holes* repeatedly echoed Alice's plunge down a hole to a wacky civilization, *The Fermata,* to leap slightly ahead here (and I should acknowledge that there's absolutely no evidence that Monica Lewinsky read *The Fermata*), proposes that the basic template of *Alice's Adventures in Wonderland* is all we really need to know about how reading and writing ought to work in the world.

To slow down a bit. Baker's sex books mostly obey the usual constraints of the pornography genre: episodic sexual encounters featuring varying combinations of participants and activities, all strung on a loose narrative frame. But while the plots of ordinary pornography tend to be throwaway or comedic pastiche, the interstices of Baker's sex books hint at aesthetic vision. For example, in addition to its series of time-stopped sexual fantasies, *The Fermata* is also the story of thirty-five-year-old temp worker Arno Strine's literary career. Like Jim recalling his pivotal moment in a video store, Arno traces his literary impulse—which results in *The Fermata*— back to a moment in college when he gave in to an impulse to share with others Lisa Alther's *Kinflicks,* a book of canonical 1970s erotica. He purchased several copies of the book and left them lying around campus like Easter eggs, hoping that someone would pick up a copy and read it. The draw of this was that it turned him into a partially empowered puppeteer. His explanation returns to Alice:

> I'm captivated by the simple idea of putting something in the path of a woman, so that she can choose to look at it and read it, or, on the other hand, choose to walk on by.

In short, Arno is more reader than writer at this stage in his literary development. We all begin as readers, trying to share our reading experiences. But soon enough Arno realizes that the pleasure he takes in distributing books would be heightened if a "woman [were to] encounter [his] very own words." He goes on to reveal that he had acted on this impulse only "quite recently," and for the rest of the book he stops time so that he has enough time to write erotic stories that he then places in the paths of a series of surrogate Alices.

Of note at this point is the character Joyce, a coworker whom Arno idolizes and to whom he eventually reveals the secret of his time-stopping power. Toward the end of *The Fermata*, Joyce acquires the power herself, and we hear of her using the ability to catch up on work, strip random strangers, and make herself a better sexual partner for Arno. Most important for our purposes:

> She talks of taking a jaunt down to Washington and sucking the presidential dick.

What's the lesson of all this? All books are written for Alices, Monica Lewinsky included—and perhaps Lewinsky more than most in that she too has come to be associated with a dress of a particular shade of blue.

38

I IMAGINED NICHOLSON BAKER OBSERVING ALL THIS FROM AFAR and snickering in a private sense of fiendish accomplishment. It *is* encouraging that a novel can still become controversial enough to amount to evidence in a legal battle with wide-ranging historical implications. But even if the ripple effects of *Vox* ought to rank it among history's most influential books, it has to be allowed that its influence, like More's *Utopia* or Machiavelli's *The Prince*, has been a function of readers not having bothered to fully understand it. This was equally true of those who liked the book and those who disliked it. On the one hand, there probably is a fruitful analogy to be made between pornography and ambitious literature (e.g., neither is driven by plot alone; both are kept in home libraries for ease of reconsultation, etc.) (sadly, before Catherine moved in I discarded my meager quartet of films, and she abandoned the sparkly, space-agey toy she'd used to get herself through lonesome times), but to completely erase the difference between the two, as Lewinsky and Clinton had done, is pretty obviously a flawed interpretative technique. And on the other hand, the reaction of those who disliked *Vox*—including many of its early reviewers—was just as flawed, though the reasons for this are somewhat more complicated.

What's the purpose of book reviews these days? Should reviews mostly summarize books so that readers can decide for themselves whether a book's contents merit further investigation (though such reviews tend to pirate books' best information and thereby become competing, condensed versions of them)? Should reviews mostly celebrate books, rouse crowds whose attention is tugged at by a whole range of less-demanding media (though the absence of any critical sense leaves even praise feeling hollow and unearned)? Or should reviews stand sentinel against mediocrity, individual reviewers accepting a kind of knighthood of taste that empowers them to scold the literary community as it strays from quality and ambition (though such power has the tendency to run amok, such that a too-strident review can both quash a promising career and make a pariah of the reviewer)? In *U and I,* Nicholson Baker advises against writers becoming reviewers at all, and in this he may have taken his cue from "The Figure in the Carpet," in which a newly successful novelist harrumphs, "I don't 'review.' I'm reviewed!" But the truth is that Baker did eventually review, albeit with more personality than reviewers are generally encouraged or permitted to exhibit. But he's kind of an exception. What reviews are still published these days tend to suffer on at least three fronts: one, they tend to be so short that thematic threads stretching between a writer's books cannot be properly addressed; two, lacking hindsight, early reviewers too often amount to a first line of defense resisting change to the status quo, and three, like Martin Amis having been compelled to interview Baker, reviewers are often conscripted into service and lack the enthusiasm of a "volunteer reader."

In one way or another all these problems manifested in the initial, poor reviews of *Vox* (which appeared among scattered positive notices). A brief sampling of the vitriol:

> *The New York Times*: *Vox* doesn't aspire to use graphic descriptions of sex to make any sort of larger point. . . . while it's titillating enough, it's not particularly revealing or emotionally involving.

> *The Washington Post*: While Jim and Abby are fully imagined, they become . . . comparatively unrealized during the more extreme pornographic parts of the novel in the hapless way that sex renders us all cartoons.

> *The Globe and Mail*: Baker is ultimately trapped by the vulgarity of his subject. Jim and Abby are obsessed by personal gratification to the exclusion of everything else.

> *The Gazette*: I . . . cannot recall the last time I was this disappointed in a writer or felt so strongly that I had better things to do than I did while I was reading *Vox*.

> *The Independent*: I hope that Nicholson Baker now moves on to matters more robust, leaving this study of infantilism well behind him.

It's too easy, I think, to chalk these responses up to jealousy of a youngish and already much-respected writer having suddenly become a best seller. The criticisms echo too closely the themes of the book itself—children's stories, titillation. The objection was not that *Vox* was obscene but that it was vulgar in Henry James's sense of the word, and the critics simply refused to acknowledge that its vulgarity reflected a culture itself becoming more obvious and simple. In other words, critics panned *Vox* because they hoped it was *wrong,* and that hope made them incapable of the negative capability that is literature's only prerequisite and to which Nicholson Baker's "negative space" had already pointed.

I thought back on my fight with Catherine over our aborted *Vox* reading. When I had argued that *House of Holes* had *not* struck her as "male jerk-off fantasy," that, in fact, it seemed to have worked just fine as an emotional lubricant, she claimed that it had been just that one time, and that it had been spontaneous. I countered that a capacity for repeated re-enjoyment with no loss of intensity or pleasure was yet another point of contact between good porn and good books, but she would have none of it. She accused me, essentially, of approaching the business with Lewinskian abandon. Untrue! Rather I had hoped that we could use the books to increase our overall intimacy. Nicholson Baker, I said, could help us redraw a line from the harmony of our intellectual lives to the sensual bond of our physical lives, enriching both like a good simile. Instead, Nicholson Baker became in Paris the name of the place we could not go.

39

PEOPLE STARTED DYING IN PARIS. OR SCRATCH THAT—PEOPLE started dying while we were in Paris. Christopher Hitchens died and then two days later Kim Jong-il died and then the day after that, combining the two, Václav Havel died. These deaths hit me with a kaleidoscopic sense of shifting history—the world was different now—which was perfect because Paris, fairly round on maps, looks a whole lot like a kaleidoscope image.

You only ever stumble across places you hope to find in Paris. In fact, you have to plan on stumbling across places because it's useless to study those kaleidoscopic maps: You look up from the map to the city and it's as though in that instant someone has twisted the tube and now it's all different. That's why Catherine and I hadn't bothered to seek out Shakespeare & Co., Paris's famous bookstore. We had planned to stumble across it, and in our second week, late at night after a long day at Versailles, we did stumble across it, by which I mean we practically stepped into a puddle of votive candles burning before the store's front door, a shrine laid out for its famous owner, George Whitman, who had died earlier that day. Whitman *did* die in Paris, and now everything was different in the literary world.

I was feeling different too. About ten days before I'd left for Paris I'd noticed that a small lump on my back—a lump that had been there for a couple years but didn't particularly bother me—had begun to grow. "Grow" was exactly the right word for it because the lump caused me no discomfort, yet I could feel it filling with something. Growing. I used a mirror to look at it, and after I looked at it I decided to get it looked at. My doctor told me not to worry.

"But I'm going to Paris for a month."

"It's no big deal."

"What is it?"

"A growth."

"I know that."

"It's a cyst. Think of it as a big pimple. It's coming to the surface."

"What if it comes to the surface in Paris?"

"It won't."

"What if it does?"

She wrote me a prescription for an antibiotic that shrank my growth for a while, but after I'd been in Paris for about a week I started to notice it again. My growth had laughed in the face of that antibiotic. My growth was like a mountain climber determined to summit the surface of my skin, and it would not be deterred by poor conditions. Before long I began to feel less a sensation of growing than a generalized twanging, and if I leaned back against anything—a pillow, say—I experienced shooting tendrils of pain that flickered out to my fingers and tweaked the base of my neck. It was my zit to bear. And I bore it. I bore it everywhere, up hills and down them—up to Sacré Cœur, for example, and back down again. Before long I wasn't merely reacting to pain, but wincing and twitching my shoulders in anticipation of it, *hunching* my back— that was the only word for it—to accommodate my ever-bulging and now quite painful growth. Oddly, the pain grew more pronounced the closer I happened to be to the center of Paris. I became more and more hunchbacked the closer I was to Notre Dame.

When I revealed this to Catherine—a text message sent from a brasserie called La Réserve de Quasimodo—she thought it was perfect because I'd been suffering from the figurative growth of my irrepressible pessimism for years now, and because I'd been crazily vaulting around Paris late at night (not to mention putting on weight, I had to admit—if I was a *Dying Slave,* I was a *fat Dying Slave*), and because it enabled her to express everything she'd been feeling in all the months leading up to Paris: She'd been kidnapped and dragged to the former bed and breakfast against her will, and she felt imprisoned and hopeless and despondent and sad.

Truth be told, Catherine wasn't feeling all that well herself in

Paris. In our second week, she'd become sick, overcome by clogs of mucus in her sinuses. I'd noticed that most sexy French women were sexy because they had a slight overbite that made them look as though they were looking down their noses at everything. Now that Catherine was having to do a lot of head tipping to keep her nose from running, she really was looking down her nose at everything, and she wound up appearing a whole lot more French as a result. This cheered her up, miserable though she was, but it was only a temporary happiness because of course she would get better. Paris was a related problem because it was temporary too. By this point we'd fallen in love with the adorable atelier, and this was sad because being happy in Paris meant that we no longer had Paris to look forward to, and before long we'd be headed back to the former bed and breakfast with few prospects for the future. Late one evening as we lay side by side on the futon, Catherine sniffling and paging through a book of Sophie Calle's Hasselblad images (which I'd stumbled across at Shakespeare & Co.) and myself terrifiedly viewing online videos of subcutaneous cyst removals (think of éclairs pounded with sledgehammers; spores bursting in slow motion; a volcano's molten belch; or, it has to be admitted, male ejaculation), we paused to consider what trip we would go on next, to plot our next escape. Paralyzed by despondency, Catherine had no productive ideas. I did, but I hesitated because it meant possibly breaking the ironclad resolution I'd made when I started writing about Nicholson Baker. Then I just said it.

"How about Maine?"

Baker was in Maine. Long story short: Baker grew up in Rochester, went to school in Philadelphia (one year abroad, in France), lived for a few years in New York and Boston before his career started to take off, spent most of the nineties in California (his father-in-law taught at Berkeley for half a century), relocated his family to England for a year for reasons that were still unclear to me, and then settled in South Berwick, Maine, where he'd lived since 1998. Even before learning all this I'd taken note of the fact that writers moved to Maine with surprising regularity. It was no Paris, but Maine seemed to rank high among desirable sites from which to conduct a literary life. Not ever having been there I had no idea why. This alone seemed worth investigating, and just before I told Catherine my idea, I told myself that being in Maine did not *require* me to profane my quest by trying to meet Nicholson Baker. Catherine agreed—not with whether I should meet Baker, but with the proposal in general.

"I'd *love* to go to Maine."

Using vacation time to plan future vacations is the state of modern life. I set to work sifting through images of summer rentals on Maine's southern coast and learned there was exactly one bed and breakfast in South Berwick.

40

THE NEXT DAY I HAD MY HUNCHBACK REMOVED. I HAD TO STUMBLE across L'Hôpital Américain de Paris because even if I could have read my Paris map the hospital wasn't on it. Happily, the hospital turned out to be located on Avenue Victor-Hugo. The hunchback removal process was made pleasant by the fact that French nurses sacrifice nothing of fashion to the sterility required of invasive surgical techniques. Scrubs turned out to be a delightful complement to the dangly earrings and artful makeup long championed by overbitten French women.

The whole episode nicely anticipated a scene near the end of

The Fermata. Arno volunteers for a medical study on masturbation-induced carpal tunnel syndrome and fantasizes at length, aloud, about his sexy doctor while she studies him masturbating in the womb-like space of an MRI machine. I say anticipated because at that point, on the day I had my growth milked, I was only about a third of the way into *The Fermata.* Preprocedure, I spent forty-five minutes reading the book in an examination room, and my laughter at the funny parts flitted out into the hallway, where elderly French people who weren't even on their last legs because they were on gurneys were being wheeled from room to room. Does the questionable appropriateness of exuberantly reading a bawdy book in the solemn enclave of an emergency room speak to the larger question of whether Baker's sex books are inappropriate, as reviewers suggested? Perhaps. It's true that the trilogy is unwilling to consider the darker side of its subject. For example, the first real-life porn star mentioned in *Vox* ("One of the tapes has got Lisa Melendez in it who I think is just . . . delightful") died of AIDS in 1999 at age thirty-five. Also, while no one tends to get hurt as a result of popular storytelling genres, there is a compelling argument to be made that pornography feeds patriarchy and that female porn stars, in particular, are conscripted into the business and compelled to have sex for pay. This is quite similar to book reviewers being forced to critique books they did not choose to read, and while reviewers and sex workers both might take umbrage at the suggestion that they have been coerced, it's worth noting that only sex workers already have, having once picketed appearances by scholar Catharine MacKinnon, who had claimed that female porn stars were oppressed and that all sex was rape. For me, though, the fact that Baker's sex trilogy was fantasy, that the books were *about* fantasy, inoculated them against that kind of vulgar criticism. We have well enough of that other, sick-souled (to use William James's phrase) view of our sexual lives. Why not a little healthy-mindedness, a little looking on the sexy side? If one of the problems of modern life is that, like reviewers who have forgotten how to fill negative space, we no longer know how to intimately empathize with one another, then perhaps a fantasy depicting intimate empathy should not be criticized for failing to represent a reality it never tried to resemble. "That's the hole you're looking for," a woman in *House of Holes* says, when she reveals that her vagina is yet another portal to the House of Holes—and what she means is that sexual fantasy is a place to which those whom modern life has left feeling abducted or conscripted or imprisoned might occasionally escape.

Or perhaps I was thinking all this only because soon, after the doctor arrived and sliced open my hunchback and pinched it empty of every last dollop of malicious infection, I was left with a quite large hole in myself. Known formally as a "cavity wound," it was tricky, this hole: Infected once, it was susceptible to relapse and needed to heal slowly, from the inside out, like the socket of a pulled tooth. What this meant was that every other day for the rest of my time in Paris I returned to Avenue Victor-Hugo so comely French nurses could lie me down and stuff medicated gauze deep into my negative space.

41

WHICH MAKES TOTAL SENSE BECAUSE ABBY OF *VOX*, OF COURSE, was another Alice en route to Wonderland, and she too has a preternatural attraction to holes. (Alice, it should be noted, is the precise opposite of Martin Amis. At the beginning of *Alice's Adventures in Wonderland*, Alice's attention diverts to the rabbit hole only because a book she has been peeking at over her sister's shoulder contains no dialogue. It's *all* prose. What, Alice wonders, could possibly be the use of a book "without pictures or conversation"?)

Early in *Vox,* Abby claims that she enjoys the negative space of dialogue, the accidental pauses into which the imagination reflexively plunges. A few pages later there comes a critical instance of just such a chat hole. Jim is describing a streetlight outside his window. The light had begun turning itself on just a moment before. He goes about his description quite patiently because the light itself doesn't just flick to life like an incandescent lamp. It's a slow process. For a time, he explains, you can't even be sure the light is coming on at all: it could be the space around the bulb getting darker. Then there's this moment, he says, when the streetlight is the exact color of the sky, and that gives the illusion of "a *hole* in the middle of the tree across the street." Then we get this:

> There was a pause.
> "Listen," [Abby] said. "This is getting expensive at a dollar a minute or whatever it is."
> "Ninety-five cents per half minute, I think."
> "So give me your number and I'll call you back," she said.

"There was a pause." What do our imaginations project into this particular negative space? After the pause Abby's voice has a tone of urgency, and her concern over the call's cost suggests that she now realizes that the conversation is going to last significantly longer than she originally planned. Jim's description of an illusory hole is neither vulgar nor obscene, yet for Abby it's decisive. It convinces her that Jim has something unique to offer, that his is a sensibility with which her own might chime. Jim talks her out of hanging up. The risk that they might not reconnect is too great, he says, and anyway two dollars a minute is a great value. Some pages further on, far enough down the road so that part of what we register is the fact that Abby stored this moment away in memory, she reintroduces the hole theme in a story she tells Jim about masturbating to a fantasy of repainting her apartment:

> And then I thought, wait, I have the money, this time I'll hire people to paint it for me. And so three painters materialized, and then suddenly there was a large *hole* in the wall, about three feet off the floor, big enough so that I could fit through so that my legs were standing in the front hall and yet my head and upper body were in the living room. The hole was finished off and lined with sheepskin. I had nothing on.

Actually this is a fantasy of a story of a fantasy because Abby is jammed into a hole like Tinkerbell and Marilyn Monroe for Jim's benefit. The scene that follows is certainly "titillating enough," as that one hostile reviewer remarked—the painters apply stripes of sun-warmed paint to Abby's butt cheeks and legs, and then there's a lengthy sequence in which the masturbating Abby envisions herself pleasuring three men at once—but to end a reading of the scene at "titillation" is to make the same mistake Jim makes when Abby's story is finished. He guesses that the trifecta of fantasy orgasms ("Then all three of them came in me, one right after another, first the one in my mouth, surprisingly enough, then the one in my pussy, then finally the one in my ass") was what permitted Abby to bring herself to actual orgasm.

The next sequence is crucial. Not at all, Abby explains. That was "just a picture," one image among many, and what had actually made her come was a pair of ideas, and for several pages she tries to communicate what these ideas are but the conversation gets sidetracked before she ever gets to them. In other words, Abby's story is an attempt to depict the working of her mind, which she can't explain in any other way. That she fails to explain it is important; but regardless, the incorporation of Jim's fantasy into her own is a tender way of answering Jim's earlier call for a "stream of confidences flowing from you to me." Stream of confidences? This is so close to "stream of consciousness" that all serious readers—perhaps not Monica Lewinsky, but certainly professional reviewers—ought to be expected to suspect from just this that while the ostensible subject of *Vox* might be phone sex, what it's really *about* is storytelling and the purpose of literature.

To make the case a little clearer: Abby's aggressive honesty ("Impress me with your candor," she says) leads to an odd admission: Not only does she like holes, she has bizarre fantasies about passing through them. Specifically she imagines getting sucked into the engine of an SR-71 Blackbird ("one of those black secret spy planes") and instantly becoming "a long fog of blood." This is a peculiar fetish, to be sure, and actually it's a subset of an even more general fantasy in which she dematerializes herself so that she can pour down into the grids of holes in telephone handset mouthpieces. Neither the plane nor the dematerialization kill her, she assures Jim, and what's important is what it feels like to be "turned into some kind of conscious vapor." The body is no longer a solid: It can fwoosh or stream. This perhaps explains Abby's unique attraction to bodies of water: "I'd put out for any body of water at all—a pool or a bath or a pond, or an ocean."

Importantly, this follows a peculiar admission of Jim's own. What he fetishizes is advances in book technology, most recently a mechanical spreading device that splays paperbacks wide for hands-free reading. Jim had masturbated, he says, while reading about the new device.

All of this is critical in the larger context of Baker's career in that what should be clear by now is that Jim and Abby embody Baker's transition from mechanical to organic cognitive metaphors.

And the fact that everyone who travels to the House of Holes does so via a process quite similar to what Abby describes—in a book published *eighteen* years later—tells us not only that the evolution is from a Jim-style worldview to an Abby-style worldview, it insists that whatever is being described is lodged deep in an abiding worldview of Nicholson Baker's.

Long before then, however, Jim returns Abby's favor. Late in *Vox,* he incorporates her spy plane into a fantasy in which he has acquired a technology that allows him to monitor global incidence of orgasm: "Maybe it's really a big black spy plane I'm in, and what's this, you're up here too, flying toward my fan-jet." But Jim and Abby do not simply play to each other's fetishes. They *complete* each other's fantasies. The listener steps in to provide details or motivations at moments when the storyteller's imagination hiccups, when the improvisation stalls. *Vox* depicts cooperative storytelling in three ways. First, while Jim and Abby do not aspire to the étude sentences of *Room Temperature,* they do deliver longish speeches that re-create lust-altered consciousness. Second, when common diction proves unsatisfying they engage in wordplay, collectively brainstorming neologisms: "yorning" for a combination of yearning and longing, "strum" for masturbation. (Incidentally, Martin Amis's claim over this word is completely false: It appears in none of the books Amis published in the twelve years leading up to *Vox.*)

And third, and most important (and despite Baker's *Paris Review* claim that writing about sex is "fun"), Jim emphasizes just how torturous it is to craft, on the fly, a fantasy in which an imagined Abby has an encounter with a mysterious stranger. Stuck at a moment of transition, he says:

> It is *work* getting the two of you together. I feel that any second I'm going to misstep in telling this. It's very stressful.

"Now listen," Abby replies, and she comes to the rescue with a segue so that Jim's story can continue.

All of this carries forward into *The Fermata,* which is an even more fantastic book, and even more a book about how literature works. And it received even more scathing reviews when it was published. "I just found it creepy," said one reviewer. "Shame on Nicholson Baker for attempting such a trite con job," said another. Nonsense! Arno spends a great deal of time preemptively defending himself against charges like these, and that fact alone should put a careful reader on critical alert status. *The Fermata* is about the process of its creation. Arno laments his inability to create a more smoothly flowing narrative, and he reviews himself in noting that his story aligns with a whole literary genre: books featuring monstrous characters invested with supernatural powers. Previous contributors to the genre include Stevenson, Goethe, Wells, Tolkien, and Mary Shelley. (Arno forgot Victor Hugo.)

The Fermata's basic premise offers the children's story counterpoint to this. The book begins with a childish scruples-testing fantasy ("What would you do if you could stop time?"), and becomes, once Arno achieves his superpower, a less allegorical version of comic books, whose intended audience was always pubescent boys catching a whiff of the occult in their newfound ability to masturbate (e.g., *The Incredible Hulk* is about getting a boner, *Iron Man* is about having a boner, and *Spiderman,* in which sticky white goo shoots from the wrists, is about ejaculation, etc.). Add to this Arno's affinity for British literature, his abandoned master's thesis on the history of Dover Books, and his claim that his erotic writings align him with Guy de Maupassant (*Tales of French Love and Passion*), and it starts to get pretty difficult to ignore the fact that *The Fermata* has a lot to say about evolving literary tastes. It should come as no surprise that *The Fermata* happily soaks in protracted, association-rich descriptions of genitalia, but these descriptions lack the wearying adult languor that Updike brought to the endeavor, nor do they exhibit the deadly import that Kundera injected into all things sexual, and nor does Baker completely pass over the matter as Ford Maddox Ford did in *The Good Soldier,* on the argument that sexual desire is a commonplace and "therefore a matter needing no comment at all." Rather *The Fermata*'s descriptions of genitalia are buoyant and gleeful, and they do what all good books do. They reveal those private truths of ourselves that become difficult to acknowledge as soon as we've lost the kind of adventurous innocence we all felt when we first had the impulse to offer others a glimpse of our own, if only they would show us theirs.

42

THAT SAID, *THE FERMATA* WAS THE LEAST COMPELLING (THOUGH the longest) of Baker's books I'd read so far. Or maybe I just had a hard time getting into it because Catherine and I were fighting. We'd been fighting with each other, she'd been fighting her cold, and I'd been fighting figurative and literal systemic infections, for years, it seemed, and what all that added up to was that I was reading about sex almost continually in Paris while having almost none of it myself. This left me in a foul mood. Not in the least because I'd been projecting Catherine into every one of Baker's sex scenes, and even though I wasn't wholly absorbed in *The Fermata,* I laughed out loud at a lot of it, which made me crave Catherine all the more.

To speak more broadly, I wasn't sure whether my frustration with *The Fermata* was a function of my innate negativity or a more general annoyance that is supposed to result from experiencing Arno's frustration as he lists the books that he consulted to help him write his own: Cardano's *The Book of My Life,* Santayana's *Persons and Places,* Baring's *The Puppet Show of Memory.* We're supposed to recognize from this list, I think, that writers overcome the obstacles of writing by reading other books. Yet here the process felt too naked. *The Fermata* seemed too normal in this regard, as though Baker bent too far toward the light of his critics in trying to prove that he could write a straightforward novel. The book contains some of the same literary lessons as *Vox* (e.g., Joyce instructs Arno on the importance of specificity of detail), but can a truly good book be made of a halting attempt to write a good book? Wasn't that a metabridge too far? Yet I sensed from the beginning that *The Fermata* was absolutely key to my coming to an understanding of Baker's underlying vision.

I began to think this when Ernest Renan popped up in chapter one. What was a stodgy old British literary critic, a sometime companion of Henry James—James once called Renan "hideous and charming—more hideous even than his photos, and more charming even than his writing"—doing popping up in a book that one critic described as "straight porn"? Furthermore, what was Henry James himself doing popping up nine chapters later, right after the come-face scene that sent Updike (and others, I now realized) into a dither? I think I actually have an answer to that last one because at this point we can hardly call ourselves careful readers if stumbling across Henry James does not inspire us to recognize, as with "stream of confidences" in *Vox,* that William James is an uncited presence in *The Fermata* too. When Arno, in the book's opening paragraph, claims that he does not "inquire into origins very often," he quietly echoes *Pragmatism*'s assertion that the truth of a thing is best measured not by an attempt to gauge its origin, but by an assessment of its practical effects. And a few pages later, when Arno poignantly admits that his ability to stop time is "the one thing that makes [his] life worth living," a careful reader hears the faint reference to what is perhaps James's most famous essay, "Is Life Worth Living?" ("The question any novel is really trying to answer is, Is life worth living?" Baker told *The Paris Review.* The savvy interviewer followed immediately with a question about James, though James's essay went unmentioned.)

These associations aren't exactly hiding in the book, but they're not a surface-level response either. If most readers these days crave a less demanding experience, the so-called beach read, then a reading of this sort might be likened to the contemplative labor of a high-tech beachcomber, one of those serious fellows who paces the dunes wearing thick headphones, trowel in one hand and metal-detecting wand in the other, sweeping rhythmically and janitorially over the sands, half-hoping for a treasure, a gold watch or a wedding ring temporarily removed and then forgotten, and the other half taking a simple pleasure in the trance state produced by the search itself. Can *The Fermata* be a "good" book merely because it repays such a reader with shiny trinkets of thought, because it has an internal rationale for what it says and does? Can we still like a book if it fails in an essential, unnameable way but steers us closer to its author's worldview? What do we mean when we say a book has failed anyway? That it has not entertained us? Why should it entertain *us,* and not the other way around? Are we not diverted by a book—"caught" by it, to use Henry James's phrase—precisely because it inspires us to entertain it as we might entertain an offer or a proposal? When did we start expecting books to entertain us without any flex of mental muscle on our part? One hears these days many citations of Coleridge's "willing suspension of disbelief," but wouldn't an even better literary world result if readers not only willfully suspended modernity-induced cynicism and negativity but actively fought and strived to believe an author's belief, if only incompletely, for an instant, and to the extent it might be fathomed through a fantasy? In other words books shouldn't entertain us, we should entertain *them,* and, in keeping with the central metaphor of *this* book, to read in any other way is to be like a sexual partner who expects to be stroked to climax while offering no strokes in return. It's only such a dysfunctional relationship—a willed *exertion* of disbelief—that explains how even a casual beach reader might avoid stumbling across the basic mission statement of *The Fermata,* which is articulated by Arno at the very dawn of his literary career.

Happily, he's on a beach at this moment. A long search for a surrogate Alice into whose path he can place an early literary effort yields a young sunbathing woman absently finger-digging in the sand alongside her towel. Arno stops time so that he can sit down beside her and peck out the first of *The Fermata'*s stories within the story: the sexual adventures of Marian the Librarian. Story completed, he plants his fresh manuscript just beneath the young woman's fingers so that it will be promptly excavated. He goes on to live out a common writer's fantasy, seeing his work read in public by a stranger. But more important than that is the thrill he feels when he first sits down to write, a treasure not even half buried in the dirt:

> Basically I was feeling for the first time that heady paired combination of satisfactions that the sexual proseur can encounter at the outset of a new enterprise, as his long-neglected artistic ambition, however tentative or internally scoffed at—the wish to create something true and valuable and even perhaps in a tiny way beautiful—combines with his basic cuntlapping lust, the two emotions reinforcing each other and making you, or rather me, feel almost insane with a soaringly doubled sense of mission.

In other words, Baker's sex writing has always been an elaborate double entendre as much about literature as about our intimate lives.

Dig in the sand a bit deeper than that and worlds open up. Marian the Librarian's adventures begin when she kicks her husband, David, out of the house. Her first adventure finds her combining the erotic possibilities of mail-order purchases and delivery men, but for now it's David who is most worth considering: David the embittered teacher of journalism who has a peculiar preoccupation with mechanical innovations. David not only adheres to a Jim of *Vox*–style worldview, he completes an intra-*Fermata* trajectory that begins with the story of how Arno originally created his time-stopping power.

43

ARNO FIRST BEGAN TO SENSE THAT HE HAD SOME KIND OF CONTROL over time when he was in the fourth grade (the same age as Mike of *Room Temperature,* when he got hot for the bagpipes). His fumbling initial experiments into how to stop and restart time focused on bits of mechanical hardware: toggle switches, rubber bands, mechanical pencils. He remained frustrated until the summer after fifth grade when he had a revelation associated with his family's basement washing machine. And where am I when I read this scene, a scene pivotal not only to *The Fermata* but to Baker's career in that it amounts to his realization that simplistic faith in machines—faster is better, progress is inevitable—is the thing he needs to outgrow? A French Laundromat, of course.

Catherine had shuttled off to Versailles again, and I'd been left with the clothes-washing duties, which I actually didn't mind because I get a little thrill out of being seen in public folding Catherine's colored bras. I'd brought *The Fermata* along, even though

I find it impossible to read while washing clothes. Some kind of puzzle-solving reflex is triggered by washers and dryers with glass doors, and the subtly altered consciousness that results from the search for pattern amid the chaos of tumbling laundry always winds up dragging at my attention, leaving me reading poorly if I attempt it at all. But for whatever reason I did wind up reaching for *The Fermata* at the French Laundromat, and good thing too: I experienced at once a version of Arno's doubled sense of mission as, against his own better judgment, he launched into an extended explanation of his own origin.

Arno's attraction to the washing machine—a belief that "untapped temporal powers resided in the spin cycle," leading to a "refining [of his] appreciation of centrifugal force"—initially sounds a whole lot like Abby of *Vox*'s hole fetish: The pattern of raised dots left on a towel wadded up against the inside of a washing machine at the end of a spin cycle made it appear as though the towel had "tried to pour itself out of the holes of the spinning basket." The young Arno had concluded from this that *he* needed to spin, and as he attempted a backyard tumble dry, he imagined projectile hemorrhaging from his fingertips, à la Abby's fog of blood. But it was no good—time didn't stop. What Arno really needed to do, he thought next, was connect himself to the washing machine. He achieved this by running a thread through holes carefully punched through calluses at the ends of his fingers, and then he tied the thread to the machine's upright agitating post. When the machine hit its spin cycle, the thread was pulled maniacally through Arno's fingers. Time stopped!

Now this didn't recall Abby at all—but it did recall film feeding through a movie projector. And Baker's "The Projector" appeared in *The New Yorker* just seven weeks after *The Fermata* was published. Notably, then, it's this cyborg-projector sequence that leads to Arno's realization that "to write [his] life" properly he needs the "entire receptacle of [his] consciousness spun." What follows next is his theory of knowledge:

> And everything in the mind—that final triumph of protein chemistry—is likewise in helpless motion, afloat, diffuse, impure, unwilling to commit to precipitation: only an artificially induced pensive force of hundreds of thousands of gravities can spin down some intelligible fraction of one's true past self, one's frustratingly poly-disperse personality, into a pellet of print.

What's notable about this is the centrifuge action itself. The centrifuge, I saw now, as I was surrounded by centrifuges in the French Laundromat, was the classic Baker machine, employed as readily at the frontiers of science as for household chores. What does a centrifuge do? Extract fluid.

This explained a bevy of watery images in *The Fermata*. Arno likens transcribing a tape for Joyce to "dog-paddling along in the moonlit scumless lily pond of her consciousness." He claims to appreciate pre-Raphaelite painter Sir Lawrence Alma-Tadema's scenes of languishing postmasturbatory Victorian ladies for their depictions of "clear water and wet tulle." And after he uses his time-stopping power to follow home the woman from the beach, he watches her masturbate in the bathtub to the recollection of his story, fixating all the while on the water flowing over her body in "riverine trails."

Of course it's this scene that culminates in the infamous comeface sequence: Arno stops time so that he can masturbate onto the woman's face, and it takes him a "good ten minutes" to clean his sperm from the woman's eyelashes and eyebrows. Once he's finished he attests to an odd feeling of companionship with Henry James and claims that he has now become "a modestly successful amateur pornographer."

44

I THOUGHT TWO IMPORTANT THINGS AS I READ THIS STRETCH, cycling through the forty-five pages from the washing machine revelation to the come-face scene.

First, I noted that Arno's story about Marian the Librarian was a whole lot better than his autobiography: Arno's writing was better than his writing *about* writing. What do I mean by better? Time stopped. That is, I stopped having the impulse to glance down at the page numbers as I read, I stopped peeking at the pages ahead for hard breaks, and I even stopped pausing to feverishly scribble the rough drafts of what I would later write about *The Fermata* in the margins. Marian was all-engrossing. I just read. That was the most important lesson of *The Fermata*. Literature has always been a time-stopping technology.

Of course that goes the other way as well. After the centrifuge revelation, when I was *not* reading about Marian, I didn't hesitate to stop time in *The Fermata* by setting it aside to check the laundry machines or move a load from a washer to a dryer. Truth be told, in books that don't divert me I almost never force myself through to a convenient stopping place before getting up to do chores or whatever. I don't wait for chapter breaks, those moments when a writer signals that it might be a good time to check e-mail or pee. In fact, in books that *do* divert me I often don't pause at *those* moments at all: I blow through text breaks like they're commas or colons. And whenever I start to feel a flagging of attention, and I'm sure that it's not just a failure of will, I'll just stop reading whenever, midsentence even, and what that means is that time in the book stops completely, everyone stands where they are, waiting for me to return, and that might be a very brief moment as I give in to a minor distraction, or it might be a much longer period as I attend to some pressing task and don't return to the book until an hour or a week or a month has passed. When I do come back I restart time by backing up a sentence or two, or sometimes a page, and I'm always surprised by how little it takes to get back into the groove of a book, to realign my consciousness with its ongoing stream of events and images. This mutual, time-stopping phenomenon of books was what *The Fermata* had been saying all along about the literature I'd realized it was about.

The second thing I thought about while I read through this stretch was that appreciation of a book does not mean you go the whole nine yards with it. If only Arno had stuck with "cuntlapping"! Sadly I have to admit to being among those who first read the come-face scene with flagging appreciation. Ditto the book's preoccupation with anuses. Arno readily admits that his autobiography is unduly preoccupied with "anes," as he says, and while I can understand the anus as a universalizing feature of physiology—among the non-gender-specific body parts put to use sexually (e.g., fingers, earlobes, lips, etc.), the anus is the only common feature routinely withheld from public view, which grants it the draw of the forbidden—I have to admit that I'd always thought of the anus as a fetish for small-cocked men, men who maybe otherwise can't achieve that wonderful sensation of feeling gripped. Don't get me wrong. I've *licked* my share of anuses, and one of the things I've thought about as I've run my tongue over the spot that has a pretty uniform texture, person to person—something like a soggy walnut—is that I've got one too, I've got a soggy walnut that others have licked. (For the record I once licked Catherine's anus, which she seemed to like okay though it wasn't anything special, and while she hasn't licked mine, I did once ask her to "fuck my butt" with her finger, which she agreed to do until the noises I made in reply, probably hammed up a bit, reminded her too much of pain and she started to cry.) So anuses *do* offer a common frame of reference, albeit a sort of tasteless one, and I suppose all this is really just my way of saying "Not interested!" which I acknowledge is problematic because I've certainly known women who attest to the joys of anal sex, and I imagine the homosexual community would want to have a general approval registered as well. But in any event, in *The Fermata,* it's not that big a deal because while there's certainly a good deal of "anal play" in the book it's not nearly as stressed or infamous as the come-face scene.

When I first read this scene in the French Laundromat, I actually stopped murmuring the words of the book under my breath and murmured "Ugh!" instead. To be fair I'd been waiting to get to this scene for more than a year, creating unrealistic expectations, and Arno himself has second thoughts about the whole thing ("I wasn't crazy about the way my come looked on her closed eyes"). Furthermore, plenty of room in the book is given over to a girlfriend of Arno's, who argues that intimacy of any kind with a time-stopped woman is loveless, at best, and at worst, necrophilic. But even so, I couldn't stop myself from thinking that *The Fermata* double-crosses itself on this point. As will be reiterated in *House of Holes,* Arno insists on a distinction between good porn and bad porn, and he assures us that he's not like the men of bad porn. But isn't a man coming on a woman's face, immobile or no, more or less a central theme of bad porn, by which I mean isn't it an exciting activity to some men precisely because most women *don't* want their faces came on? Isn't there just no way around the fact that it's more about power than intimacy? As I dug back into my mental archive of Nicholson Baker, the only relevant tidbit seemed to come from *The Mezzanine,* when "Howie" describes his solution to public urinal stage fright. To get his juices flowing, he imagines peeing on the head and face of men whose only crime happens to be that they have sidled up beside him. One poor imagined sap "fend[s] the spray off with his arm, puffing and spluttering to keep it from getting in his mouth." This clearly *is* about power, and nakedly so. That in mind, a careful reader seems invited to conclude that *The Fermata*'s come-face scene tips the book's balance toward Arno's monstrousness, pushing him beyond redemption.

45

I DIDN'T START RETHINKING THIS UNTIL THE BOOK RETURNED to Marian the Librarian, and this was long after I'd come to terms with the fact that I wasn't going to be having Baker-inspired sex in Paris. It wasn't an unhappy time though, because Catherine and I had settled on two weeks in a Maine beach cottage for the coming June, to be followed by a week in South Berwick's lone bed and breakfast, and even though we weren't having sex, Catherine was letting me lotion her entire body every morning, head to toe, after she sit-down showered. Her cold had cleared up, and I'd cleared up too, though not as a function of my codeine prescription, but as a function of what the hole in my back represented: the removal of an affliction of which I'd only ever been spectrally aware. Even Catherine seemed aware of this, and one morning after *I'd* sit-down showered and descended the spiral staircase naked, she glanced at me walking across the room and said, a little slowly and thoughtfully, "Paris seems to agree with you!" This instantly made me think of *The African Queen,* and all journey romances like it, in which two completely incompatible people are thrust into a wandering adventure that first sets them raging against each other, but then there's always some kind of pause in the action, a hesitation of reflection when Hepburn begins to appreciate Bogart, or Bogart begins to appreciate Hepburn, and one of them says to the other, "Africa seems to agree with you!" Love is blossoming! I was so overwhelmed at Catherine's comment that I could think of no better reply than "Well, I agree with *it*!" We nodded awkwardly and I kissed her on the cheek and headed to Montmartre to read more about Marian the Librarian.

Marian's second adventure—David is now a forgotten memory—finds her luring a young neighbor and his girlfriend into a threesome in Marian's garden. The two young lovers approach the garden in all innocence, and Marian is surely playing a faint serpent role here. There are two central points to the seduction. First, language. Marian appeals to the young lovers with an explanation of what she calls "dildo talk." Simply put, dildo talk is how human beings employ language when lust so addles the mind that elegant phrasing and sophisticated sentence structure become neurologically impossible. "It's dildo talk, frankly," Marian explains, and it's the "frankly" that is of interest because it suggests that we're only rarely capable of being honest about this particular use of words. "'God, I wish I could show you what I have up my ass right now. It feels fucking hot.' She paused. 'See, that's a sample of dildo talk.'"

What's in the pause? For me, the pause is filled with *my* history of dildo talk, recollections of moments when I risked "talking dirty," as is more commonly said. Catherine, actually, is particularly receptive to this kind of language, though timing is everything. Start in too soon with things like "Fuck that cock, I love you!" or "Jesus God, your big witchy tits!" (Catherine delivered her Catholic college valedictorian speech as a practicing Wiccan) and she shrivels up like a salted snail. But time it right, and it's exactly what she needs to vault past her sexual tipping point. (This, of course, is the only real tipping point, and I imagine it was just this sort of tipping point that had earned Malcolm Gladwell, author of *The Tipping*

Point, the rare honor of becoming a dick synonym in *House of Holes*: "Dave angled out his Malcolm Gladwell . . .") I liked it that Baker avoided the word "dirty" in his discussion of dildo talk (though he indulges in it elsewhere), because I'd always thought that "dirty" was a counterproductive term. Consult any soil expert, and what he or she will tell you is that "dirt" describes no actual category or state of earth (e.g., sand, clay, mud, etc.). "Dirt" is a judgment—and hence a danger. Ought it not be possible to arouse ourselves without risking a term that, once the spell of lust has faded, may trigger retroactive shame? One of the more difficult truths of Baker's sex books is that no matter how much we enjoy the études of James or Bach, there will always be a part of us that responds to a simple, vulgar, primal beat. Hence, dildo talk.

Marian doesn't put it quite like that, but it's an argument along these lines that first draws in her neighbor and his girlfriend. But that's not the only hurdle that the youths need to clear before they can open themselves up to desire. The young neighbor's girlfriend, Sylvie, in particular, needs more—and that's the second point to the seduction.

A convenient happenstance offers the solution. After the encounter is well under way, Sylvie claims that she "*need*[*s*] to use the bathroom"—defecate. Marian refuses to let her rush into the house for privacy. The case Marian makes for being permitted to watch and even assist with Sylvie's bowel movement builds off her earlier claim that if her young neighbor, Kevin, were to piddle in front of the two women it "would help Sylvie relax."

Both Kevin and Sylvie have difficulty with this, and the difficulty is the whole point. Virtually all of the body's holes—the Baker hole theme returns—are controlled by muscles that are both voluntary and involuntary. That is, they are linked biochemically to whatever constitutes the conscious and unconscious minds and therefore offer a kind of theoretical nexus if what you truly hope to address is the negative effect of modernity's hatchet job on thought and sensation—the so-called mind-body problem. This is Marian's argument. The fact that we have difficulty exerting our will over muscles that ought to respond to voluntary mental command—call it emotional constipation—reveals the inhibitory impact that cultural values may exert over the pursuit of pleasure. Marian's solution is to become a kind of biofeedback coach. "Once you do that," she tells Sylvie, meaning shit semipublicly, "you'll feel free to do anything that feels good, anything you want, and you'll come extra hard."

That's pretty much what happens from there. And it's precisely because this is kind of a sweet moment (a faux-birthing sequence, spare on details: "[Marian] felt the weight drop in her hand and immediately folded the napkin over it and sprayed Sylvie clean") that I reflexively leaped back to "going big job" in *Room Temperature*. *The Fermata* depicts what might be termed "shit intimacy." This may seem like an odd pairing, but haven't shit and intimacy always tended toward harmony? Does not a parent's love trace back to having changed a baby's noxious diapers, and does not a child's love remain incomplete until he or she is called upon many years later to return the favor? Isn't fondness for household pets a function of coaching them through the management of their "business," cleaning up after them as the need arises? And even if we do manage to shut our bathroom doors, do we not gird our romantic love when we are called upon to clean a toilet we did not deface ourselves, and is not our love enhanced when a toilet we *did* deface is cleaned by another without reproof? At the risk of investing the cosmos with an intelligence it surely lacks, it seems to me that embracing nature's most profound juxtaposition—it's not some cruel joke!—is the surest and quickest route to happiness.

It's all this that got me rethinking the come-face scene. Why, exactly, did I see this particular activity as being more about power than intimacy? Doesn't an aversion to come faces—or scratch that, because this is probably true even for people who are pathologically drawn to come faces—rely on the insulting suggestion that semen is "dirty," good enough for the womb and perhaps the torso and breasts, but repugnant in this one case? Even if that argument fails, I have to admit to not having initially read the come-face scene in the context of Baker's career. Doesn't the sequence change a bit when we recognize that Arno's orgasm rides the same rhetorical thrust as Jim of *Vox*'s ejaculations? Hadn't I stopped myself from considering what he might have been trying to passionately profess here? That was probably why Martin Amis and all the other hostile reviewers had a hard time reading these books: they had neither the space nor the inclination to link them to earlier work. And that's why Catherine couldn't read them either: she hadn't read the earlier books, and the mistake was mine in thinking she could hop aboard my whitewater descent through the rapids of Baker's career. For some, I'm sure, I've crossed a line, the line between "read" and "torturous read," but I reject that—I reject the idea that a muscular, strenuous interpretation in any way amounts to torture. Because what I was feeling now was the opposite of torture: a sense of freedom, the same freedom that Sylvie feels once she craps out her inhibitions. I *was* having sex in Paris. I was having exactly the kind of Emersonian sex that had been my goal since the first moment I'd considered reading Nicholson Baker.

46

BUT THERE'S A PROBLEM WITH THIS SEX. IT'S EASY ENOUGH TO recognize that *The Fermata*'s beach scene juxtaposes writing and taboo sex for the purpose of mutual illumination. With a little mental effort we can recognize that Arno's orgasm in the come-face scene contains the seed, if not the dirt, of an ideal writer-reader relationship: seeing your work put to exactly the kind of use you'd like to see it put to is kin to the most transgressive of sexual acts. The young woman is Arno's ideal reader, and this aligns perfectly with Baker's having once said that his ideal reader is probably a woman. The problem, of course, is that I've set out to be something of an ideal reader myself and I'm not a woman.

Compounding things, it's not at all difficult to fathom a current of ambivalence toward male homosexuality in Baker's work. It first appears in *The Mezzanine* with "Howie"'s peculiar observation about men almost bumping into each other in bathroom doorways. "Average men," he claims, excuse themselves with "Oop," while gay men and women use the plural form, "Oops." In *U and I,* a book about a man loving another man's work, you might expect to find some ecstatic homoerotic play, but that thought gets tamped down before you even have it: Baker makes a somewhat derisive reference to Henry James as "William's gay brother." Arno's girlfriend in *The Fermata,* the same one who chastised him for preferring helpless partners, forces him to consider the prospect of the time-stopping ability being used on him by a man. "I admit that's not something that appeals to me," Arno says. "But to be consistent I suppose I would have to say, fine, if the gay man means well, and he wants to give me a blowjob without my knowledge, it wouldn't be the end of civilization." This same strained sense of fair play is palpable in Baker's review of homosexual British author Alan Hollinghurst's *The Folding Star,* published just a few weeks after *The Fermata* appeared: Baker notes that "mutually baffling pornography" is the lone bridge spanning the "chasm" between the "gay cosmology" and the "prevailing straightgeist."

And it's not just gayness. Nicholson Baker doesn't seem to like men much, gay or straight. This terrified me. Baker had repeatedly allowed that he was not particularly comfortable around men, and I was frightened because it suggested that he might not like me trying to be his ideal reader. And now there was a chance, an outside chance, that I would encounter him in Maine. The only solace I was able to take in the matter was in imagining the quandary Baker must have found himself in with the 1993 birth of his second child—a son. The boy was named Elias, and I wanted to believe—I *had* to believe—that the anagrammical similarity of his name to his sister's was an admission that men can be Alices too.

Of course they can! And I'll go even farther than that—farther than Baker. Not only is the thought of a man having sex with another man not the end of civilization, it may well be the beginning of it—and I don't just mean boring old Greek cultural homosexuality. If what civilization has been trying to say by making the study of literature an important spoke in the wheel of humanist and liberal arts educations—part of the curriculum of society, as it were— is that books serve an important cultural function, and if literature really is a kind of intimacy that echoes what we're supposed to feel during physical love-making, and if "ejaculate" really does mean that you feel something very deeply and are compelled to shoot it ecstatically forth into the world, then how can I possibly avoid the conclusion that what I've been hoping for all the while I've searched for a new sense of literary purpose is for Nicholson Baker to spray his literary come all over my face? Yes! That *is* what I want, and not in some glib, halfhearted Arno way either. Metaphorically speaking, I want Nicholson Baker to come on my face, and to keep coming on my face, again and again—and isn't that all any reader should want, isn't that the explicit lodged way deep down in the implicit? Wouldn't that—same-sex trust and acceptance,

particularly among aggression-prone men—amount to the beginning of a better civilization? I want Nicholson Baker to ejaculate all
over my face, and I don't care if it's about power, and I don't care if
I'm left puffing and spluttering to keep it out of my mouth. I want
Nicholson Baker to keep spewing all over my face until I can't possibly take it anymore.

47

WHICH INFORMED MY REREAD OF *HOUSE OF HOLES* IN PARIS.
Rereading the book in light of Baker's earlier career let me tap into
its seamless snatching up of threads dropped eighteen years earlier.
In its first few pages there is another clear instance of shit intimacy.
A short time later a character fwooshes into a gaseous, semicon-
scious vapor. And on page eleven a man groans like one of Baker's
critics ("Just plain disgusting") at another man banging his erect
penis against a woman's face.

And then there are the holes. One character streams down into
a straw that is practically a citation of the lengthy description of
straws in *The Mezzanine*. Another climbs into a Laundromat clothes
dryer to have his consciousness centrifugally spun. The pleasure
of *re*reading is discovering how incomplete your pleasure was the
first time around. Like sex it gets even better when the participants
know each other a little.

House of Holes is a book of stories as Arno of *The Fermata*
might have written them. But, as with Wonderland, there is no
clumsy attempt to explain its origin this time. *House of Holes* is a
simpler machine. Unlike *Vox,* it has a setting, a zany combination
of a free love commune and a voc-tech college, but like *Vox* there

is a background dystopia populated with lonely people who find it hard to be truthful about what they really like. The world outside the House of Holes, *our* world, is overrun with pornography that is "depressing and drowns out good porn," the kind of porn *House of Holes* aspires to be. That "good porn" exists is perhaps proved by the book's reception. It was not a best seller (it spent a couple weeks on the extended list), but reviewers struck a far more pleasing chord:

> *The New York Times Magazine*: It's as funny as it is filthy and breathes new life into the tired, fossilized conventions of pornography in a way that suggests a deep, almost scholarly familiarity with the ancient tropes.

> *The Boston Globe*: Brilliant, absurd, puerile, depraved, and completely enthralling.

> *The Toronto Star*: After more than a decade as a reviewer . . . I thought it was safe to assume that I'd experienced every type of literary pleasure. . . . *House of Holes* proved me wrong.

Where had this come from, all of a sudden? It wasn't, I thought, that the world had spontaneously changed between *The Fermata* and *House of Holes*. It was that Baker helped change the world, through those who had read his books and understood them and those who had read only imitators, like me—those who had surmised only remotely that such writing was now possible and necessary.

Which is not to say that *House of Holes* proposes an easy solution to the broken world from which it offers relief. That broken world is embodied in the book by a litany of broken figures: the manless arm of page one, and later headless men and jars full of stolen clitorises, all evidence of how modernity and bad porn chop us up into objects. The book's bad porn subplot climaxes when a brave young woman—another Alice, if we're paying attention—confronts the bagpipe pornmonster. The pornmonster is a giant assemblage of parts, a seething, oozing chimera, a motile blob of dirtiness. The pornmonster can speak, and it is sad. It knows no better than to immediately water-cannon its visitor with "sexual splatterment," head to toe. The young woman refuses to be disgusted. She even likes it a little. And from there it's the most innocent of associations that leaps from the pornmonster to Humpty Dumpty and the scattered shards of a shattered cultural sexuality, and hence a suggestion that a fantasy book ought to be able to put a fantasy egg back together again. The pornmonster repents, the stolen clitorises are returned, the arm finds its man, and we are all reborn as *House of Holes* ends with a young man and a young woman making love in a tiny silver egg: the womb of a better world.

48

IT WAS NOT, I'M FAIRLY SURE, JUST AS I REREAD THE END OF *HOUSE of Holes* that I one day returned a bit earlier than planned to the adorable atelier. I know that it was our third week in Paris, because we'd hit a dull rhythm of living in Paris sometime before, and after I'd begun having my hole stuffed in the mornings, we had stopped taking our walks together along the Seine and had settled into separate routines. Even the street market salmon dinners we had enjoyed sharing so much in our first days—candlelight, wine, quiet music—had become perfunctory: We ate silently, musing over solitary adventures. And I know too that on this particular occasion I failed to text Catherine to let her know that I was headed home. It *was*, however, in the spirit of *House of Holes*, its general ebullience, that I rode up the waggly elevator, earlier than planned, and strode toward the studio. I surprised Catherine before she had a chance to react. She was on the half toilet, plywood door open as wide as a child's smile! She squinted at me but couldn't quite figure out how to blame me for the intrusion.

"I was hoping," she groaned, "to take care of all this before you got home."

She twisted sideways on the seat so she could crimp shut the door.

We said nothing more of this. But that night, halfway through dinner, Catherine spotted a drop of wine sliding down the outside of our seven-euro bottle, and in one fluid rattlesnake motion she snatched up the bottle and caught the trickling drop with her tongue, licking its mauve trace from the bottle's shoulder to its neck and letting the very tip of her tongue flick at the raised rim of the bottle mouth where the drip had first dribbled out the top. Oh, glory day! She set the bottle down again and glanced at me, silent and aslant, and in an instant our mood was no longer a bad habit.

In response I thought of two separate scenes from books: a quite similar interval in *Madame Bovary* ("She bent back to drink, her head thrown back, her lips pouting . . . while with the tip of her tongue passing between her small teeth she licked drop by drop the bottom of her glass"), and a moment in *Lolita* when Humbert Humbert uses his tongue to pluck a speck from Lolita's eye ("Gently I pressed my quivering sting along her rolling salty eyeball"). This was terribly exciting, but I knew better than to act on this new momentum. The next day we went to Parc de Sceaux and to the Louvre again, and then on the ride home, veiled as an afterthought, Catherine commented on how happy I seemed, a positivity that was in large part a result of having read Nicholson Baker well, though she attributed it to my codeine prescription. She suggested the

possibility of trying one of the pills herself, perhaps later, perhaps
back at the atelier.

"You mean codeine sex?" I said.

"Maybe," she said.

Back at the atelier we played music for a while and Catherine
took one of my pills and we nibbled on the macaroons that we
had splurged on at Paris's famous macaroon store. Earlier in the
day, the store had been crammed with Parisians, but somehow
we had slipped to the front of the line, which added to the sense
of its being a very special day indeed. Then, after the macaroons,
during the wine, Catherine said, a little sheepishly, "So—do you
want to try?" Yes, I wanted to try. She disappeared downstairs, and
I wasn't allowed to descend until she was ready, and when I did
she was wearing the lacy red bra that I'd washed and folded for
her—that was part of the excitement, recollecting that in the French
Laundromat I had carefully nested one of the bra cups inside the
other—and as well she had on a pair of the heavy dangly earrings
favored by French women, which she had purchased even before I
arrived in Paris. We kissed for a long time, and while we were kissing I thought of Arno's observation that there is no good autoerotic
substitute for kissing. True, true. And then I thought, while I was
in the process of making Catherine come with my mouth, that it
was exactly these kinds of moments that we're not supposed to talk
about in books about writers, except, I guess, if our goal is Rabelai-
sian abandon, which is monumentally sad because that too cleaved
the work of the mind from the work of the body. Yes, of course, an
orgasm is a sort of stoppage in time, a rejuvenating period in which
we seem to relinquish consciousness—which Catherine did now
at my touch, not with fanfare and great quantities of fluid production, but with a kind of blessed absence, a hole that opened in her
self—but it's also true that thinking of sex only in this way ignores

all the time around orgasms when our minds are at work both reflexively and voluntarily, as we wade through thoughts that arouse
us, thoughts that are every bit as important as the thoughts we
think when we're not under the intoxicating influence of being part
of an organic machine, one body joined to another. It occurred to
me, after Catherine's orgasm was complete and we rearranged ourselves on the futon so that I could enter her, that it might seem odd
that I'd have borderline analytical thoughts during intercourse, but
that's wrong, I thought, that's *part of the problem,* both with how we
think about books and how we think about the world. And for me,
anyway, some of those borderline analytical or even critical thoughts
are among the most exciting of thoughts, like the thought I sometimes have of my sperm shooting up into a womb and beginning
a grand doomed quest—I think of Lucian's *True History* and envi-
sion little Argonauts. Exciting! Or I think about how it's possible
to insert fingers in a woman's vagina and anus at the same time and
almost touch them together through an impossibly thin membrane
between the two passages. On this particular occasion, as I moved
slowly in and out of Catherine, I held on to both her earrings in
my fists because they were heavy on her earlobes and pulled more
than she thought they would when she bought them, so it was a
favor I was doing her, I suppose, but the earrings in my palms felt
like gathered-up rosaries, fistfuls of sharp pebbles, and it wasn't really irreverence that accounted for my excitement at this so much
as the trust Catherine was showing me because of course I could
have just ripped the earrings from her ears—even accidentally, if
I wasn't careful. I recognized this to be a much more Updike-style
thought than a Baker-style thought, but even that was kind of exciting because it got me thinking back on Baker's claim that Updike's
writing about literature wasn't ecstatic enough and of that snarky
comment that had been made about autobiographical criticism: I

pee, therefore I am. *No, no, no,* I thought. *I come, therefore I am.* It's only such an existential motive that can explain the success of everything from traditional aphrodisiacs to the latest spectrum of erectile dysfunction cures, as pleasure alone can't possibly account for the wild calisthenics that people—okay, men   will perform so that they can go on being able to come. That seemed completely true to me. And it was *this* thought, not the thought about being able to come, but the thought that I might really be onto something true, that got me close to coming with Catherine. That and the fact that she was now moving her hips in concert with mine: I love looking down at her little hula wriggles, and the resulting puckering and unpuckering of her stomach, which always makes me think of the muscles of a snake moving in ripples as it tugs itself along. This, I always conclude, is the best explanation for why there's a snake in Eden, but that's not what made me come, now. This time the thought that sent me over the orgasmal edge was one I often have during sex about how the penis and the clitoris in the pregendered fetus start out as pretty much the same thing, so that coitus is a sort of romantic return to a common origin. That did it! And this time, because Catherine had told me that lately she'd been having some pain when I came inside her—a hard truth made beautiful by its confession—I pulled out and spilled onto her stomach. She held me in her hands as I came, and there was something about how she stroked me during this orgasm, something that she'd never done before, and which I never do when I masturbate because when I masturbate I always just go for the best spurting sensation I can muster, but whatever it was made my orgasm particularly prolonged. Not only that, but toward the end of it, my entire penis attained for a good fifteen seconds a wildly intense sensitivity, and what I thought about during that period, in some deep part of me—it felt almost as though my consciousness and unconsciousness had swapped places—was how women describe their clitorises during orgasm, a point of prolonged, intense sensitivity, and now my own prolonged intense sensitivity was prolonged further by the deep background thought that my cock felt like a big vibrating clitoris. Catherine was stroking my big clit! A Baker-style thought if there ever was one. And I didn't share it with Catherine after I'd rolled off her and collapsed onto the futon for the deep-breathing postsprint interval we always observe before one of us, usually me, gets up to retrieve the necessary tissue. I didn't say anything because my thought was already transforming into this: *That's* what we should be when we read, not some passive receptacle, not some spurting lecturer, but a precise point of prolonged and intense sensitivity, caught in time and reading.

49

IN SEPTEMBER 2012, ABOUT THREE MONTHS AFTER I MET NICHOLSON Baker in Maine—to spill my beans here a bit—Baker was interviewed by the *New York Times* on the occasion of the release of his second collection of essays, *The Way the World Works* (in which he finally touched on his bassoon-playing days, though only briefly). In the interview Baker admitted to being so disheartened by the United States' ongoing drone war in Pakistan that it made him want to quit writing. It was a strange thing to say in that he offered it in response to a question about whether he'd ever met any authors who impressed him. I held my breath reading his reply because I'd just met him and I'd hoped to be impressive myself. But Baker named no names—not me, not Updike—and instead offered a non sequitur about the "presidential administration," assassinations, and how it all sickened him and made him "want to quit writing altogether." Less than a month later, he posted online several protest songs he'd composed and written himself. A book he'd been writing, he explained on *The New Yorker* blog, had "stopped working," so he'd started composing protest songs instead. He hadn't played music for thirty years, but he bought a keyboard and set up a modest recording studio in his barn in South Berwick, and there he was—a musician once again.

I listened to the songs and liked them well enough—I thought I heard some *lectio divina* in there—but still I worried. It's always a cause for concern when a mid- to late-career writer takes up a whole new medium. D. H. Lawrence's paintings come to mind, and Eudora Welty's photographs, and I was once able to finger through clippings in a collage studio in Mark Strand's house when a friend who was housesitting for him gave me a tour. Writers like hobbies, of course, like stringing sticky strands of connection between literature and the adjacent arts, but when they go public with this work—even when prose writers publish their poetry, or critics try their hand at a novel—what sometimes looms even larger than the new work is the sudden recognition of the limitations on the genius that created the old work. Even worse, the new work may seem like a critique of the old work, as though the old work had failed in some way. This is particularly so when the writer in question has also been saying that he might well quit writing altogether.

But I didn't really think Baker was planning on quitting writing. He also said he was listening to his songs while he wrote, so at worst he seemed to have suffered a sudden onset of ambivalence and dread. And, for me, what these latest appearances of Nicholson Baker in my life really did—appearances that now came *while* I was writing about him—was reveal the shortcomings of my critical methodology. I'd known for a long time that I was bending the rules by intending to read *The Anthologist* last: *House of Holes* came out two years later, and *The Way the World Works* a year after that (though it includes pieces published as early as 1994). But that wasn't the problem. The problem was that breaking authors' careers into subject-themed subsections, as I'd been doing, as libraries and bookstores do, and even as Baker's essay collections do, creates an artificially orderly impression of the mind at work, as though writers are like shrewd generals dispassionately dispatching regiments of intellectual resources, mentally sculpting passions and interests into the kind of neat colored rectangles used on battlefield maps to represent squadrons or battalions, blocks that get meaningfully nudged about as battles are planned and waged. Even the publishing industry feeds this false impression. Books themselves segment up passions and interests into rectangular book-shapes, and the fact that some books sell exceedingly well and come to stand for writers' careers while others underperform and fall by the wayside throws off our bottom line of who a given writer is as a person. The methodology I had devised to combat this, reading all of Nicholson Baker's books in the order of their publication, can be only a partial solution to the problem because by the time a book has been published, often a year or more after it has been completed, its author has moved on to other things, other books. Reading suffers from interest lag. Add to that the fact that a real writing life is nothing at all like being a callous general or admiral shifting regiments or fleets about like pieces in some ugly game—rather it's like being one of the pieces, a lonely trench soldier charging into the no-man's-land of each new project with scant sense of purpose and perhaps only a prayer for survival—and what you realize is that even a carefully devised system of reading overlooks crucial turns in a writer's intellectual development.

True, I had sensed an emerging political conscience in Baker. There was that early, anonymous plea about the Gulf War, and I'd known from the beginning that there was a presidential assassination book coming, and there was still the mystery regarding Baker's stance on the Holocaust. And actually by the fall of 2012, I'd read nearly all of Baker's books. All but *The Anthologist*. But even reading Baker had turned out to be an obstacle to understanding him because as I set about writing I came to realize that my methodology had warped into the evil twin of memory criticism: I wasn't struggling to remember books, as Baker had, I was struggling to remember what it had been like *not* to have read books I'd read months earlier.

Really the whole chronological reading thing broke down not long after Catherine and I returned from Paris. We crash-landed back at the former bed and breakfast and stumbled out from the wreckage to the heavy workloads of our non-Parisian lives. I was about halfway through reading Nicholson Baker at that point, and I vaulted back into the work system I'd devised in the fall, writing about Paris and Baker's sex books in the mornings and then reading books from later in his career in the afternoons. Now, though, the balm and refreshment of Baker's midcareer essays produced craving for more, particularly when I had just woken up and was preparing to sit down to write, and reading a little Nicholson Baker seemed like the perfect tool to use to poke a hole in the dike of my imagination. One day this longing won out, and after that I read Nicholson Baker indiscriminately, at all times of day, sampling pieces from throughout his career on a whole range of subjects. For a while I was concerned about this because Baker's many interests got all jumbled up in my mind. It's just this kind of jumble that triggers in critics the taxonomical reflex—jumbles must be ordered and cataloged—and I did not stop being concerned until I realized that it was just this sense of *jumbledness*, of books seeming to clamber all over one another, that was the best possible portrait of Nicholson

Baker's, or any writer's, mind. If Baker's run of books, taken as a whole, tells the story of how he untangled his own jumble, like a man painstakingly unknotting a giant wad of Christmas lights, then a reader's job, I thought, should be less to assist with the straightening and hanging of the wire than to undecorate the tree and rewad the string back into its original, brain-shaped clot.

Writing about him was even better than reading him. I loved the struggle of moving slowly through the books, massaging out trajectories and associations the early reviewers had overlooked. It was a fine time, for a time, and I reveled in a renewed sense of purpose that held all the way through my meeting Baker in Maine and my writing about his sex trilogy. It may have been precisely because the sex trilogy ends on such an upbeat note that I was surprised—even though I knew it was coming—to discover that all along Baker had been having dark thoughts. And even though I'd set out to use Baker as a savior—meaning that on some level I knew he would have to make a sacrifice in the end—I experienced a sad lull as my joyous renewal came at just that moment when Baker was considering abandoning writing, when he appeared to have been left spent.

I felt even guiltier when I realized that apotheosizing an author does not render all their books gospel truth. You'll never believe who helped me understand this. Martin Amis! In a review of Don DeLillo published in *The New Yorker* just before Catherine and I went to Paris, Amis claimed that when we say we love a writer what we really mean is that we love about half their work. I'd quibble with "love"—lust and arousal are more natural metaphors—and I'd argue too for somewhat more than half, with the added observation that we cannot reject books by writers we admire simply because they do not inspire in us fawning emotions. If books fail, they must fail in response to muscular attempts to help them succeed. That is, or ought to be, what it means "to read."

In any event, it was Amis who gave me license to depart from my critical methodology by deciding not to write about two of Baker's books, both of which failed despite my muscular attempts to help them succeed. *The Everlasting Story of Nory* and *A Box of Matches* failed to my mind because they did not rise to the standard Baker himself set for the critic of a poem. The critic, Baker once wrote, must present "hard evidence that [he] has really grunted and sweated over this single lump of poetry." *The Everlasting Story of Nory*, a third-person account of a young girl with literary ambitions spending a year in England, written in a narrative voice that to all appearances is the same girl, and *A Box of Matches,* a series of early-morning meditations in a Maine farmhouse by another Baker-figure, Emmett, a forty-four-year-old editor of medical textbooks, are not "grunt and sweat" books. They are books that *could* have been written, and perhaps even needed to be written given that Baker was now raising two children, but they were not books that needed to be written in the sense that they stemmed from a burning core of passion and interest. They read like books written in Baker's spare time. As well, they attempt a return to innocence—*The Everlasting Story of Nory* defends Baker's literary aesthetic, and *A Box of Matches* strives to complete the trilogy begun with *The Mezzanine* and *Room Temperature*—but they're too late: Baker is no longer an innocent. In fact he's begun a private passion. In *The Fermata,* Arno only toys with thoughts of suicide ("I immediately realized how laughably far I was from actual suicide"), but for Emmett of *A Box of Matches,* it's a steady ominous thought ("It isn't a subject I take up every day, but it does recur").

The larger goal of *B & Me* demands a caveat here: Nicholson Baker is not, and has never been, the true subject of this book. If I've been correct in suggesting that there's something wrong with the state of modern literature, that the state of modern literature is like an aberrant state of mind, a state on the brink of breakdown and despair, then the problem is not simply that Nicholson Baker's work has gone overlooked, however celebrated it might be. It's that the whole world is slowly going mad and forgetting writers like Nicholson Baker, writers whose *books truly need to be books.* Nicholson Baker need not serve as savior for anyone other than me. It is not that all readers should be of one mind in choosing the writers they read. Rather, what needs to be said is that the literary world has set itself on fire, and as a result it has become more and more difficult for any reader to find *their* Nicholson Baker, to find the writer who will become Nicholson Baker for them. A world without Nicholson Bakers is a scorched world. And that, more or less, is the trajectory that runs through the rest of Nicholson Baker's books—the ones I took with me to Maine.

20

THE FIRST LINE OF THE PREFACE TO NICHOLSON BAKER'S *DOUBLE Fold: Libraries and the Assault on Paper*—published, it's worth noting, just a few months before the 2001 attacks on the World Trade Center (and a further note: *The Everlasting Story of Nory* was the last novel Baker published before 9/11, and *A Box of Matches* was the first after it)—lies twice:

> In 1993, I decided to write some essays on trifling topics—movie projectors, fingernail clippers, punctuation, and the history of the word "lumber."

Okay, maybe "lie" is too strong a word. But "decided" is definitely misleading. It implies that Baker, in the lag period preceding the publication of *The Fermata,* simply turned his attention to other things. That's not really true. He'd been toying with the history of punctuation at least since *Room Temperature,* and his essay "Lumber," which charts a shift in the word's definition from "junk" to "raw material" as it sailed from England to America, traces back to an interest that began percolating in the early eighties. "Trifling" too is a bit of misdirection. Movie projectors and fingernail clippers may seem like trifling subjects to an audience that hasn't read Nicholson Baker, but anyone familiar with his work—*like* Nicholson Baker—knows full well that one of its central tenets is that trifles hint at truths. Trifles are not trifling at all.

The preface goes on to explain that at around this same time, 1993, Baker suggested to *The New Yorker* a piece about card catalogs ("Discards") that he at first thought would be "brief [and] cheerful," but which grew less brief and less cheerful once he threw himself into the work. This is misleading too, however, in that too tight a focus on this one piece, crediting it with generating the angst that resulted in *Double Fold* a number of years later, overlooks a whole set of pieces, "The History of Punctuation," "Discards," "Lumber," and "Books as Furniture," that all grew out of a single motive and rubbed up against one another with enough friction to nick to life an ambitious ember in Nicholson Baker's mind.

What's this motive? In short, a good chunk of Baker's career has been dedicated to assessing the damage that has been inflicted on the literary endeavor by the advent of the digital age. Or wait. Because now it's me being misleading, or at least getting ahead of things. Like pretty much all writers these days, Baker was and is hardly a Luddite. And particularly early in his career, perhaps because he so spectacularly leaped from writing on a typewriter to writing on a screen, his initial impulse was to regard computers as helpful tools, a bit of progress no different from a better drinking straw. This is most apparent in "Lumber," which employs neonatal search engine technology to semiotically sift through a couple centuries' worth of uses of "lumber," and Baker goes out of his way to agree with one critic's claim that literature databases offer "the most significant development in literary scholarship since xerography." Reading "Lumber" was critical for me in that it revealed that I might have been wrong to criticize *U and I* for undervaluing research. When "Lumber" quotes Jonathan Swift using "florilegias" in 1704—meaning *U and I* repeats an error rather than makes one of its own—I got my first glimpse of the true jumble of Baker's mind: Memory criticism and what might be called "Random Access Memory criticism" emerged at the same time.

"Lumber" is a mostly cheerful work, but "Books as Furniture" is vastly more so. Early in 1995, having noticed that home décor mail-order catalogs had begun to display furniture provocatively decorated with books—rows of books neatly shelved in blurry backgrounds, or books left open on coffee tables, forgotten by interrupted readers—Baker did what he'd always done when he found his interest piqued. He began an investigation. He amassed a small library of mail-order catalogs and devised a forensic system to identify the books in the pictures. The fact that big-box megamarts using books as props amounts to a kind of book pornography did not bother him at all. Indeed, still drunk on *Vox* and *The Fermata,* Baker's attention fixated on a single image of two books positioned on a bed, one called *Tongues of Flame* and the other *A Rose for Virtue,* the latter "leaning fondly, or even ardently" against the former. The "catalog's clinch" was a shot of the virtuous rose deflowering the tongue of flame with an act of "fleeting flammilingus."

Baker found and read *Tongues of Flame.* It wasn't a great book, he reported, but it was "more flavorful, perhaps, for having been found circuitously." Then he subjected "tongues of flame" to a slightly repurposed RAM criticism methodology. What this revealed was that "tongues of flame," too, was a phrase that occurred across history, from early eighteenth-century poetry to Eco's *The Name of the Rose*. It had been pretty much exclusively used to describe a fire's first hot licks of books doomed to burn.

Now to my mind the image of a burning book, whether in a library catastrophe or an ideological bonfire, is one that should simply and always spark in us a correspondingly fiery passion to extinguish the blaze. Burning books are the symbol of civilization's tendency to implode, due to an obscenely willful devaluation of human intellect. As it happened I had a little pre-Baker experience with the fact that this devaluation of intellect is foreshadowed by books employed as decoration.

51

IN 1992, AT ALMOST THE SAME TIME BAKER WAS TURNING HIS attention to truthful trifles, I visited my sister in Minnesota for Thanksgiving. The timing offered anthropological adventure: a visit to the Mall of America, the nation's first megamall, which opened that August, on the occasion of its inaugural Black Friday, tradition-ally the nation's heaviest shopping day. What better time or place, I thought, to reflect on the American devaluation of intellect? We braved the Midwestern cold and crowd, and then, in a shoe store as my sister was attended to by an already exhausted, crimp-backed salesman, I indulged in the first chance I'd had to soak in the at-mosphere of the state-of-the-art sales milieu. What drew my atten-tion? Books. As though they were marked with a reflective dye that glowed under the light of my vision, I saw books placed all about the store in an attempt to invest the sterile space with a bit of faux hominess. But what ugliness. Books doomed to remain unread. Books like unbaptized babes drifting through a frantic limbo, un-coddled and unnursed. One sat just next to my hand. I picked it up: a tattered, unjacketed collection of poems by E. E. Cummings. It was a first edition, I discovered, and on the title page, in a slightly wavering hand, someone had written "William Stafford." William Stafford! Who else but William Stafford could possibly have writ-ten "William Stafford" in a book that had found its way to a glass-topped table in the Mall of America, placed there as garnish for a row of six chic boots? Unless some wacko had been going around writing "William Stafford" into every book he found, even valuable first editions, I had miraculously stumbled across William Stafford's own copy of *95 Poems*.

I stifled a victorious shriek and for anyone who might have been spying on me, I put on the literary collector's equivalent of a poker player's inscrutable visage: *book face*. And then in one smooth motion I reached down for my satchel and slipped the book in-side—cool and clean as a glass of milk! Not even my sister noticed, and when her attendant shuffled off for another size of something she'd tried on, I leaned over and bragged of my conquest in a cocky whisper.

That was my undoing. My sister had only recently passed the Minnesota bar exam, and she panicked because were she to be caught in the company of a shoplifter she would be disbarred even before beginning to practice law. We fought a hushed battle there in the store. I tried to argue that you can't steal something that's not for sale, and that any sane judge would weigh the merits of the case and rule her crime, at worst, an instance of accessory to ethical theft. But even before I completed my argument, my sister began a core meltdown, hacking up fragments of spittle-flecked Latin, and flushing with such intensity that I feared an appearance of stigmata. I returned the book to the table, to my shame, and I did not achieve redemption until several years later when I liberated a first edition of *Underworld* from an Ikea in New Jersey. It was like cutting a barely breathing mouse from the gut of the serpent that had swallowed it alive.

It's the righteousness of these memories that explains my initial reaction to the cheerfulness of "Books as Furniture." Baker had linked mail-order catalogs to book burnings, but was he troubled by it? Not really. "Books as Furniture" insisted on seeing books in catalogs as evidence contrary to the argument that book culture was in decline. *Tongues of Flame* had triggered for Baker a happy stream of associations, so shouldn't we be grateful for "reading suggestions that fall unsolicited through our mail slots"? Might not "a mail-order catalog be sending us to graduate school"? No! It mightn't! "Books as Furniture" was entirely enjoyable, funny, and whip smart, and to readers of *The New Yorker* its stance in relation to the world around it was surely familiar: a kind of haughty imperviousness, a willed and ironic indulgence in the obliviousness of the frog whose bath will boil.

But here's the thing. I'm not sure even Nicholson Baker bought this at this point. "Books as Furniture" appeared a year after "Discards," the piece he'd hoped would remain cheerful but didn't. In the larger context of Baker's career, "Books as Furniture" reads like a forced laugh, a desperate attempt to keep light a story already turning dark.

"Discards" and "Books as Furniture" are about two kinds of catalog: card and mail-order. And the central difference between the two pieces is that the latter left Baker sitting at home as he'd always done, waiting for beautiful frivolity to fall into his lap, while the former shoved him out the door. In September 1993, Baker visited the private company in Dublin, Ohio, that had been tasked, almost exclusively, with converting the varied and widespread card catalogs of the country's public libraries into a unified computer database of holdings. This process had begun in the late seventies when the New York Public Library blazed the trail of catalog renovation, and it climaxed in 1993 just as Baker locked on to it as a subject. What he found in Ohio was even worse than grunt work: It was a sweat-shop of undereducated temp workers inundated daily with heavy boxes of cards destined to be destroyed and born anew as cereal boxes and insulation material. The company had good intentions, Baker allowed, but he found himself outraged at error rates of tran-scription. Each typo wiped a book from the library record, leaving it in a purgatory not so different from a shoe store.

"Discards" begins with a description of a 1985 junk-the-catalog party at a University of Maryland library: Attendees tied hundreds of cards to balloons and released them all at once in a rubber-and-helium debauch. One of the essay's central mysteries is why so many people regarded catalog recycling as a cause for celebration. I had almost the exact opposite thought: Why had it been this, and not the Gulf War or the history of movie projectors, that finally ignited in Baker a burning core of passion and interest, the heat of which radiated out from his protest songs even many years later?

52

THE HISTORY OF CARD CATALOGS, AS BAKER TELLS IT, IS THE creation story of information retrieval technology, of search engines. It's the history of how we look things up. This was Baker's wheel-house in that, experiments with memory criticism aside, he *was* a search engine. I'd begun to notice this as early as page sixteen of *The Mezzanine*: "I tried to call up some sample memories of shoe-tying . . ." What's interesting about this otherwise innocuous line is that I initially read "call up" as an early instance of a hard-drive-as-memory cognitive analogy: A willed attempt to remember something is like keying into your computer a command to search its disk. This made complete sense as even then Baker was writing on a computer. But it was wrong. These days we certainly do use "call up" to describe hard-drive data retrieval, but that's a metaphor too. Computers have always poached from books to help the uninitiated make sense of digital information (e.g., web "pages," text "scrolling," etc.), and what "call up" really is is a faint and fading reference to library searches, in particular to searches for rare or obscure books: Having found a book in a card catalog, you submit to the page desk a request that is sent down to a team of troglodyte librarians who elevate desired volumes via mechanical conveyor. "Call up" is a metaphor of the mind as a library.

The Mezzanine ends with just such a search: "Howie"'s piqued interest in broken shoelaces sends him on a miniquest to a library to investigate whether anyone else in the world ever wondered over the same thing. To the extent that *The Mezzanine* can be said to have a climactic moment, it's the instant when "Howie"'s exhaustive thumbing-through of called-up materials turns up a study of shoelace breakage in an obscure Polish journal, conducted by a researcher named Z. Czaplicki. "Howie" admits that his joy in this discovery might be hard to understand, but I understood it just fine. He cares about shoelace breakage because the search for the study enables him to touch another active mind in the world. "Howie" repurposes the study (which is real: Z. Czaplicki completed a number of other studies as well, of yarn, of carbon-coated fibers, of composite filtration materials), making of it an unlikely source of comfort and solace. "I left the library relieved. Progress was being made."

This explains the discomfited Baker of "Discards," in that his investigation of card catalogs revealed that progress was not being made. Actually it was being *un*made. The objets d'art of card catalogs contained a host of human information—from the hand-written suggestions of generations of librarians on subject catalog cards to the cards themselves, which after having been fingered for decades upon decades became a pleasingly fuzzy record of library user interests—but now they were all being junked. That was the flabbergasting part. Valuable records of minds at work in the world were slipping away, and people were happy about it. Baker took it personally because his own worldview, his career, owed everything to the idea that with a little effort you could look up even trifling information.

Which isn't to say he didn't give the new technology a chance. Beyond Baker's experiments with RAM criticism, "Discards" re-cords hours and hours spent dabbling with online catalogs that turned out to be sluggish and not very helpful. In comparison, a visit to a still extant catalog at Berkeley offered immediate, tactile reward: the wear on the "Censorship" and "Children's Literature" cards revealed them to be common user topics, and for each subject Baker found a helpful handwritten list of "See Also" suggestions.

"Discards" doesn't say it directly, but its central fear is that what information-retrieval technology actually automates is the basis of human intelligence: the ability to propose creative associations. To be fair Baker was reacting to a technology in its infancy, and he acknowledged that it would get better, but even a high-speed digital catalog wouldn't make better suggestions than the librarians who crowd-sourced the originals. Card catalogs were a machine that had not needed repair, yet a vast national renovation of public holdings had been initiated without any kind of vote or debate, and the result was that generations of effort were tied to balloons and released to thermal whim. In reply, Baker struck an indignant tone not uttered since his initial reaction to the Gulf War. "What we have already begun seeing . . . is a kind of self-inflicted online hull." "We should know better than to do this to ourselves." He wasn't alone in his distress. "Discards" quotes a medieval-studies historian who likened the junking of catalogs to the burning of the library at Alexandria. This inspired the grimmest statement of Baker's career so far: Catalog conversion was "a kind of incidental book burning that is without flames or crowds and, strangest of all, without motive."

He was right about all but the last. There *was* a motive—he just couldn't yet bring himself to say it.

53

THE INSTANT CATHERINE AND I WALKED IN THE DOOR OF OUR Maine beach rental, I spotted a classically Bakeresque device on the kitchen counter: a corkscrew from fifty or sixty years before, a wood handled tool with a floppy cap to generate leverage and nothing more. It was elegant testimony to human ingenuity, and the fact that corkscrews had not stopped there, had continued to evolve away from elegance and simplicity such that these days you practically feel obliged to invest in unwieldy corkscrews that look like surgical rib spreaders and require sets of instructions to operate, illustrates a principle that Nicholson Baker had hinted at in "Rarity," and played a supporting role in *The Fermata,* but didn't truly get under his skin until "Discards" and then *Double Fold* revealed that the same awful thing was happening to books.

The Maine beach rental was a studio apartment above the detached garage of the home of a now-dead engineer, built on the ocean side of a precarious, peninsular squiggle of land that swooshed out from the coast of southern Maine like a graphological flourish at the end of a signature. There was a fat central fireplace, a great old hulking log-burning stove, furniture worn comfy through decades of use, and books on shelves hung in every available nook with a sailor's sense of economy of space. The studio was itself a simple machine that had not needed improving, and no one had tried. The same was true of the town. Hidden a few miles north of the commercial vomit puddle of Kennebunkport and a few miles south of a giant litter-soiled sandbox—Maine's Ocean City, Maryland—the little community was an ongoing experiment in auto-Rumpelstiltskinism, a groggy miniburb with one small grocery and a mysterious convent that every morning deployed a recon platoon of power-walking nuns. Maine too, or at least parts of it, was like an elegant machine that had avoided unnecessary renovation, and perhaps that explained why Nicholson Baker had moved here. The rental was only thirty-five miles from South Berwick. At that point, I still hadn't decided whether I would try to meet Baker, and as far as I knew Baker was sitting at home writing as Catherine and I unpacked our bags, used the corkscrew to open a bottle of wine, and consummated Maine with the patient, syrupy tenderness that had flowed between us ever since we'd returned from Paris. We settled in for two weeks of beach walks and ocean sounds. It was in a place that appeared to have been overlooked by the apocalypse that I read Baker's account of the calamity that befell everywhere else.

All of Baker's writings about books and literature (a number of essays followed *Double Fold,* and as well there were the introductions to *A Book of Books,* which I'd now read in earnest, and *The World on Sunday,* a collection of newspaper images Baker had compiled with his wife) obliquely pinpoint the onset of bibliogeddon in the early nineties. This made complete sense. Reagan hadn't undone all the progress of the sixties and seventies, but he did unleash an aesthetic end times, failing to repel and even abetting the attacks of Mallthra, the corporate beast that wiped away what remained of Main Streets and town squares nationwide, replacing them with gargantuan commercial hives and farted-out strings of giant slimy strip-mall eggs. The end of the Cold War heralded about ten minutes of peace—or actually less, as the USSR wasn't officially dissolved until Christmas 1991—and at a distance of two decades the Gulf War now gives a report like the first sneezing fit of a global flu, an infection of schlock imperialism as the world's last superpower desperately tried to go viral. Then the digital tsunami: Computers finally started getting smaller, and as a direct result everything else, stores, people, started getting bigger. We could see it all coming—the writing was on the screen—but no one did anything about it, least of all Nicholson Baker, whose career pinnacled at just this moment.

Or that's not fair. From the perspective of his later work, Baker's early books look like a fledgling attempt at an antidote, vaccination through minutiae, a desperate plea that we recall that life's most intimate pleasures stem from inconsequential things. It was only when this started to go wrong, when Baker's casual stroll through the card catalog of his mind tripped over a subject booby-trapped with consequence, that his career tacked hard toward the vulgar utility of history. He didn't go down without a fight. Not long after "Discards," Baker got a call from the Rochester Public Library, whose resources he had used as a child. They were junking their catalog. Did he want it? He said no. Then, a year later, he was contacted by a group of librarians at the San Francisco Public Library, far closer to where he'd been living since the beginning of *U and I.*

Their catalog was going too, scheduled to be discarded as part of a move to a newer, much-celebrated facility. These librarians noticed what Rochester missed: Baker had come to look a bit like a wan Obi-Wan Kenobi, that desert mystic whose special warrior powers offered him no defense against a flattering plea.

"You are the only one who can save it now," they told him.

Baker's career would never be the same. The writer who might have preferred an endless stream of mail-order subjects found himself flying into action, making formal legal requests to inspect the catalog in question, and then filing a lawsuit when the request was denied. The lawsuit worked. In September 1996, the San Francisco Library Commission voted to keep their catalog after all, but the victory was short-lived because when Baker finally got a look at the catalog he noticed that there were far more books on cards than there were in the digital record. That's when he realized "the real story . . . [was] only incidentally about catalogs."

The SFPL was dumping books. As everything else got bigger, the new library was actually smaller than the old, and they had begun culling their collection so it would fit. Books that had been checked out only infrequently were pulled and sent to a "Deselection Chamber" at an abandoned and decrepit medical facility. Many rare and valuable books wound up in landfills. Library administrators, the real villains of the saga, claimed that the weeding of the collection was part of a pragmatic reorganization undertaken in the wake of the Loma Prieta earthquake of 1989. Baker wasn't fooled. The tragedy had been used to justify a long-standing plan the full scope of which he only now began to glimpse: The once simple and elegant machines of libraries were being turned into something far less efficient and far more expensive. And it wasn't only catalogs being eliminated—it was books.

Did the librarians who impressed Baker to duty to save a single catalog know they were recruiting a reluctant commander for a much larger conflict? Impossible to say. Others are implicated too. Baker's wife having once worked as a reporter surely helps explain why his attention soon turned to discarded newspapers. And his father-in-law, another medievalist, once called Baker's attention to a new library practice of discarding books after their texts were preserved electronically, as though the books themselves were not of historical significance. Regardless, Baker soon found himself described as a "ringleader" in news stories. Just a short time after depicting the erotic blossoming of Marian the Librarian, Baker became an activist with, as one journalist described it, "an almost mystical sway over a ragtag collection of feisty librarians." Even before Baker got involved, these librarians had been practicing "guerrilla librarianship," secreting off books consigned to the Deselection Chamber. And perhaps because all this sounds a whole lot less like a rebel force mustered to combat an imperial army than an aboriginal resistance brigade smuggling away pockets of the oppressed, Baker soon found himself accused of anti-Semitism. Anti-Semitism? *Yes.* Didn't "Deselection Chamber" sound a bit too much like a gas chamber? Wasn't Baker—or whoever coined the phrase "Deselection Chamber"—guilty of hyperbole, of diminishing the suffering of the actual victims of the Holocaust?

54

AT LAST! THE MYSTERY RESURFACES. METAPHORICALLY, AT LEAST.

The charge of anti-Semitism must have stung because Baker, via Mike of *Room Temperature,* once speculated that some of his "Quaker forebears were assimilated Jews," and he "treasured" a hope that the shape of his nose was evidence that he was still "somewhat Jewish." On a slightly related trajectory, I noticed when I reread *U and I* (as I wrote about it) that Baker had made fleeting reference to having read a partly fictionalized autobiography by Harold Nicolson. I wondered: Was *Harold* Nicolson related to *Nigel* Nicolson, Baker's first publisher? I looked it up—yes, they were father and son. And beyond writing a book that had helped Baker refine his views on autobiography, Harold Nicolson had served as a junior minister of information in England during the years leading up to World War II. It got a little confusing from there because there was *another* intelligence field–related Harold Nicholson—this one with an *h*, like Baker—who worked for the CIA until he was convicted of spying for Russia in the 1990s, but it was Harold Nicolson, no *h*, who turned out to be one of the many historical threads running through Baker's *Human Smoke*, which is, among other things, a history of war mongering during the 1930s. As it happened, Harold Nicolson had been privy to a number of the secret peace plans that had been proposed to avoid World War II, plans that might have prevented the Holocaust but that all failed because they attempted to avert violence by committing it: The German generals in secret contact with the Allies refused to go along with any plan that required the assassination of Hitler.

All this got me wondering about Baker's given name. What if it wasn't just fortuitous, as I'd originally thought, that Nicholson Baker had the same name as his publisher, *h* or no *h*? What if Baker's father, or his grandfather, had been *named* for Harold Nicolson as a result of some old promise or heroic act? It wasn't that far-fetched because even Mike of *Room Temperature* attests to "English Protestant" origins, and Baker, from where we sit with him in 1996, just as he was being sucked into the dark world of library activism, was already looking forward to shoving off for his mysterious year

in England. To do what? Beyond write *The Everlasting Story of Nory,*
I had no idea. But even if Baker hadn't been named for Harold
Nicolson—and I admit it's a long shot—it was clear that the most
direct route from the vast slaughter of Jews during World War II
to Nicholson Baker ran directly through Harold Nicolson, whom
Baker had long held in mind and whose son, for all I knew, was
solely responsible for ensuring that *The Mezzanine* saw the light of
day (in his *Paris Review* interview, Baker admitted that *The Mezzanine* was originally rejected by "nine or ten publishers" who "didn't
get the footnotes").˙

---

*Some time later, as I was writing this portion of *B & Me,* I stumbled across another
uncollected story of Nicholson Baker's—I almost missed it completely—that shed
more light on all this and demonstrated just how easy it is to slip into the weeds of
an author's life. In 1995, Baker published "My Life as Harold" in *The New Yorker,*
a short contemplative piece in which a Baker-figure named Harold, married to a
woman named Margaret, wanders Boston during a three-day period of uncertainty.
Harold is a writer, and his funk begins a day after he falls "asleep while reading [Har-
old] Nicolson's 'Peacemaking 1919.'" *Peacemaking 1919* is Nicolson's account of the
forging of the Treaty of Versailles, and the book is worth noting because it reveals
that Baker's family line *did* converge with Harold Nicolson. Baker's great-grandfather
was Ray Stannard Baker, who had already become a successful author of books for
young boys when he launched a career as a muckraking journalist. He went on to
become a trusted adviser of President Woodrow Wilson during the treaty negotiations. Ray Stannard Baker later dedicated much of his career to repairing Wilson's
tarnished reputation, and he won a Pulitzer Prize for his biographical work in 1940.
Ray Stannard Baker appears a number of times in *Peacemaking 1919* (Nicolson
attended the negotiations too), but I found no account of friendship between the
two men. Nicolson allows that Ray Stannard Baker's depiction of the negotiations
is closer to the truth than others produced at the same time, but he laments Baker's
more emotional appeal.

Notably Ray Stannard Baker also produced a brief narrative history of one of
his, and hence Nicholson Baker's, more colorful ancestors, a man with the perfectly
unusual name of Remember Baker. Ray Stannard Baker's "Remember Baker" tells
the story of Remember's life as a captain in Ethan Allen's Vermont militia unit, the
Green Mountain Boys. Recalled as "a tall, slim fellow with a sandy complection,"
Remember Baker was known as intrepid and courageous, and was among the first to
volunteer for service at the outbreak of the Revolutionary War. He was also one of its

It was around this time, 1996, "in the middle of the controversy," as the preface to *Double Fold* has it, that Baker was contacted by a man named Blackbeard, who claimed to have a library story to tell. That's pretty enticing, but Baker was already weary of the war. He didn't return the call for several weeks. What Blackbeard eventually told him made it clear that the SFPL was the tip of yet another iceberg: research libraries all across the country, and even the Library of Congress, were in the process of discarding rare books and newspapers, on bogus claims about the durability of paper. The book burning, if it was that, was not a small wildfire in a remote canyon, already surrounded by smoke jumpers—it was a massive conflagration, out of control and spreading in all directions. The holocaust, if it was that, was not some rogue state genocide conducted by a bankrupt tyrant already crippled by international sanctions—it was an ongoing global extermination executed by a superpower acting with impunity. At first, Baker "couldn't quite comprehend" what Blackbeard told him. It didn't come at a convenient time. The legal "squabble" was ongoing, he was packing for England, and he was trying to keep on an even keel by writing upbeat essays like "Books as Furniture." Anyway, the subject had left him frayed: "I was tired of finding fault with libraries; in theory, I loved libraries."

It wasn't until two full years later, after England, and not long after his family moved to Maine, that he sat down and thought, "Why not find out what's happened to the newspapers?"

---

earliest casualties. Serving as a scout in the far north, Remember Baker was shot dead by Indians and beheaded. Ethan Allen later said that his death "made more noise in the country than the loss of a thousand men towards the end of the American war." Remember Baker was thirty-five years old.

In my frenzied research into all this, I couldn't help noticing, given the direction Nicholson Baker's career had taken, that a number of both Harold Nicolson's and Ray Stannard Baker's books were among those that had been discarded after having been scanned and made available digitally.

55

OR SO HE CLAIMED THERE WAS SOMETHING ABOUT THAT
"Why not?" that didn't sit right with me. It was too flip and casual.
Those two years passed in the preface to *Double Fold* just as I've depicted them here, with a paragraph break, a strike of the return key,
but what else was happening between Baker's first chat with Blackbeard and his decision to follow the man's story?

Well, *The Everlasting Story of Nory* was published, which in addition to not feeling like a particularly inspired book contains hints
of Baker's growing malaise. Nory's writer-father is described as a
man whose sole contribution to the world is "books that help people go to sleep." And a hint of frustration over readers who prefer
first-order plot anxiety to books that celebrate the ordinary pokes
up as the precocious Nory struggles to articulate her own emerging
critical sensibility:

> Sometimes the problem with telling someone about a book was
> that the description you could make of it could just as easily be
> a description of a boring book. There's no proof that you can
> give the person that it's a really good book, unless they read it.
> But how are you going to convince them that they should read
> it unless they have a glint of what's so great about it by reading a
> little of it?

It's ironic that Baker doubts his methods and impact as a writer
now—if that's what he's doing here—because *The Everlasting Story
of Nory* was published in May 1998, and the Monica Lewinsky
scandal, which is the other significant thing that happened during
these two years, broke that January. By April people were suggesting

Vox had something to do with it. And now, a bit farther on with my Baker study, I realized that even if the Lewinsky Affair did in fact demonstrate the ongoing power of books, albeit tragically and accidentally, Nicholson Baker probably *wasn't* snickering about it from afar because for him it all would have been part of a larger crisis, just now emerging. Baker had no real love for Clinton (he would soon criticize Clinton for waging war in Bosnia, and for having too blithely accepted the bunkum of corrupt library administrators), but even a profound dislike for Clinton wouldn't have shielded Baker from disappointment over the fact that *Vox* appeared to have failed for Clinton and Lewinsky as readers, even though they *had* read a little of it.

How could Nicholson Baker not have been suffering through these years? He'd just gotten the first clues that a library drama he'd allowed himself to get dragged into was part of a crime so big he couldn't even comprehend it: It was like digging up the first body of a serial killer only to have that body yank up another, and then another, like a long grisly string of paper-doll victims. And pretty much at the same time he'd learned that a book that he'd written with the simple hope of being funny and perhaps making the world a more honest place had backfired so badly that it had become evidence in the most famous legal case ever about *dis*honesty. In other words, how could Nicholson Baker not be in the process of concluding that something had gone terribly wrong with the state of books in the world, with libraries, with modern literature? And for me, from there, it got kind of meta- and time travelly, because of course I'd had my own thoughts about libraries, or at least what I'd thought were my own thoughts about libraries as prisons, thoughts that had gotten me thinking about reading Nicholson Baker. And as I'd been reading Baker for the past twenty months or so, I'd been thrilled to see those thoughts repeatedly echoed, as when "Lumber" summarizes Pope's characterization of a critic's personal library as a "gilded prison"; as when "Books as Furniture" notes that it was once common for books to be strung together on "Jacob Marleyesque chains"; and as when Baker, after coming into possession of twenty to thirty tons of rare first-run newspapers (more on this shortly), went shopping for a place to store them and was shown an abandoned naval prison near Portsmouth (he was "tempted," but leased a renovated mill closer to home).

At first I regarded these echoes as additional confirmation of Naipaul's claim that we read to confirm what we already know, though I recast it in Jamesian terms: As readers we're like adventurers seeking the source of our streams, and when our river collides with other rivers we infer a great collective headwater and continue upstream, chugging bravely forward on our voyage. But when Baker turned his attention to libraries, and when I started to sense him sinking into negativity, suffering as I'd suffered before I started reading him, it began to seem as though my stream had no current of its own, that I flowed only as a function of the mind of another. Was that even possible? Could I have started thinking about reading Nicholson Baker not because he wrote an important book of memory criticism, or a book about an anthologist just as I'd become an anthologist, but because his thoughts on libraries were not the echo of my thoughts because *I* was the echo? Or more simply put, could my crisis of 2010 have been the resurrection of Baker's midnineties crisis? If so, then I had a whole new crisis. The angst I'd hoped to cure with Baker had been caused by Baker. Could a weapon that inflicted a wound also heal it?

In any event, it was clear that "Why not?" was an insufficient explanation for why Nicholson Baker had turned his attention to the history of libraries. He knew, I believed, that he was making a formal declaration of hostilities in a private Cold War. But "Why not?" was less a false statement than a note of reluctance. What seemed obvious now was that *Double Fold* was Baker's revelation, both in that it stemmed spontaneously from a deep hot cinder of concern, and that, as with prophets, he hadn't asked for the job and didn't particularly relish it when it arrived.

26

SO WHY DRONES? WHY, IN 2012, WAS NICHOLSON BAKER INSERTING drones into peculiar interviews and writing protest songs, most of which were about drones? It wasn't a new concern, as even *Checkpoint*, the 2004 assassination book, lashed out at drones, meaning Baker was well ahead of the drone curve. But why drones and not nuclear proliferation, or cluster bombs, or land mines, or any of a whole host of weapons stored in the well-stocked arsenal of needless death innovation? Partly it was the cavalierness of it that bothered him—a president could sit in an office and decide who lived and who died—but that still didn't explain why a drone attack was a particular problem for a pacifist.

That's the other thing: Nicholson Baker was now a pacifist. "Why I'm a Pacifist," published in *Harper's* in 2011, reads as though it's been stitched together from scraps salvaged from *Human Smoke*'s cutting room floor, and like "Discards" it's a much more ideologically forthright document than Baker has generally produced. I reluctantly add that "Why I'm a Pacifist" credits Baker's pacifism to his wife—reluctant because when I met Baker he told me that his wife was an extremely private person. The more I had learned about her, however—for example, the playful tidbit she added to Baker's midnineties keep-the-chin-up piece about gondolas: *"Come into my gondola, I'm going to fondle ya"*—the more she seemed to rank right up there among influential literary spouses.

Yet the question remained: Why, if you're going to kill someone, was it better to do it with a simpler and more elegant device like a club or a manned aircraft, something that might get *you* killed too? Sure, a degree of attendant personal risk might reduce the chance that you'll follow through on your murderous impulse. Or you can make the argument, as Baker did, that computerized weaponry leads to higher body counts, so that if your measure is total quantity of death then drones pose a problem. But wasn't the real problem why anyone would want to be killing people in the first place? Shouldn't we be trying to figure out how to stop *that*? Drones don't have anything to do with that, one way or the other. What they do have something to do with, in the context of Nicholson Baker's career, is *Double Fold* and libraries and the Holocaust.

57

DOUBLE FOLD IS A BLEAK PORTRAIT OF MODERNITY VIEWED through a translucent paper lens. Early in the book, Baker uses a pocket history of Egyptian mummies to link civilization's devaluation of human intellect to the evolution of print technology. For many years, as though they were an inexhaustible resource, mummies were used to power Egyptian trains, the ancient corpses shoveled into locomotive ovens. In 1847, a geologist proposed importing mummies in bulk to the United States as part of a scheme to make cheaper newspaper stock from the linen wrappings. Only one newspaper ever used the linen in significant amounts, but Baker speculated that for a time mummy wrappings were an

ingredient cooked into the stew of many newspapers, including the
New York Times.

But mummy paper didn't last. Around 1870 an even cheaper
paper product came along: ground-wood pulp paper, one of those glorious innovations that didn't really need any further adjusting. It was
inexpensive and it came from a benign, sustainable resource. Hence
the golden age of newspapers and later the egalitarian paperback.
A cynical mind might see these developments as steps on a slippery
slope: Cheaper paper leads to cheaper thoughts. But Baker didn't.

As he saw it, the problem didn't begin until just after World
War II. His deep historical soundings pinged back to the surface the
outlines of modern library philosophy: Cheaper paper meant many
more books and newspapers being published, all of which needed to
be archived and stored, and that meant not only bulging catalogs,
but bulging buildings and budgets as well. What to do? There were
two choices: miniaturize or digitize. Or three really, as what *Double
Fold* emphatically proposed was that the best choice was to leave it
all alone: build a few more buildings and hire a few more people,
which was the cheapest option anyway.

But that's not what happened. *Double Fold* is really a double
narrative, a tragicomedy of errors that reads like a bad joke (the
history of miniaturization) followed by its worse topper (the history of digitization). Sure, microfilm and electronic scanning were
a big initial investment, but didn't they offer a permanent solution?
No, they didn't. But before you even got to that problem, you en-
countered a perfect doublethought of midcentury library science
philosophy: the only way to pay for the upfront costs of miniaturization and digitization was to reduce the future costs of ongoing
book ownership by dumping books. Some plans looked forward to
libraries eliminating as much as 95 percent of their holdings—in
order to preserve their holdings.

Nationwide, library administrators recognized that without a crisis like a recent earthquake to justify a massive reorganization, they would need a phantom crisis to explain why it was necessary. Hence Baker's subtitular "assault on paper," in which a range of forces conspired to depict ground-wood pulp paper as hopelessly flawed, as having "inherent vice." Paper was doomed, administrators claimed. High acid content meant that everything printed after 1870 was slowly eating itself up. Whole collections of books would spontaneously crumble before the year 2000. Not only was this false, it wasn't hyperbolic enough. An extremely influential 1987 documentary, *Slow Fires,* stoked fears with a metaphorical description of a catastrophe that wasn't happening: "These precious volumes are burning away with insidious *slow fires.*" Following suit, the chairperson of the National Endowment for the Humanities made books sound like victims of a firebombing: "As we speak, the war continues, and every day . . . 6,000 more bodies [are] brought into the Library of Congress."

The only way to save books was to use them, like the Egyptian mummies, as fuel for the engines of progress.

28

IT GOT WORSE FROM THERE. A FEW YEARS LATER, THE CHAIRPERSON of the NEH resigned and joined the board of directors of defense contractor Lockheed Martin. Who was the chairperson? Lynne Cheney. *Double Fold* barely mentions Cheney, probably because at the time she was merely the wife of former congressman and President George H. W. Bush Secretary of Defense Dick Cheney. In *Checkpoint,* however, published just three years later, she's the subject of an ugly gush of vitriol.

"That woman," the book's would-be assassin claims (note the Clintonian echo), "is the real obscenity."

Cheney resigned from Lockheed Martin when her husband was elected vice president and she became Second Lady, but what was Lockheed already pioneering while she was on the board? Drones. These days, among many other nefarious things, Lockheed makes assassin drones like the scary flying wing–style RQ-170 Sentinel (nicknamed the "Beast of Kandahar"), and they make cute little drones like the Samurai, which is about the length of your forearm and flies by imitating the most elegant flight design ever stumbled across by nature: the maple seed. Lockheed doesn't get mentioned by name in Baker's work until *Checkpoint* ("'Lockheed! The vileness of what they do. It fucking buggers understanding'"), but the company, along with a sustained interest in aeronautical engineering, is a peculiar common denominator in Baker's work:

1939: *Human Smoke* documents Lockheed's activities in the years before World War II, doing business with all sides of the coming conflict and delivering planes and parts to Japan as late as May 1939.

1967: Mike of *Room Temperature* recalls playing with plastic warplanes as a boy and attests to a "fierce appreciation of [a] plane's swept-back airfoils and cockpit canopy."

1989: Of the many models Baker purchased for "Model Airplanes," only one was a Lockheed design, but the exact plane is of interest: the F-117A Stealth Fighter was first built by legendary Lockheed R&D outfit Skunk Works in the 1970s, but the plane's existence did not become common knowledge until its high-profile deployment during the Gulf War.

1992: The SR-71 Blackbird that figures in Abby of *Vox*'s fantasy was also designed at Skunk Works. Baker's use of the plane came after its initial retirement in 1989, but the Blackbird was recommissioned in 1993 and remained operational for another five years.

2001: "No Step," in which Baker strives to retain an innocent appreciation of airplanes by fixating on fragments of language printed on wings, appeared in the Autumn 2001 issue of *The American Scholar*—that is, pretty much coincidentally with the first use of commercial aircraft as weapons of terror.

September 11 was a loss of innocence for Baker, as it was for everyone else, and for that reason among others the story of Baker's career is really the story of all writers who came of age during the digital age. Baker was preoccupied by drones not because they were particularly heinous, though they may well be, but because they insulted his personal history, our collective history. We come innocently into the world, grow curious about how things work, and we explore that curiosity having faith that those who invented the latest machines did so because they too were curious and because they hoped to make the world an incrementally better place. If that's how things ever worked, and perhaps it's naïve to think so, then it wasn't what was happening now, and what Baker gravitated toward in the work that ultimately led to *Double Fold* was those facets of modern life that trace back not to creative individuals working out of a benign spirit, but to government departments and think tanks following a heinous directive: The surest route to peace was war preparedness, mutual assured destruction. *Human Smoke* begins with Alfred Nobel's 1892 claim that his explosive factories would lead to a more peaceful world.

How do libraries fit into all this? Baker had no trouble with that. Microfilm technology descended from techniques developed for use in espionage, and miniaturization was praised as a "secret military weapon" in 1942 by influential library administrator Vernon Tate. Tate's career trajectory arced significantly from the Office of Strategic Services (precursor to the CIA), to the National Archives, to head librarian at MIT. And he was just the beginning. *Double Fold* tracked down a whole crew of shifty "Cold War librarians," administrators with ties to the intelligence community. The names read like a character list from *Get Smart* (e.g., Verner Clapp, Merrill Flood, Fremont Rider, etc.), and the whole thing would be funny if it didn't add up to a plot to systematically exterminate books.

If that's hyperbolic, then that's the point of *Double Fold,* which responded to the duplicitous argument that books were burning themselves up with a radical extension of the same fiery metaphor Baker had already deployed once. He noted that the Library of Congress experimenters who tried to deacidify books by exposing them to a chemical more commonly used in flame throwers thought of themselves as "book burners," and Baker described the cabinets in which books were treated as "gas chambers." He spoke to a microfilmer who happily accepted the moniker "the butcher of books" (filmed books needed to be "guillotined"), and he corresponded with a former Kansas State Historical Society employee who told him that a great quantity of the society's post-1875 newspaper collection had once been made to "disappear." Baker's informant "saved a small stack and tried to avoid looking at the column of smoke rising from the sawmill."

This last surely explains what Baker did when he heard, four-fifths of the way through the research and writing of *Double Fold,* that complete runs of a number of very rare newspapers were on the chopping block in England. Literally. The newspapers had been offered up to other libraries, but if none accepted them, then twenty to thirty tons of newspapers that were supposed to be spontaneously crumbling would be auctioned off, sold probably to a "book breaker," who would market individual pages as novelties, profiting from the purchase precisely because the newspapers were *not* crumbling spontaneously. The news of the endangered papers came just as administrators were telling Baker that the worst was over, that the great purges of catalogs and the wanton dumpings of rare holdings were things of the past. That was a lie. And maybe that made writing a book about the whole thing seem like an incomplete response. Baker had been drawn into a conflict and so far his response had been limited to a valiant attempt to demonstrate that pens were still as mighty as swords. The future pacifist became a figurative soldier, and *Double Fold* is the story of fighting one metaphorical fire with another. What he discovered was that in order to battle duplicity you had to become a bit duplicitous yourself. Yet when the English newspapers went up for auction—actually American newspapers held by the British—he couldn't let pass a chance to save what could be saved. He and his wife drained their retirement accounts, put their futures and the futures of their children at risk, and bought all the rare newspapers and stored them in a mill. And Baker *meant* the echo: The time had come to put his money where his metaphor was, and if it was an insult to victims of the Holocaust to liken himself to those who had risked life and limb to rescue the few who could be saved, then so be it.

But why was it happening at all? Mystified by administrators' antagonism toward books, Baker ventured a guess here and there: blind faith in progress; inept former spooks trying to profit from obsolete skill sets; and, most disturbing, digitizers who knew full well that searchable electronic databases would make it easier to monitor who looked at what.

But the newspapers themselves were the most compelling motive. At first it seems odd that a writer who had placed such a high premium on truth would invest so much in a medium prone to inaccuracy and propaganda. Did it matter that newspapers frequently lied? "No matter what is in a newspaper, even if every word is untrue," Baker writes, "we know for sure that these particular words and drawings and pictures happened . . ." Why was that important? Because even their "exaggerations now have truths of their own to tell us." Can't you get that from a scanned copy? No, because "their oldness and their fragility is part of what they have to say." It was a rough draft of history argument. Newspapers were the record of what people believed was happening while whatever was happening was happening. A history of lies was an even more important truth to never forget. And if you were an intelligence operative, and what you really wanted to do was control history, control the narrative of your society if only to cover your ass, then what you just might attempt to engineer, long before that society's intellectuals have begun to suspect that anything was amiss, was a system that would let you dispose of whatever evidence of your malfeasance had managed to trickle out into the mainstream, burn it all up before some fascinated-by-minutiae nerd went picking around the ground-wood pulp lumber yard of a library. In other words, erase history *before* it became history.

Only one thing could go wrong: If just one meddlesome bookworm slipped between the cracks and figured out what you were up to, figured out that pens weren't as mighty as swords anymore, then what he just might do is give up his pen and paper and reach for a sword of his own.

59

SOMETHING ELSE NAIPAUL SAID: "TO TAKE AN INTEREST IN A writer's work is, for me, to take an interest in his life." Yes, I agree, but there's a danger there too. A critic who slips from being an interpreter of texts, in which what gets depicted is the mental process by which stories come to have meaning (and what stories do in the minds of readers *is* what they mean), to a surveyor of biographical facts risks sidestepping the only reason a writer's life is interesting in the first place. All the things I've been doing with Baker's life since he turned to the vulgar utility of history—summarizing complex arguments, manipulating incomplete information, struggling to further compress a life already compressed once—are the things that make biography a minefield of perils. As a general rule the shortcuts that biographies take to make incompletely recorded lives seem whole are the reasons they're not. Or more elegantly put, biography is but the clothes of the man, a phrase generally credited to Mark Twain, though that too may be a tie or a hat—or better, an accessory: a cuff link—with which Twain has been outfitted by an exuberant critic-haberdasher.

Which maybe explains why Henry James once refused when he was asked to write a biography of Hawthorne:

> It will be necessary, for several reasons, to give this short sketch the form rather of a critical essay than of a biography. The data for a life of Nathaniel Hawthorne are the reverse of copious, and even if they were abundant they would serve but in a limited measure the purpose of the biographer.

What life data there are of Hawthorne offer a perfect example of the kind of mistake James hoped to avoid. In 1850, a young and enthused Herman Melville descended on Hawthorne in Massachusetts, not long after he had expressed admiration for the older writer's work with some particularly suggestive language:

> I feel that this Hawthorne has dropped germanous seeds into my soul. . . . He expands and deepens down, the more I contemplate him; and further, and further, shoots his strong New-England roots into the hot soil of my Southern soul.

I'd had this passage in mind—for reasons that are probably clear—ever since Catherine and I arrived in Maine, and the problem, James's problem, is what biographically minded critics had tended to do with these lines in the years since. These days it's common to find tedious scholarly works with titles like " 'The Ugly Socrates': Melville, Hawthorne, and the Varieties of Homoerotic Experience" and "Alienated Affections: Hawthorne and Melville's Trans-Intimate Relationship." Preposterous. Naipaul may be right, but to take an interest in a writer's life answers a siren's call in that there's a temptation to leap to wild conclusions that accidentally say more about a critic's state of mind than they do about the writer under consideration. This, actually, is the idea behind Tommaso Landolfi's wonderful short story "Gogol's Wife," which I'd also had in mind as Baker's wife kept turning up in his work (e.g., "How I Met My Wife"). And speaking of Baker's work—or rather, speaking of not speaking of it—it may be that I was now guilty of having hung out the shingle of my own critical haberdashery, but I don't think it's entirely my fault. Baker's early work had always stood in defiance of that old saw "Boy, have I got a story for you!" He didn't. Nicholson Baker had desperately tried to avoid having a story for us—and that was the best story of all. But now, in this later part of his career, he really did have a story to tell, and at the risk of seeming a little unhinged myself, it started to drive him a little crazy.

His wife was the first to notice.

The title of *Double Fold* came from a page-folding paper test, repetitive dog-earing, that library administrators dreamed up to measure the "brittleness" of books. It was more absurd duplicity. A book was deemed "unusable" when a concerted effort to break one of its pages succeeded in breaking it. Baker's madness began to poke through when he tried the test himself:

Late one night, after the children were in bed, I began some random experimentation at the household bookshelves. My wife asked me what I was up to.

"I'm—I'm performing the fold test," I said.

"Please stop breaking the corners off our books," my wife said. "It can't be doing them any good."

If a stammer ("I'm—I'm . . .") in an otherwise non-speech-impaired person indicates psychological duress, then it wasn't doing Baker any good either. He went on to devise his own readability test, repeatedly turning page 153 of an 1893 edition of Edmund Gosse's *Questions at Issue* to determine whether it could survive the rigors of simple reading. He began to enjoy this repetitive action—surely a sign of mental buckle—and he topped out at eight hundred turns. The upshot? A one-hundred-year-old leaf of ground-wood pulp paper, the same piece of paper that failed a double-fold test, could be read many times over.

I thrilled at the next bit. Baker noted that "one root of the word 'duplicity' is *duplicitas,* 'doublefoldedness.'" This sent me vaulting back to connections I'd anticipated more than a year before: the unfolding mind metaphor in *U and I,* and *I and Thou* as well. Baker was less thrilled. A fissure had opened up in the middle of his psyche, and though it seemed light and funny at first, it stopped being funny two years later with the suicidal ideations of *A Box of Matches*: "This morning I woke up writing an impassioned petition in my head, but impassioned petitions do nothing."

Was Baker sad that *Double Fold* had done nothing? The book wasn't a best seller but it did win the 2001 National Book Critics Circle Award for nonfiction, to date Baker's only major literary prize. Even critics who panned his other books lauded *Double Fold.* But praise didn't heal the wound, and a certain doublefoldedness would be palpable in Baker even years later. On the one hand, "The Charms of Wikipedia" (2008) would celebrate the oft-maligned web resource for its communal nature and resuscitate a favorite allusion: "I clicked the 'edit this page' tab, and immediately had an odd, almost light-headed feeling, as if I had passed through the looking glass . . ." And on the other, "Kindle 2" (2009) would lash out at Amazon's unnecessary invention of Vizplex, electronic paper: "The problem was that the screen . . . was a greenish, sickly gray. A postmortem gray."

But does duplicity alone explain why an otherwise polite, law-abiding writer would soon fantasize at length about murdering the president of the United States?

60

THAT'S ABOUT WHEN I DECIDED TO BREAK MY IRONCLAD resolution and meet him. Not to plug the holes in his biography— the 1982 professional crisis, the year in England: these were more enticing as mysteries, I decided—but because I thought he might be the only person in the world who could understand the crisis *I* was now in. I had followed his exact footsteps, and I'd hoped to write a brief and cheerful account of renewing my literary faith, but now it was all darkening again. Plus, I'd rejected my original assumption that it was better not to meet a writer as you read him. The whole point was that it was important to be reading living, noncanonical writers, and wasn't the main difference between a living writer and a dead writer the fact that the living writer was still around and might be willing to talk to you? That was the suggestion of Henry James's prefaces, I thought, and that was the premise of "The Figure in the

Carpet," too. The story's narrator-critic is hermeneutically aroused when he meets a famous writer at a party, and the writer baits him with a suggestion that there is something in his work that no reviewer has ever seen:

> It stretches, this little trick of mine, from book to book, and everything else, comparatively, plays over the surface of it. The order, the form, the texture of my books will perhaps some day constitute for the initiated a complete representation of it. So naturally it's the thing for the critic to look for.

The critic does look for it—by doing just what I'd been doing: reading directly through all the writer's books. To "meet" a writer, in "The Figure in the Carpet," is to meet a challenge. It's an occasion that musters dormant energies. And that's what I mustered when I finally decided to meet Baker, and I didn't care that the "little trick" in James's story, when someone finally glimpses it, becomes a sort of pharaoh's curse, killing off critics and destroying marriages.

I should admit that by this point, after about a week at the beach rental, I'd driven over to South Berwick a couple of times. I had Nicholson Baker's phone number and address—he wasn't listed, but it wasn't hard information to find—and I'd even driven past his house to a little park just down the road, where I sat for a while on a bench thinking that it might be nice if Baker were to take a midafternoon stroll and stumble across me reading *Human Smoke*. That obviously didn't happen. And after I decided to out and out approach him it took me several days to figure out how to do it.

"Should I just knock on his door, do you think?" I asked Catherine. "Catch him flat-footed? Get the *real,* unscripted Baker?"

"No, don't do that," she said. "Just call him. You're being weird."

"And say what? What would I say?"

"Jesus! Say what you always say when you're writing about someone. You do this all the time. Quit whining."

Poor Catherine. Here she was trying to have a vacation, probably beginning to regret that she'd done anything at all to help bring about this whole Nicholson Baker thing, and when I wasn't bothering her with silly questions I was periodically bursting our beach-side idyll with shocking bits from *Double Fold, Checkpoint,* and *Human Smoke.* "Those motherfuckers!" I'd say. "You can't imagine how bad it is—listen to this!" Every afternoon we were taking long walks on the beach that were restful and rejuvenating until I started to use the time to mull what I'd read, sink back into negativity, and plot how to meet Baker. To spare Catherine, whenever I sensed that a particular stream of thought needed to be voiced aloud, I let go of her hand and told her that I wanted to walk in the surf. Then I made long, mumbling speeches about how bad things had gotten or tried out what I might say if I called Baker and he simply picked up the phone.

That didn't happen either. When I finally called, his voice mail picked up. Strange as it seems, I hadn't anticipated this. I froze because I realized that what I had prepared to say if he picked up would sound completely stupid on a voice mail message. I panicked and hung up. I hate doing this, these days, because you know that if you call once and hang up and then call back and leave a message, the person you called will be able to tell that you called twice and will assume you panicked. But there was nothing to be done. Before I called back I wrote out a quick script of what I would say to Nicholson Baker's voice mail, a thing I never do, and then I called and read my script and hung up the phone. Done!

Baker didn't call back right away, which made me nervous and insufferable. I often get nervous when people don't call me back, but this was much, much worse. I kept having to remind myself—or rather, Catherine kept reminding me—that for all I knew, Baker was off on a research trip or he was visiting family somewhere and might not get my message for several days. That didn't help. Staring at my phone didn't help either, but that's what I did. I stared at my phone and tried to will an incoming call. I'd left my message at ten o'clock in the morning, and by five o'clock I was a despondent mess. He wasn't going to call. I wondered aloud whether I should leave another message—maybe the first had vanished into the digital ether—but Catherine talked me out of that and the next morning she wisely suggested that we drive to Portland to get our minds off Nicholson Baker.

That's when he called. The phone rang while I was driving, and Catherine and I looked at each other in a way that made me think of the last scene in *Bonnie and Clyde*, that moment of locked eyes before they're riddled with bullets. Should I answer while driving? I answered the phone. "This is Nick Baker," the voice said, and that was the last coherent thing Baker said for quite some time.

We generally use the phrase "words fail" for those moments when we're so overcome by emotion that we are reminded of the inability of language, even artfully constructed sentences, to do justice to the full breadth and texture of human experience. But there really ought to be a "words fail"–like phrase for moments when even simple thoughts like "Hello!" or "Nice to speak with you!" or "Of course I'd like to meet you, come over at four o'clock!" get all screwed up in transit from our neurons to our vocal chords. Baker didn't have a speech impediment like Updike, but he did seem to have something like a mental stammer, which actually we all have from time to time and which is maybe the real reason written language evolved from recording data—warehouse inventories, I once read—to forming complex thoughts. When you write down your thinking you can edit out all those mental hesitations—or scratch that, misfirings—and project a version of yourself that isn't more intelligent than you are, exactly, but is a self strained clean by the puffy gauze of prose. I listened to Baker for a moment and thought, *He really should have written down a script before he called!* That set me at ease. I realized I had an advantage. I had read almost everything Baker had written, and what that meant was that in communicating with me he was in competition with his more perfect written self. As far as I knew Baker hadn't read anything I'd written, so I had nothing to live up to. All of which is to say that Nicholson Baker didn't have any idea what to say to me, and that calmed me down. I got the sense that he was willing to meet with me, though, and after he offered to drive to wherever we were staying—he said he liked to travel—I tried to be gracious and suggested a restaurant near his house that I'd reconnoitered when I drove to South Berwick. Baker said he would prefer to avoid "the whole restaurant thing." I thought, *What restaurant thing?* But no matter, he was being incredibly gracious with his time. When he said, instead, that I should come to his house for an hour or so and started in on a fairly complicated set of directions, I interrupted in a slightly ominous voice, "I know where you live." "*You idiot! You sound like a stalker!*" Catherine hissed beside me, loud enough so that Baker might have heard, but if he did he let it go and told me to come at four o'clock.

61

CATHERINE WAS GROPED BY A STRANGE MAN ON THE STREET IN Portland—this happened once in Paris too—but apart from that we had a fine time in the city. Nicholson Baker had called! Even

Catherine was relieved because it meant she would have some time
to herself, and after lunch I drove her back to the beach rental and
then set out for Baker's house in one of those curious moods that
descend when you realize that you are living out a sequence of
events that might become a story you will later tell, when the usually crumpled tapestry of life unfurls and for a time you can make
out figures and patterns that otherwise remain unintelligible. This
was true even though I was not at all sure that I would tell the story
of meeting Baker—I planned not to write about meeting him, in
fact. When I spoke with him on the phone, I specifically said that I
hoped our meeting would be as far from an "interview" as was humanly possible, given the fact that I was writing a book about him.
I didn't record our conversation—it was the first of two; for the second we did the restaurant thing at a diner—and I didn't take down
any notes about it either. I was a memory journalist.

Mostly I remember what I said. I told Baker that I thought
there was a connection between his work and Martin Buber's.
Baker hadn't read Buber, as I had feared but expected, but he
liked the idea of remote influence. We chatted about chess and
trombones and bassoons and ampersands and my father, who as a
young physicist had worked for a company that subcontracted for
University Microfilms, the organization whose role in the history
of miniaturization Baker had skewered in *Double Fold*. The truth,
my father had told me, was even darker than Baker suggested. Poor
microfiche image reproduction quality was not a result of University Microfilms having failed to invest in better technology. They
had the technology, they just chose not to use it; it wasn't greed, it
was neglect. Baker was duly shocked at this, but he had clearly left
all that behind him; he'd taken his hill and earned his medals, but
he'd been left wounded and the war would be won by some other
general. He shrugged shyly when I flitted out a few names of writers

even more contemporary than Buber. He hadn't read them, and he admitted this as though it were a flaw, as though he'd not gotten around to them yet, but I knew it was probably more complicated than that, that there were writers he hadn't read because, for him, literature seemed to have taken a wrong turn sometime around the turn of the twentieth century, and if you were a writer picking up the threads of one of the wrong-turners, then you weren't likely to be of interest to a reader like Nicholson Baker. But Baker gave no sign of this, seeming to wish not to weigh anyone down with unhappy knowledge, at least not in this context, a noninterview that was beginning to seem a whole lot like an interview.

To change the tone of our chat, I told Baker than while I'd been in Maine I'd thought about driving around to look for Stephen King. King had lived in Maine for years, and my plan, I said, was to finish the job of the careless driver who had once struck King on a country road but failed to kill him. Earlier I allowed that people don't generally get hurt as a result of popular storytelling genres. Let me qualify that, because *I* do. I get hurt every time I hear that Stephen King has served up yet another regurgitation of the same meal he's been scarfing down and puking up for decades, with nary a moment between feedings. There is probably no better measure of how low the literary world has sunk in recent years than the desperate attempts that have been made to bring King into the canonical fold, not for his writing but on the hope that a few of his zombie army of readers might be tricked into buying the books of any other writer. It hasn't worked. And it wasn't an entirely random subject to have broached with Nicholson Baker, because King had once lashed out at Baker, likening his first two books to "fingernail parings," an unprompted and unjustified attack to which Baker calmly replied with his essay on fingernail clippers ("Clip Art"), which turned out to have a very interesting history that traced back to Baker's hometown, Rochester. Baker chuckled at my murderous fantasy, and said that he'd once tried to read King only to find him too frightening. King must be "some kind of genius," Baker said, at which I scoffed until I recognized it as a moment of lingering Bakerian duplicity. Of course a writer steeped in so much Victorian thinking would slyly use "genius" in its nineteenth-century sense! It had been a while since William James popped up in Baker's work—I had bolted upright when *Double Fold* gave one of its paper villains the three-name serial killer treatment, William James Barrow, though there was no connection, I checked—but clearly Baker meant "genius" in the sense that William James had meant it when he included it in a series of lectures on abnormal states of mind alongside "Demoniacal Possession," "Witchcraft," and "Degeneration."

We chatted at a table just outside Baker's house. Baker had put out a couple plates of snacks for us, and two warm beers. I drank one, he ignored the other. We talked for more than an hour beyond the time he allotted for the meeting. Baker sighed a lot. When he spoke, his sentences came out in long slow tumbles that were probably designed to let someone who was writing down what he was saying keep up, but since I wasn't writing anything down, their only effect was to slow down my thought process in listening to him. This, actually, confirmed the first flash of thought I'd had when I drove up his driveway. And it was this thought that was all I really needed to come to an understanding of Baker's own murderous fantasy, *Checkpoint,* which I'd finished reading a week earlier. Baker was waiting for me outside when I pulled up the driveway. He was a quite tall man, as I'd read, but he hid it by slouching his shoulders, and the wall of trees that served as backdrop gave him an ancient, gnarled look.

That was my thought: Nicholson Baker looked far less like a hobbit or a wizard than an ent.

62

TOLKIEN, AS A SUBSET OF THE CHILDREN'S STORY THEME, IS ANOTHER thread woven through the carpet of Baker's career. Mike of *Room Temperature* admits that all he'd ever learned about coziness came from descriptions of Bag End. Arno of *The Fermata* lists Gollum among the literary monsters he might be said to resemble. "Lumber" notes that Gandalf used "lumber" in its original sense, and as a cognitive analogy to boot. And in "Thorin Son of Thráin," Baker tells the story of his mother having once read aloud to him the entirety of *The Hobbit*. It was Baker's "most emotional early reading experience."

But Tolkien is a betrayal too, isn't he? If Baker had felt that a rug had been yanked from beneath him when his long-standing love of libraries was upended by the actual history of libraries, and if a boyish fascination with fighter planes had transposed into horror as remote-control toys evolved into amoral robots, then wouldn't he have felt similarly juked as Tolkien shifted from the childish innocence of *The Hobbit* to the more adult vision of *The Lord of the Rings,* in which disdain for all peoples east of the Promised Land is only too apparent, in which the simplistic duality that characterizes Western thought is uncritically celebrated, and in which the sturdy resilience of the "Englishman" is heralded as being of ongoing importance to world history despite Britain's marked reduction in global stature? In other words, *The Hobbit* is an adventure story and *The Lord of the Rings* is a war story, and this might be relevant if you were a writer suffering a prolonged period of disillusionment and you had begun to contemplate violence even as you were on course for publicly professed pacifism.

What are the ents if not the pacifists of Middle Earth? Like Baker, the tree shepherds have a preference for slow and careful progress, and it takes some tricky tactics to even convince them to sign up for Middle Earth's latest conflagration. It's the hobbit Pippin who does the convincing (in "Kindle 2" Baker compares himself to "Pippin staring at the stone of Orthanc"), and the way he makes his case fits nicely with Baker's career. *Double Fold* briefly turns its lens upward to the iconic Holocaust imagery of a horrible smoke rising from an infernal chimney, and this image returns in *Human Smoke,* the book itself named for concentration camp ash. Likewise, Treebeard refuses to intervene in the war for Middle Earth, and so Pippin turns him south, toward Saruman. "There is always a smoke rising from Isengard these days," Treebeard says.

I'm relying a bit more on Peter Jackson's film trilogy here than on Tolkien himself, but even that fits because the release dates of all three films nestle snugly between the publication dates of *Double Fold* and *Checkpoint.* What else was happening during these years? *The Two Towers* was released a little more than a year after the Twin Towers fell. The Patriot Act, signed into law six weeks after 9/11, turned every electronic device with an Internet connection into a stone of Orthanc: You could remotely view the world, and the world could peer back at you, legally. *The Return of the King* pleased audiences in December 2003 with a wide range of spectacles, among them the carbuncly Orc captain Gothmog, who at the beginning of the siege of Minas Tirith barks, "Release the prisoners!" an order to catapult into the city the severed heads of several dozen Men of the West. Just six months later the ongoing occupation of Iraq produced a series of beheading videos, insurgents recording the gruesome crimes and catapulting the footage onto the Internet, though it was widely considered wrong to watch for free what had only of late been sold as entertainment. And finally, the ultimate message of *The Lord of the Rings*—civilization is weak without a strong monarch—aligned perfectly with the concerted effort to expand executive power in the world's mightiest nation.

Of course, it's easy to dismiss this kind of parallel drawing between world events and the worlds of books and stories, and this has become only easier as storytelling has plummeted to the status of entertaining diversion. And in a way, that's what happened to Baker, too. In 2002, not long after *Double Fold* appeared, a professor at the University of Pittsburgh's School of Information Sciences published a hostile book-length response (so poorly written it seems less an earnest rejoinder than a piece of hastily produced propaganda) that criticized Baker for having pointed out that many influential library administrators had ties to the intelligence field. Baker was out of his depth, the book suggested. He *must* be a conspiracy theorist. Baker denied the charge. There was no conspiracy, he insisted, only collective incompetence. Nevertheless, even before the critical work was published, the darker suggestions of *Double Fold* began to echo in the Bush administration: the use of private companies to digitize public card catalogs foreshadowed the rise of military contractors in the so-called War on Terror; the seductive algebra that made book dumping look profitable reappeared as the claim that the invasion of Iraq would pay for itself with oil revenue; and 9/11, like the Loma Prieta earthquake, was an atrocity used to justify a wholesale reorganization of society, the blueprint of which had been sketched long before the attacks occurred.

It wasn't until *Human Smoke* that Baker turned his gaze to a broader history: the use of atrocities for ideological ends. It's difficult to pinpoint exactly what Baker has to say about these usages, as the book, which I finished a day before I met him, is a collage of clippings, partial vignettes only slightly molded into narrative shape. *Human Smoke* includes bits from obscure memoirs and histories but is mostly composed of borrowed newspaper accounts of the long, slow buildup to war, all of it arranged chronologically and each snippet outfitted with a flatly stated date marker, as though the book has a pulse: "It was March 1, 1938," "It was September 3, 1939," "It was October 21, 1941."

Baker appears not at all in *Human Smoke*, but as I read the book—his longest—I felt him constantly in the background, on the lookout for facts cut from history books, facts that without him might have wound up in a landfill. I imagined him sitting alone in his rented mill, a little cold and his breathing audible in the cavernous room's acoustics, paging slowly and horrifically through his twenty to thirty tons of newspapers (all of which, actually, had been moved to Duke University by 2004), and as I took in what amounted to a *lost* draft of history I caught myself turning the leaves of the book as I might have turned that old newsprint, pinching up the corner of a page and sliding my palm beneath it, faceup, cradling the paper and lifting it gently and spilling it into my other open palm, which caught and laid the page in place and then smoothed over its surface to nudge out the air between it and the sheet beneath it. Despite Baker's absence, *Human Smoke* is an extremely personal document. The extensive citing of Harold Nicolson links it to the earliest stages of Baker's career, and its embedded history of a mostly forgotten pacifist movement reaches back even farther: The pacifists whose stories Baker tells either taught at Haverford or prominently visited his alma mater. The book completes a forward evolution as well. During the minor media tempest generated by the publication of *Checkpoint*— Knopf originally planned the book release for the eve of 2004's Republican National Convention—Baker described himself, in an interview, as "practically a pacifist." This contrasts with his author's note on Amazon in 2012, written in refreshing first person and completely lacking caginess or guile:

I've written thirteen books, plus an art book that I published with my wife, Margaret Brentano. The most recent one is a comic sex novel called House of Holes, which came out in August 2011. Before that, in 2009, there was The Anthologist, about a poet trying to write an introduction to an anthology of rhyming verse, and before that was Human Smoke, a book of nonfiction about the beginning of World War II. My first novel, The Mezzanine, about a man riding an escalator at the end of his lunch hour, came out in 1988. I'm a pacifist. Occasionally I write for magazines. I grew up in Rochester, New York, and went to Haverford College, where I majored in English. I live in Maine with my family.

63

SO DID *HUMAN SMOKE* DENY THE HOLOCAUST? NOT IN ANY WAY. The rumor I'd heard was a measure of collective human crassness. The book did deny a range of accepted facts, however. It denied that Hitler was bent on war any more than were Churchill or Roosevelt. It denied that the slaughter of Jews was unavoidable, and that no one saw the Holocaust coming. Most of all it denied that World War II was a war that had to be fought, which is the foundation for the widely held, oxymoronic belief that World War II was a "good war." Perhaps Baker's point was that as long as this remained acceptable, as long as we allowed that any war had been good, a door would be left ajar for other wars on the chance that they too might be judged to have been good. But haven't we ever since borne witness to a long series of conflicts, all of benign intention, each demonstrating that war is not so very good? Until we've gone back and demonstrated that World War II wasn't particularly good either, or even necessary, we offer aid and comfort to those who would employ atrocities, even atrocities they saw coming, to push through that door once more, to justify another indulgence in humanity's most grotesque instinct. These days, in the face of mounting evidence, it's not too shocking to point to Pearl Harbor or the bombing of Coventry, as Baker did, and suggest that the powers that were had some intimation of what was coming, didn't do much to stop it, and planned to use the aftermaths to sculpt public opinion.

It's probably clear by now that I'm suggesting that *Human Smoke* has a ghost subject: the Bush administration, the ignored forewarnings of imminent attack, and the predrawn plans to exploit the heady nationalism that would erupt in the wake of some new atrocity. Notably only a few of the early reviewers of *Human Smoke* even mentioned that it followed on the heels of *Checkpoint*. No one bothered to wonder whether there was a "little trick" stretching from book to book. And only one interview I found took the time to ask Baker why he'd written *Human Smoke* at all. It wasn't puzzlement at the West's reaction to Hitler, Baker claimed, though that was part of it. "Then I had the Iraq war," he said. "I was in Washington when the Pentagon was flown into. I said, 'I just hope we're not bombing some place any time soon.'"

I *love* this quote—the tortured sentence structure of a man suffering genuine pain.

64

NOW I REALIZE THAT IN HAVING "GONE THERE," AS IS FREQUENTLY said these days, that even in having entertained the idea that the accepted history of the time leading up to and following 9/11 is, at best, conveniently incomplete, what I've done is jack into the worldview of Jay, the would-be assassin of *Checkpoint,* one of two characters who make up the short novel's *Vox*-like all-dialogue structure. Jay really is a conspiracy theorist—he says only a little about 9/11, but claims that "all the totally off-the-wall conspiracy theories, all of them, are true"—and that makes my "going there" totally appropriate. It is, or should be, the job of readers to exuberantly tap into the worldviews of whatever characters they read about. "If you read a book and let it work upon you," wrote Goethe, "and yield yourself up entirely to its influence, then, and only then, will you arrive at a correct judgment of it."

I'll go even farther. A critic aspiring to conspiracy theory makes complete sense because readers and writers have always conspired to create what books are "about." More broadly, writers conspire, as I've already suggested, with editors and jacket designers and interior designers, to create the "book," and particularly with first editions it's fair to assume, at least with a writer of Baker's caliber and interests, that an author has at least offered input on everything that makes up a book—hence what I've been doing in *this* book, mining just about any of a book's features for its meaning. Is there a danger to this? Of course. In the analysis of books, as in the analysis of complex world events, we hover between two kinds of error: ascribing too much meaning where there is little, if any, to be found, and ignoring meaning that stares us right in the face.

What stares us in the face when we pick up a first edition of *Checkpoint?* Admittedly the red, white, and black target motif of the dust jacket didn't make a whole lot of sense to me. It's not a book about archery. But a little weirdly the book has two title pages, both of which precede the front matter and the dedication (*"For Carroll, and in memory of Bob,"* Baker's parents-in-law—Robert Brentano died in 2002), and that's where it starts to get interesting. On the first of these the title is printed across the top in extra wide–spaced letters, and a little ways down there is a single black dot, like this:

C   H   E   C   K   P   O   I   N   T

•

This is a recto, a front page, on your right-hand side as you hold the book. What this means is that the next page, a verso, is the same piece of paper. Actually it's more complicated than that because most books are really stacks of large sheets of double-folded paper called quartos, each of which, counting fronts and backs, become eight pages of a book. But you know what I mean. Our tactile experience of a book is that each of its "pages" has a front and a back, and these fronts and backs, somewhat confusingly, are also called "pages." The next page of *Checkpoint,* or rather its next two pages, is another title page, though this time the title, much larger, begins on the left-hand verso ("CHECK"), hops the gutter in the middle like a *Playboy* centerfold, and continues on the right-hand recto ("POINT"), which also lists Baker's name, the publisher, and the year of publication.

Back on the verso, though, something tugs at your attention. There's *another* black dot. It appears like a floater on the surface of your eye until you focus on it. And when I focused on it I felt a chill, as on reading an unexpected rhyme, because I realized at once that this dot aligned with the dot on the reverse face of the same piece of paper. I was sitting in the sun on a plastic chaise longue on our deck in Maine, happy to be about to dig into Baker's most controversial book, and I was already applauding myself for taking in all of its one hundred and fifteen pages in a single draught. But I stopped before I started. I held that page up to the sun, which revealed not a perfect eclipse of dots, but it was close enough that the suggestion was clear. It was a *hole*. Another Baker hole, a hole that I hadn't stumbled across since *Vox*, but that I knew was lurking in Baker's mind because in a few years' time it would reappear in force in *House of Holes*. And of course this was a very specific kind of hole: a bullet hole.

On a hunch I flipped to the end, to the page after the last page of text. Aha! Here was the same black dot on another recto, but *not*, this time, on the corresponding verso. What did that suggest? The hole-making bullet had not penetrated all the way through. It was still lodged inside the book. Next I removed the ugly dust jacket and found a similar clue. The book's black, blank front cover board was cool to the touch and had a vague pattern of faint, squiggly lines evocative of the surface of Mars, broken only once by a circle in the middle, half an inch across, a perfect hole revealing a glossy polished disk. As with the black dots there was no corresponding hole in the book's rear board. I held *Checkpoint* out at arm's length and looked at it anew. Before you even begin reading it, you know that this is not a book that fires a bullet. Instead, like a book that has been stuffed into a breast pocket and miraculously foils an evil design, it stops one.

Which means that almost right away I was forced to conclude that I'd been way off base in thinking that Baker was falling away from literature. Now that I thought about it, I had to admit that a book that only *contemplates* violence—*Checkpoint* is less about assassinating Bush than failing to assassinate him—has not yet given up the pen for the sword.

Not that any of this went discussed in *Checkpoint*'s early reviews. The mud once slung at *Vox* and *The Fermata* turned out to be only a primer for the ordnance that would be launched at *Checkpoint*: "A quickie polemic that masquerades as a novel"; "This odd, abortive, short yet desperately rambling little playlet . . ."; "This scummy little book . . ." Again and again in the dozen or so notices I later read, reviewers refused to yield an inch to its influence, even reviewers who claimed to admire Baker's "trifling" work. It's commonplace enough to note that book reviewers often get it wrong. Books that reviewers ignore or malign go on to be classics, and books for which reviewers toot joyous kazoos fade into silence. Even before *Checkpoint,* Nicholson Baker's career had stood as a kind of high-water mark in the history of reviewers getting it wrong. Baker books, whose hearts were pincushioned with the wooden stakes of zealous, self-consecrated book slayers, rose up uncannily from their premature tombs and batwinged their way to audiences. But the reaction to *Checkpoint* was something new. Reviewers noted that it was a smart and funny book, but nevertheless judged it laced with an unspeakable serum. It wasn't just a bad book. It was a book that, good or bad, it was wrong to have written. Even before *Checkpoint* was published, when feature writers were putting in calls to the Secret Service to see what *they* thought of it (wiser than most, the agency spokesman reserved judgment: He hadn't read it yet), it was clear that the book might not have a chance to stand up on its own. Baker fought back for a while. "*Checkpoint* is an argument against violence, not for it," he told one interviewer. And when "scummy little book" started to get quoted in other articles—when, that is, the story of the book began to overwhelm the book's story—Baker tried reversing the barb's trajectory with the argument that "scummy" was a perfect adjective to have chosen, because wasn't recent history an agitation of the cultural pond, and what rose to the surface when you agitated ponds? If this was a coy reference to Baker's muckraking great-grandfather, no one heard the echo. The verdict: literature oughtn't rake muck. And maybe Baker agreed, ultimately. By the time of his *Paris Review* interview, he'd given up. The book was a failure, he allowed. He wished he hadn't published it. "It was an argument for nonviolence that people took to be an assassination fantasy," he said.

But that's a false distinction, I think. It *is* a fantasy. And maybe even more than *Vox, Checkpoint* is about the role and purpose of fantasy in the world. How do you get there? You read the book.

65

IN QUICK ASIDES, A FEW OF *CHECKPOINT*'S EARLY REVIEWERS DID note that its all-dialogue structure linked it to *Vox*. That's true and important, but distinctions between the two books appear right from the start. *Checkpoint* begins:

> May 2004
> Adele Hotel and Suites
> Washington, D.C.

> JAY: Testing, testing. Testing. Testing.
> BEN: Is it working?
> JAY: I think so. [*Click . . . click, click.*] Yes, see the little readout? Where'd you get it?
> BEN: Circuit City.

What do we already know from this? Two men, Jay and Ben, are fiddling with some kind of recording device, and before we know anything about them we can tell they are sort of hapless types, men unsure of how to operate a simple machine. We probably know, in approaching *Checkpoint,* that it is a book that will meditate on the assassination of a president—when was the last time you started a book having no inkling of its contents?—and if that has been of concern to us, if that has steeled us against the book because we generally agree that there are just a few things that nobody ought to be allowed to say, then even these few lines should offer reassurance. This is no straight-faced intrigue story. This is no wishful thought trying to smuggle itself into an impressionable mind. These guys *can barely turn on a tape recorder.*

More important, they're not alone. Like *Vox, Checkpoint* is only mostly dialogue, and right away, if we hope to avoid Martin Amis's error, we must ask who it is that has affixed a date to the front of this document. Actually the fact that it's a document, a transcript, is the first thing we should register, and this makes it totally unlike *Vox.* And that, in turn, should get us wondering about who's typing inside the brackets ("[*Click* . . .]"), brackets being the way that context, commentary, or, in this case, ambient noises are introduced to all kinds of records of human interaction. Who does the introducing? Authors or editors. So there's an invisible author/editor of *Checkpoint,* and just why would anyone go to the trouble of typing up this conversation? There's no indication that *Checkpoint* is a post–successful assassination story in which the killers' plotting has become part of some morbid historical record. No—the more natural conclusion, which you can and probably should draw in your first ten seconds of reading, is that Jay and Ben have been apprehended. *Vox* had become evidence in the Lewinsky Affair. *Checkpoint is* evidence.

Or maybe that's being too literal, as the whole thing is pretty absurd. Jay announces that he plans to murder the president on page two, and Ben's immediate response is to assume that this is one of Jay's "little flippancies." What does this tell us? Ben knows Jay well. This is confirmed over the next forty pages or so, as we get hints as to the nature of their relationship. Ben and Jay are middle-aged men who once attended high school together. They're like-minded souls, and they are mostly in concert as the conversation drifts to Lynne Cheney and Lockheed Martin and the current political climate, but their lives have diverged in the years since their friendship was formed. Both men have worked as college professors, but while Ben makes casual reference to the "honors seminar" he coteaches every spring, Jay can look back only on an aborted career as an adjunct. Ben is a successful historian and the author of several books; Jay "get[s] jittery" whenever he tries to write. Ben is a family man, happily married and father to a fourteen-year-old son; Jay can't sustain a relationship and admits that his personality tends to drive women away. The men no longer live in the same town, and that's important to the basic occasion of the book. It's been several years since Jay and Ben have spoken—pivotal years, politically speaking—and out of the blue Jay has contacted Ben with an urgent request that Ben meet him, at once, at a hotel in Washington, D.C. And please bring a tape recorder. It's testimony to the depth of their friendship that Ben drops everything and makes the journey, stopping at a Circuit City along the way.

As a committed Bakerite I felt something of a tingle on recognizing that *Checkpoint*'s entire focus was an intimate, male friendship. Hadn't Baker ruled this out for himself? When I met Baker for the first time I sent up a kind of trial balloon by sneaking in a reference to Abelardo Morell, with whom Baker *did* have a long-standing friendship. In addition to the author photos and the two men having produced *A Book of Books* together, Morell makes an appearance in *The Mezzanine*, first as "Abe," "Howie"'s boss, then as "Abelardo." But I didn't get much of a response from Baker. No "Oh, yes, old Abe, great chum of mine—need to give him a call!" I took this as confirmation that Baker did not have many, if any, intimate male friends. To my mind, that demands a reading of *Checkpoint* that stretches beyond the realism you'd expect of a writer drawing in any way on personal experience.

It's easy enough to recognize that Ben is another Baker-figure, a stand-in for Baker himself. The details of Ben's life read practically like Baker's author's notes, and when Jay asks Ben what he's been working on lately—there is a surprising amount of small talk in *Checkpoint*—the answers, the Office of Censorship and "Cold War Themes," put an attentive reader in mind of *Double Fold*. And once we recognize that Ben is Baker, the entire book changes, or it should change, because in a nutshell *Checkpoint* is the story of Ben talking Jay out of his wacky plan. The conversation is literally an argument against violence.

To be fair, though, Jay too puts an attentive reader in mind of Baker. Jay's life trajectory, now in an emotional tailspin, seems pretty close to the troubled Emmett of *A Box of Matches*, published only twenty months earlier. And tellingly, when Jay finally does allude to 9/11, he directly anticipates what Baker, speaking for himself, would soon say of the attacks: "I knew, I knew when those towers came down, I knew we would be bombing somewhere very soon."

Throughout this study I've been more or less operating on the assumption that Baker's many Baker-figures are interchangeable. And that's pretty much true, but it's not entirely true, and *Checkpoint* is unique in that it's the only time two different versions of Baker, one of them approaching fiction and a somewhat more non-fictional edition, appear on the page at the same time. *Checkpoint*, then, is an exercise in self-dialogue, a depiction of Baker's chronic, duplicitous ambivalence. Or, given the absurdity of Jay's planned assassination methods—remote-control flying saws and programmable bullets: a boy's fantasy of drone technology—the two men represent Baker's inner comedy team.

The early reviews of *Checkpoint* do not note this aspect of the book at all. From here on we're in uncharted *Checkpoint* territory. So what does Baker chat with himself about? Jay has a lot to say about Ben's work. Ostensibly, he's called Ben in to serve as confessor, and though there's a lame attempt to recruit him as an accomplice, Jay knows full well that there's absolutely zero chance Ben will participate in the scheme. Curiously, then, not long into the discussion, Jay begins to press Ben on why he tends to write only about the past. History. Isn't the present, these days, a more pressing concern?

Jay's point is a little similar to an observation leveled by one of Baker's hostile reviewers, writing about *A Box of Matches*: "It's a particularly disposable artifact from a pre-9/11 world that willfully celebrate[s] the trivial and minute." Hasn't the world changed? Don't we now need different kinds of books? Ben grows defensive on this point. Historians can't really study the present, he claims. They don't have access to the kinds of documents they would need. As well, Ben admits that he doesn't really want to spend his career mulling the political scoundrels of his time. The Gulf War "really undid [him]," and if getting "interested in the Second World War" means he's hiding in the past, then fine. Jay argues that Ben could "at least map the old onto the new," as *Human Smoke* sort of does, and this activates, from Ben, a rant on how the current political climate has already mapped the old onto the new in that the political scoundrels of our time, those who fomented the Iraq War, were the same scoundrels who had mucked things up thirty or forty years before.

Eventually, and this is the crucial moment, Ben appears to recognize that all this chatting about his work has distracted him from his mission, which is to distract Jay from *his* mission. To get the conversation back on track, Ben initiates this exchange:

> **BEN:** You know, this isn't frivolity.
> **JAY:** I'm not being frivolous. There is zero frivolity in my outlook right now.

That's the problem. Ben uses "frivolity" here as we all might, as a synonym for "trifling," as a way of disparaging thoughtlessness.

But in the context of Baker's career it's a double entendre: Frivolity is what the book *should* be, what *books* should be. All of us in the post–9/11 world, even characters in post–9/11 Nicholson Baker books, have forgotten how to appreciate frivolity.

66

THERE ARE TWO WEAPONS IN THE ROOM. OR SCRATCH THAT—THERE are two *tools* in the room, one that can be employed as a weapon but is designed for other uses, and one that is designed for violence alone and can serve any other purpose only awkwardly. A hammer and a gun. Jay and Ben, we know, are tool-challenged men, so it should come as no surprise that the tools trigger abstract reflection along Bakerian lines. Jay notes that the value of a hammer, as opposed to a gun, is that it is a "basic tool." He reminds Ben that a similar cudgel-style implement was employed in a famous nursery rhyme to delivery "forty whacks."

This links nicely with *Vox*'s allusion to children's literature, and in general Baker's sex trilogy is close at hand throughout *Checkpoint*. For example, shit intimacy reappears as Jay and Ben try to get their heads around the motivations of war-mongering scoundrels:

JAY: . . . The thing I can't figure is, military men seem to want to spend their lives living with other men. Can you make any sense of it? They're out there on some desolate airbase in the middle of nowhere, protecting some future pipeline—eating with other men, shaving with other men. And then actually defecating with other men.

BEN: It's a puzzler.

JAY: Shitting with them, day after day after day! How can they
       endure it?
BEN: I guess it's like professional football.
JAY: Excuse me for a second, I've got to take a dump.
BEN: Sure.
JAY: No, I'm just kidding.

That's more than coincidence. Baker can't have produced this exchange without hoping that some reader somewhere would reflect
back on Sylvie and Marian and conclude that Marian's claims about
shit intimacy—"You can do anything now"—has a dark equivalent
when applied to heterosexual men who prefer shit intimacy with
other heterosexual men.

More notably, near the end of the book, when Jay's madness begins to spiral out of control, it's hard not to hear Jim of *Vox* climbing to his feet and roaring out his orgasms:

JAY: . . . So then the desire for justice starts moving through
       me. It's like a huge paddlewheel, it just churns up all of
       this foam and fury. VENGEANCE.
BEN: Please don't stand up! I mean it, this will invalidate any
       point you will ever want to make.
JAY: This *is* the point I want to make. You're blocking me.

It's worth tracing this scene through to its conclusion. Ben man-
ages to keep Jay in his seat, but he realizes that Jay is experiencing
an uncomfortable buildup of churned foam. Ben tries a conces-
sion. He allows that murderous emotions can't be suppressed: "Feel
murderous, by all means. Rage inwardly. Just don't actually attempt
the murder." But it doesn't work. Nor does Ben's claim that assassinating the president could have wide-ranging implications that
Jay can't anticipate: "You don't have any idea what you might set in

motion, what kind of uproar, what kind of clamping down would follow." I didn't fully understand what Ben meant by this until I read *Human Smoke,* which tells the story of Herschel Grynszpan, the Jewish assassin who murdered Ernst vom Rath just three days before Kristallnacht. Vom Rath's death was immediately employed by Goebbels to crystallize Germany's already hardening anti-Semitic spirit.

But Jay is unimpressed with the argument. He offers a counter-example: Dietrich Bonhoeffer. I *knew* this was coming! Bonhoeffer's appearance, however, makes exactly the opposite point I'd thought it would make: Even a good man can get sucked into a bad plan. Regardless, it's a surprisingly lucid argument for Jay to make, as his diction ("penisfucker," "peckerfuck," the angry correlate of dildo talk) has begun to suggest that he is beyond the reach of reason.

At the brink of disaster Ben strikes on an idea. He asks to see Jay's hammer, which has been hidden under the bed covers, and on taking it up he claims to recognize it as a tool of voodoo-style magical potential: "Whatever harm you inflict on an evildoer's image with this hammer will also be visited upon the evildoer himself." Jay agrees to play along with this immature fantasy. A printed headshot of the president happens to be near at hand, and they position it on the bed. Jay proceeds with a bludgeoning. The scene echoes the corresponding climax of *Vox*:

BEN: Just lift the hammer. Good. Now when you bring it down, put your whole strength into it. Really kill him. Ready? Now, GO!	"Oh, I'm starting to come for you, my cock is pumping inside you."
JAY: HHHHHHHRRRRRRRA-AAAAGH! [*Flump!*]	"*Oh!* Nnnnnnnn! Nnn! Nnn! Nnn! Nnn! Nnn! Nnn!"
	"It's spurting out! I can't help it! Ah! Ah! Oooooo."

BEN: And again?

JAY: DAMMIT! [*Flump!*]
BASTARD! [*Flump!*]
RRRRRRAAAAGH!
[*Flump!*]

BEN: Okay, okay. Wow. So how
do you feel now? Any better?

There was a pause.

"Oh man," she said. "Wow. You
there?"

"I think so." He swallowed. "Let
me catch my breath."

That's pretty much the end of *Checkpoint*. Ben now has the gun and
the hammer, and they're leaving the hotel, and, apprehended or no,
the solution to Jay's assassination fantasy has been another fantasy,
a story, a Shakespearean king-slaughter that enacts Susan Sontag's
paraphrase of Aristotle: "Art is useful . . . in that it arouses and
purges dangerous emotions."

Not only is *Checkpoint* about the role and purpose of literature, it's a fervent defense of art for a post–9/11 world. And for my
money it is not only a book that ought to have been published and
celebrated, it's perhaps the only book of that time that needs to have
been published at all.

67

U AND I IS PRETTY SPECIFIC ON ONE POINT: UNDER NO CIRCUM-
stances does Baker want "to see the techniques of 'closed book
examination' applied to any other novelist." So no following in his
footsteps. I thought about this as I was driving to meet Baker for
the second time. En route to the diner where we would have lunch,
I noticed that Baker was driving the beater car ahead of me. He was
swerving a bit. That's why I noticed him. Until now, I'd followed

his biographical footsteps, but now I was literally following him—warily, and with an extra car length between us for safety's sake.

At that point it had been a little more than two years since I'd first read *U and I*. Since then my paperback copy of the book had sat smooshed between other books in what I now thought of as my Baker library, which filled a shelf near at hand as I sat and wrote. The book's having been smooshed meant that when I plucked it out again in late fall 2012 to reread it once more—abomination or no, I intended to teach it—its cheap-stock cover had lost all its sexy, questioning curvature. It was once again a flat book. I snapped the spine when I read it this time—I find that to be a weirdly satisfying sensation—and about a third of the way through I discovered what I now recognized to be a description of "the restaurant thing":

> Indeed, all male friendships outside of work sometimes seem to be impossible: you look at each other at the restaurant at some point in the conversation and you know that each of you is thinking, man, this is futile, why are we here, we're wasting our time, we having nothing to say, we're not involved in some project together that we can bitch about, we can't flirt, we aren't in some moral bind with a woman that we need to confess, we've each said the other is a genius several times already, and the whole thing is depressing and the tone is false and we might as well go home . . .

He goes on for a while longer, but he doesn't need to—because this is *exactly* what having a public lunch with Nicholson Baker is like. Or not quite, because Baker couldn't tell me that I was a genius because he hadn't read anything I'd written. He did, however, not long after we sat down, ask which book of mine he should begin with to get a sense of my work. My heart soared at this! Baker would read something I'd written. But then I realized he was just being polite.

I hedged for a while over an answer, and I thought over the connections between his career and my life that might occur to him if he *were* to read my work, even the connections that I haven't shoehorned into this study because there were finally so many it became embarrassing. But I didn't mention any of that. Nor did I say what I was thinking, which was this: *Nicholson Baker, you have no idea. Scratch me anywhere, and I'll bleed* your *blood, man!* Instead I got a little shy, or I faked shyness, and I asked him how he would answer the same question. Baker saw right through this ploy. I had inverted the polarity of our discussion, and in so doing emphasized once again what we were both trying to forget: This was an interview. He must have wondered if I'd been lying or at least wrong when I'd said that I didn't plan on writing about meeting him.

The real truth was that I had a pang of concern. What if Baker wrote about meeting *me*? What if that was the only reason he had agreed to meet with me in the first place? It was just the sort of metatwist that was always popping up in his work, and he could totally get away with it because I'd written far fewer books than he had, and even though I had a big head start on him, he could probably skim through everything I'd written in a few afternoons and then write some pithy thing for *The New Yorker* and beat me to the punch. Nothing doing! Answer your own question, Nicholson Baker! "I have no idea how to answer that question," Baker said, and that slammed the door on that particular line of mutual interviewing, and we were left for a time in the droll, stagnant stasis of "the restaurant thing."

It might have stayed like that, tense and uncomfortable, had Baker not begun to be made even more uncomfortable by something he noticed over my shoulder. His eyes darted past mine several times, as though he couldn't stop himself from visually confirming some private dread, and soon he recognized that his distraction was itself a distraction, and he explained that he knew a woman sitting a few tables away from us. He couldn't recall her name. This made him anxious because he was anticipating that the woman would spot him and stop by our table, and there would be the awkwardness of his not being able to properly greet her or introduce her to me. If you plan ahead, moments like this are easy enough to navigate. You can prepare something warm but inconclusive: "Hello! Good to see you! How *are* you?" Or, because people are generally pretty forgiving, you can acknowledge the slip: "I'm sorry, you've caught me off guard. I'm Nick—what's your name again?" I might have earned Baker's goodwill had I offered, as newish romantic couples sometimes do when one partner meets the poorly recalled acquaintance of the other, to aggressively introduce myself if the woman did approach. But that didn't occur to me because now I was distracted. *The Fermata,* I was in the process of recalling, describes at some length the "name problem," moments when Arno fails to recall people's names. "I will so much want to remember his or her name!" he says. "They usually remember my name, and in some cases I can detect a faint hurt look in their eyes when they perceive, through my joshing and bluster, that I don't remember theirs." Of course Arno has a solution. He stops time to dig through people's purses and wallets for identification. But Nicholson Baker could not stop time, and it was absolutely killing him. He practically writhed in his chair, like a piece of popcorn shriveling under hot butter or an ant fried by a ray of sunlight focused through a magnifying glass. I didn't have to wait long for the coup de grâce, as the woman had caught Baker's eye as she had begun to stir. She did not approach our table. Rather, on her way out the door she called out to Baker from across the room, in a friendly voice loud enough to turn the heads of several people between us: "Hey, Nick! How are you?"

Baker dissolved. He glanced briefly in the woman's direction, made only the tiniest of gestures toward josh and bluster, and then turned his head toward the wall and blocked his face with his hand, as though to throw up what shield he could against an avalanche of bullets and blows.

That's when my heart just about melted for Nicholson Baker. It was a rude thing for him to have done, an incredibly rude thing, but more important was the fact that Baker loathed himself for his mind's failure to have performed the very simple task of recalling the woman's name. It was the mental stammer, it was the one thing about human interaction that literature truly can ameliorate, and it was the absolute worst thing, I realized, that Nicholson Baker, accused by turns of perversion and violent designs, was capable of doing to another person. That moment was a backward measure of Baker's goodness. But instead of consoling him, or doing anything at all to help him recover, my mind reflexively called up a panel discussion I'd stumbled across a few months earlier, a public conversation in which Baker had participated along with several other writers. Baker responded to a question about interviewing people:

> There's always a moment when there's some little piece of that person that sums him or her up completely. There's some little moment of vulnerability often, or a mistake, or a piece of something that he or she had on the mantel that somehow sums the person up and that becomes the proxy of the whole individual.

68

AFTER LUNCH BAKER SURPRISED ME. HE SUGGESTED THAT WE GO to another restaurant for dessert. Two restaurants in one day! But when we got to the second restaurant it was unexpectedly closed. Baker shrugged at our misfortune. It was unclear what we should do next. A heavy rain had begun to fall, and for a moment we made a very odd couple there on the sidewalk, he quite tall and me dwarfed beside him, both of us crouched under undersized umbrellas in a downpour.

I had a realization and an idea. I realized that I was glad the second restaurant was closed because the first restaurant proved that I was never going to be able to be a simple friend to Nicholson Baker. I could stifle it, but in listening to him I was always going to be in the process of connecting whatever he said back to things he'd written six or fourteen or thirty years before, and even though that might honor him in a way, might even be a form of friendship, it also meant that in interacting with his less than perfect, unwritten self, I would forever be overlooking the simple courtesies of human intercourse.

But Catherine could be his friend! She could have good intercourse with him! That was my idea. A few days before, Catherine and I had said good-bye to the Maine beach rental and relocated to South Berwick's lone bed and breakfast. It was a sad departure. Not long after we had consummated Maine in the beach rental, Catherine had downloaded Cole Porter's "Let's Do It, Let's Fall in Love," and we had happily danced to the tune and then spent the rest of our time at the beach walking, reading, and doing what the educated fleas, the romantic sponges, and the lazy jellyfish do. Leaving it behind made us realize that we absolutely had to leave behind the plague-ridden former bed and breakfast. In fact, maybe we were done with bed and breakfasts entirely. But nevertheless Catherine was now back at South Berwick's bed and breakfast, waiting for me to be done with Nicholson Baker, and my idea was to invite Baker back there so that Catherine could be nice to him. Clearly I didn't know how.

Of course all this put me in mind of a Baker story. "Subsoil," from the midnineties, is set in a bed and breakfast. A man doing research at a railroad museum close to a quaint little inn becomes preoccupied with a small, desiccated potato he finds in his room's closet. Why had the famous Mr. Potato Head toy, the man gets to wondering, shifted from using actual potatoes that were perfectly serviceable as playthings, to the turd-like plastic molds that forced all children to play with the same fake spud? "Subsoil" is a cautionary tale. The man's growing obsession with needless innovation is symbolized by the desiccated potato, which begins to grow. First modestly with little nodules poking out its sides, and then monstrously as the lengthening tendrils creep out of the closet and slither all over the inn like the tentacles of a Lovecraft squid god. The moral? It's possible to get so caught up in a troublesome idea it overwhelms you.

That's true of authors too. You can get to the point where you've simply had enough of them. I don't mean me. I mean Catherine. That was the risky part of my plan. For two years now Catherine had been listening to me prattle on about Nicholson Baker. It had gotten to where she didn't even flinch when I stormed out of my office, tossing my hands in the air, and blurted out things like, "Nicholson Baker is fucking brilliant! He should win a goddamn Nobel Prize! The *Peace* Prize!" In other words, even before we got to Maine, Nicholson Baker had become the spooky tater slinking all over the former bed and breakfast, like one more plague upon us. I couldn't get enough of him even though I'd clearly had enough already, and Catherine had had more than enough before she'd had any at all.

I invited Baker back to the bed and breakfast anyway. He was happy to oblige. It was midday and the overly decorated living room was vacant, and as Baker took a seat I rushed up to our room. "Baker's *here*," I gurgled out. "Holy shit!" Catherine said, and she bounced off the bed. We descended the staircase together. The ace up my sleeve was that Ben of *Checkpoint* had taken up photography as an emotional balm. Photography is yet another medium that has been subjected to needless digital innovation, and the techniques Ben preferred—which Baker himself employed for the book he produced with his wife—were kin to the processes that Catherine had perfected in our bathrooms. I introduced them and watched them talk. We had a lovely chat that lasted until the rain stopped. It wasn't a threesome, but it was excellent human intercourse, and I do think that for a moment Nicholson Baker forgot that all this might one day wind up in a book.

After Baker left, Catherine went back upstairs for a sunhat, and we walked into South Berwick, toward the Sarah Orne Jewett House, which stood on a prominent corner. We stopped at the restaurant where I'd first thought that Baker and I might do the restaurant thing. But we didn't do the restaurant thing—we did the bar thing. We had a jubilant drink, and we toasted having had a lovely visit with Nicholson Baker, and even though I hadn't yet read all of his books it did feel as though something was now complete. We made a pact then and there to move to New York, and toasted again, to our less plague-ridden future.

Something fortuitous happened on the way back to the bed and breakfast. We were walking, hand in hand, along the street, and Catherine paused to smell some flowers planted below the windows of a house, one of those New England homes whose front wall extends all the way to the sidewalk. We were both smelling those amazing flowers when a woman—the owner of the house—came around the corner in gardening clothes, carrying a pair of shears. I recognized her at once. It was the woman who had called out to Baker in the restaurant. She recognized me too.

We complimented her flowers, her house, her town. What was remarkable about the woman was how very happy she seemed to be. She loved living, she said, in a town where Jewett had lived, and where Baker lived, and where, she revealed, Robert Pirsig also lived, though he was rarely seen. But that didn't matter, and nor did it seem to matter that Baker had been unable to acknowledge the woman's innocent greeting with anything like aplomb. She had absolutely refused to be made unhappy by it, perhaps because she had known that she would be headed home to tend these wonderful flowers. The woman did not invite us into her garden, but she did voice a preference for Baker's sex trilogy—and this reminded me that no matter how dark Baker's career had become, there had always been this happy nugget at work in the back of his mind. *House of Holes* was perhaps the happiest note of Baker's career, and it had been published in close proximity—jumbled up with—some of his darkest work. Before we walked on, the woman told us that we looked happy too. And we *were* happy—and being told we looked happy made us happier still. We bade the woman farewell, and we walked back to the bed and breakfast, remarking repeatedly on those amazing flowers.

69

AND NOW IT'S THE BEGINNING OF 2013. CATHERINE AND I ARE IN Brooklyn. We've been visiting through the holidays, and we have finalized our plans to move, come summer. Guess who else is here. Martin Amis! A few months after I met Baker, Amis publicly broke with the London literary scene and decamped for Brooklyn. He'd had enough of it. Or maybe the scene had had enough of him. I learned of the move when I stumbled across a blog post headlined, "Martin Amis Moves to Brooklyn, Sounds Like Jerk." Amis is now an Englishman who has mistaken himself for an American.

Nicholson Baker hasn't ever sounded like a jerk. Even when responding to unjust criticism, he has always been a model of politeness. Nevertheless it's possible to have had enough of him too, and this seems especially true if you've lived with him for most of your adult life. That's what *The Anthologist* is about.

Paul Chowder is a Maine poet who lives in a house with a nearby barn to which he occasionally retreats to sing to himself. He's not an insignificant figure—he's had poems in *The New Yorker,* he won a Guggenheim, and he has published at least three books— but he's come to have doubts: "My life is a lie. My career is a joke." The problem is poetry itself. Paul argues that literary modernism, having taken its cue from the technological advances of the late nineteenth century, forgot the brief and cheerful thing that ani- mated poetry in the first place: rhyme.

In other words, there was something wrong with the state of modern literature. It too had been subjected to needless innovation, and Paul's problem is compounded by the fact that he himself is not a rhyming poet. He has, however, managed to convince a publisher to let him edit an anthology of rhyming verse. The basic conflict of *The Anthologist* stems from Paul's inability to write the book's intro- duction. More pointedly, Paul's resistance to finishing the task has made him so insufferable that Roz, his girlfriend of eight years, has had enough of him. She has moved out.

There's a lot that ties Paul to Nicholson Baker. Many years be- fore, Baker had claimed in "Reading Aloud" that the clumsy and off-putting cadences of modern poetry readings are a result of "the absence of rhyme." And *The Anthologist* was published eleven years after Baker moved to Maine with his wife.

But there are differences between Paul and Baker too. And just as I had expected, the things that made Paul less Baker-like made him more like me: He's edited an anthology; he doesn't want children; he complains that teaching undergraduates has ruined lit- erature for him; and he even longs for a moment of finally reading a writer of whom he'd frequently heard but had never sat down to read. What I didn't expect was my reaction to all this. I didn't really care. *The Anthologist* was about me in almost every possible way, yet my reaction was about as far as you could get from Naipaul's claim about reading to confirm what we already know. Naipaul, I realized now, was completely wrong. Or perhaps I'd misunderstood him. If we only read for what we already know, Naipaul went on, then "we can take a writer's virtues for granted. And his originality, the news he is offering us, can go over our heads."

When Catherine and I had first arrived in New York, just before Christmas, I went to the Strand Bookstore to buy a copy of *The Anthologist*. They had a first edition—it was the only first edition of Baker's books on the shelf. Then I went down to Wall Street to try to find the building where Baker had worked during his yearlong stint in the financial world. The firm was long defunct, but I'd found an address for their offices. I was hoping to ride the escalator of *The Mezzanine*. But the building had no escalator. These days it's all elevators in New York, which I suppose makes it easier to track comings and goings in a post–9/11 world. Anyway, the escalator was in my satchel. The "steeper escalator of daylight" from the first paragraph of *The Mezzanine* repeats on page two of *The Anthologist*:

> So I'm up in the second floor of the barn, where it's very empty,
> and I'm sitting in what's known as a shaft of light. The light leans
> in from a high window. I want to adjust my seat so I can slant my
> face totally into the light. Just ease it into the light.

I read this a few days ago, on January 1, 2013, in the Rose Main Reading Room at the New York Public Library, a cathedral-like space laid out with a huge washboard of sturdy and impossibly long wooden tables. I had taken a seat across from an old, shaggy-haired, warlocky fellow with several large thesauruses stacked in front of him. The man made a repetitive lip-smacking noise as he scribbled in a notebook, as though his thoughts were tart. He was either a crank or a mystic. That's where I was when I first leaned into Paul's shaft of barn light, and for a while, for me, *The Anthologist* worked just like that: by seeming to cite all the little tricks that have leapt from book to book throughout Nicholson Baker's career.

When I had first spoken to Baker on the phone, as Catherine and I hurtled toward her groping incident in Portland, I tried setting him at ease by revealing that I'd reread "The Figure in the Carpet" just that morning. This was true. I'd been convinced that Baker wasn't going to call, but I knew that if he did call, it would probably be that morning, and I imagined it would set his mind at ease about me if he thought of me as the kind of guy who occasionally dedicated mornings to reading nineteenth-century fiction. Baker got the suggestion of the reference but denied its validity: "Well, I assure you, there is no figure in *my* carpet." Hogwash! I knew it then, and I confirmed it when I read *The Anthologist* and discovered that "The Figure in the Carpet" was *one* of the figures in Baker's carpet.

About two-thirds of the way through, Paul tries to win Roz back by making her a bead necklace:

> I started to bead. The verb made sense. I was beading. What you do is pick up a bead and . . . turn it until the shadow of the hole, or the light appearing through the hole, comes into view, and then you know where to insert the end of the wire. As soon as it's on, you lose interest in it and let it slip down and away and you're on to the next one. Revising is difficult. . . . I could string beads for a living. I kept thinking of the phrase "beads on a string."

Beyond the reappearance of the Baker hole theme, this passage describes how a writer's little tricks add up over the course of a career.

"The Figure in the Carpet" offers two metaphors for this. One comes from James's narrator-critic: The tricks form "something like a complex figure in a Persian carpet." But the famous writer offers a better analogy: "It's the very string . . . that my pearls are strung on!"

So Baker was indulging in a bit of Jamesian evasiveness. And *The Anthologist* turned out to be a veritable gumball machine of tricky beads. Paul addresses his audience in *Vox*'s virtual arena: "You're out there. I'm out here." His description of poetry strikes a familiar orgasmic note ("the shudder, the shiver, the grieving joy of true poetry"), as do his darkest thoughts ("What if I just loosened my grip, and fell to one side, and just—*fffshhhhooooow*"). Appearances by Updike and Gosse link the book to *U and I*, Isherwood and Auden link it to *Human Smoke*, and Pound and MacLeish link it to *Double Fold*. There's even a reference to Tolkien in a passage on the difficulty of writing: "It's a terrible struggle; you fight with the Balrog through flame and waste and worry and incontinence and tedium. The Balrog of too-much-to-say." In this way the book cleaves itself in half for two different readers. For the casual reader Paul must write his introduction, and long before he confirms it, you suspect that the book itself is the introduction. But for the committed Bakerite another read emerges as Baker's many pearls line up along the book's taut string: It's not an introduction to an anthology, it *is* an anthology, and all a writer can ever hope to be is an anthologist of his or her self.

There's more. In the Rose Main Reading Room, a great sucking sinkhole of concern opened up in my chest as I realized what was at stake in *The Anthologist*: Baker's wife may have had enough of him. Maybe she had moved out like Roz, or maybe she hadn't, but either way the book seemed to chronicle a period of marital strife.

What was interesting about this, for me, was not whether Baker and his wife went on living together. I knew they did. It was my reaction to the proposition that they might not. When was I ever, outside of a book, so moved for a stranger that my emotions triggered physiological reactions no less profound than had I been struck or stroked? Never. *The Anthologist* was entirely agitating as Paul began to flirt with his neighbor and Roz went out on a date. I did *not* want that to happen. I wanted them back together, right this instant. I tried talking to the two of them, out loud. That story is not you guys, I said. That's *Updike*. Evil, evil Updike, and even though Updike is a wonderful writer to whom I've dedicated many hours of satisfying reading, I don't want real people to be like Updike. Not even Updike wanted people to be like Updike. You know this from his story "Gesturing," which is about how unhappy an Updike-figure is with his Updikian life, and when you consider the implications of Updike having chosen this story for self-anthologization in *The Best American Short Stories of the Century*—well, tears just fill your eyes. Don't go that way! Roz, Paul is obviously a challenge. He's a monomaniac with delusions of grandeur and loads of negativity, and it's probably no garden party putting up with him, day after day. But he loves you, and he does good work. Please go back to him. And oh, by the way—Updike was an anthologist too!

All of this was more or less confirmed eight months or so later, after we'd moved to New York, and a draft of *B & Me* was complete, and Catherine had read through the book to exercise her veto power over passages that were too explicit or revealing, when Nicholson Baker published *Traveling Sprinkler,* a sequel to *The Anthologist.* Even more than *The Anthologist, Traveling Sprinkler* is characterized by its jumbled delivery, its associative progression of thought to thought, and it too is a compendium of Baker thought: Paul tells us about his penis ("My penis is soft and it doesn't make a scraping sound"); he reveals that he had an early career as a bassoonist; he has an intimate male friendship with Tim, a drone protestor; the hole theme reappears (" . . . the moon naked like a white hole in the sky"); a lengthy metaphorical scuba sequence ties the book all the way back to "Snorkeling"; and the "traveling sprinkler" of the title is another simple tool driven by water and centrifugal force, the sort of thing, Paul admits, that he was greatly interested in "before [he] got distracted by the wars in Afghanistan and Iraq." Most important, *Traveling Sprinkler* ends with the happy suggestion that Paul and Roz will reconcile.

"Do you want to take a ride in my boat?" she asks him.

70

BUT LONG BEFORE I READ THAT, I *DIDN'T* READ ALL OF *THE Anthologist* in the Rose Main Reading Room at the New York Public Library. I stopped about a third of the way through and read the rest of it on the subway, not because trains are good cognitive analogies—they're not—but because of something I noticed early one morning, during rush hour. The car, headed into Manhattan, was packed. What was striking was the pure silence of the crowd. Of course many people were wearing earbuds, subjecting themselves to private cacophonies. But that's a little like reading, isn't it? That was like me in the Rose Main Reading Room, sitting still but spasming with concern for a person I may never meet, a fictional character I *can't* meet. Our libraries may be vanishing, but there are still a few quiet spots left in the world, and a crowded train may be one of the last places left, outside of books, where it is possible to feel the warmth of a stranger, to literally have their thigh rub provocatively against your own, without anyone's feeling groped. Ours *are* accursedly interesting times, but we can still touch each other.

Baker taught me that. And perhaps it's that kind of moment, when you've finally realized what it was you were looking for in an author, that signals when you've had enough of them. One day headed back to Brooklyn, before I'd even finished *The Anthologist,* I realized I'd had enough of Nicholson Baker. I'd moved on. Curiously, I was thinking of Martin Amis instead. It occurred to me, who knows why, that I'd been thinking a whole lot about Martin Amis these past couple years. He'd kept popping up, making appearances in my life. Once when I went to a library to find an obscure Baker story, there was Martin Amis on the next page, hanging ten on the media wave he'd churned up for *The Information.* And when I went looking for reviews of *Human Smoke,* there was Amis again, getting reviewed right alongside Baker because he'd written a similar book at just about the same time. And when I finally went digging around for *Vintage Baker,* a premature Baker anthology published in 2004, there was *Vintage Amis,* published the very same year.

Maybe I had done wrong by Martin Amis. I'd been cruel. And wasn't that what I now understood literature to be about—cultivating an ability to transcend our ugliest emotions, the ones that can turn us against ourselves and those we love, that can result in horror and even slaughter? Maybe I was wrong about Martin Amis. Maybe he was a nice but misunderstood fellow, like Nicholson Baker. I wouldn't know until I read him. That was my thought, even before I finished *The Anthologist.* Perhaps I should read Martin Amis. Perhaps I should anthologize him.